ADVANCE PRAISE FOR

INTRA-PUBLIC INTELLECTUALISM: CRITICAL QUALITATIVE INQUIRY IN THE ACADEMY

"In this contemporary era of racialized and political reckoning and welcomed civil disobedience globally, the editors and contributors of this book offer unique insights that inspire new and radical ways to engage in intra-public intellectualism. Through contemplative and decolonizing imaginaries, dialogues, and interludes, each chapter disrupts boundaries and expands possibilities for re-envisioning the role of academics and critical qualitative research in theorizing and transforming public social spheres. This edited book is a must read for those seeking a compelling and diverse compilation of perspectives on public intellectualism."

Michelle Salazar Pérez,
Associate Professor of Early Childhood Education,
The University of Texas at Austin

"In a world that too often seems beyond resuscitating, *Intra-Public Intellectualism: Critical Qualitative Inquiry in the Academy* is an injection of hope for critical qualitative inquirers committed to public causes, no matter how lost. While offering plenty of provocations, interventions, and lines of flight, in sync with the post-philosophies prominent throughout the book, each edited chapter is also a demonstration of how to (still) think and do responsive and responsible public critical qualitative work that matters. It is a positive reminder that the public is still worth fighting for and we critical qualitative researchers have and must soldier on."

Jennifer R. Wolgemuth,
Associate Professor of Measurement and Research,
University of South Florida

"This powerful and timely collection of essays answers the call for a critical inquiry that advances a long over-due public social science."

Norman K. Denzin,
Distinguished Emeritus Professor of Communications,
Sociology, and the Humanities, University of Illinois

INTRA-PUBLIC INTELLECTUALISM

INTRA-PUBLIC INTELLECTUALISM

Critical Qualitative Inquiry in the Academy

EDITED BY TIMOTHY C. WELLS,

DAVID LEE CARLSON, AND MIRKA KORO

Myers Education Press

Gorham, Maine

Myers Education Press

Published by Myers Education Press, LLC
P.O. Box 424
Gorham, ME 04038

Myers Education Press is an academic publisher specializing in books, e-books and digital content in the field of education. All of our books are subjected to a rigorous peer review process and produced in compliance with the standards of the Council on Library and Information Resources.

Library of Congress Cataloging-in-Publication Data available from Library of Congress.

13-digit ISBN 978-1-9755-0248-5 (paperback)
13-digit ISBN 978-1-9755-0247-8 (hard cover)
13-digit ISBN 978-1-9755-0249-2 (library networkable e-edition)
13-digit ISBN 978-1-9755-0250-8 (consumer e-edition)

Printed in the United States of America.

All first editions printed on acid-free paper that meets the American National Standards Institute Z39-48 standard.

Books published by Myers Education Press may be purchased at special quantity discount rates for groups, workshops, training organizations and classroom usage. Please call our customer service department at 1-800-232-0223 for details.

Cover design by Teresa Lagrange

Visit us on the web at **www.myersedpress.com** to browse our complete list of titles.

Contents

Acknowledgments

Timothy C. Wells, David Lee Carlson, and Mirka Koro

IT IS HARD TO ACKNOWLEDGE all the people, conversations, experiences, and ideas that went into this book. Certainly, the book would not have been possible without the generous contributions of all the contributing authors to this book, those who wrote a chapter, those who created interludes, and those who granted permission for their work to appear in this book. We acknowledge your time and efforts and thank you for your willingness to contribute. We similarly want to thank Chris Myers, Gaile Cannella, and Myers Education Press for their interest, guidance, and insightful feedback throughout the process of the book.

As we note in the Introduction, the idea and initial development of this book emerged from an interdisciplinary reading group at Arizona State University. This group provided the dialogue, constructive support, and space to work out ideas, which proved vital in the development of the book. We thank everyone who participated, past and present. On this note, we appreciate all those who served as reviewers for the chapter submissions, many of whom were active members of the reading group. Those reviews were extensive and certainly made this book better.

Finally, we want to thank all those who created the conference proposals, participated in the panels at the American Educational Research Association (AERA) and the International Congress of Qualitative Inquiry, and provided reviews of our initial exploration into the topic of public intellectualism. Before the COVID-19 cancellations of conferences for this spring, some of the chapters in this book were going to be presented as a panel at the AERA. These conferences would have made for fruitful discussions and enriched the book. Regardless, we thank those who were willing to contribute their time and expertise to create those panels and extend the reach of this book.

Map to the Interludes

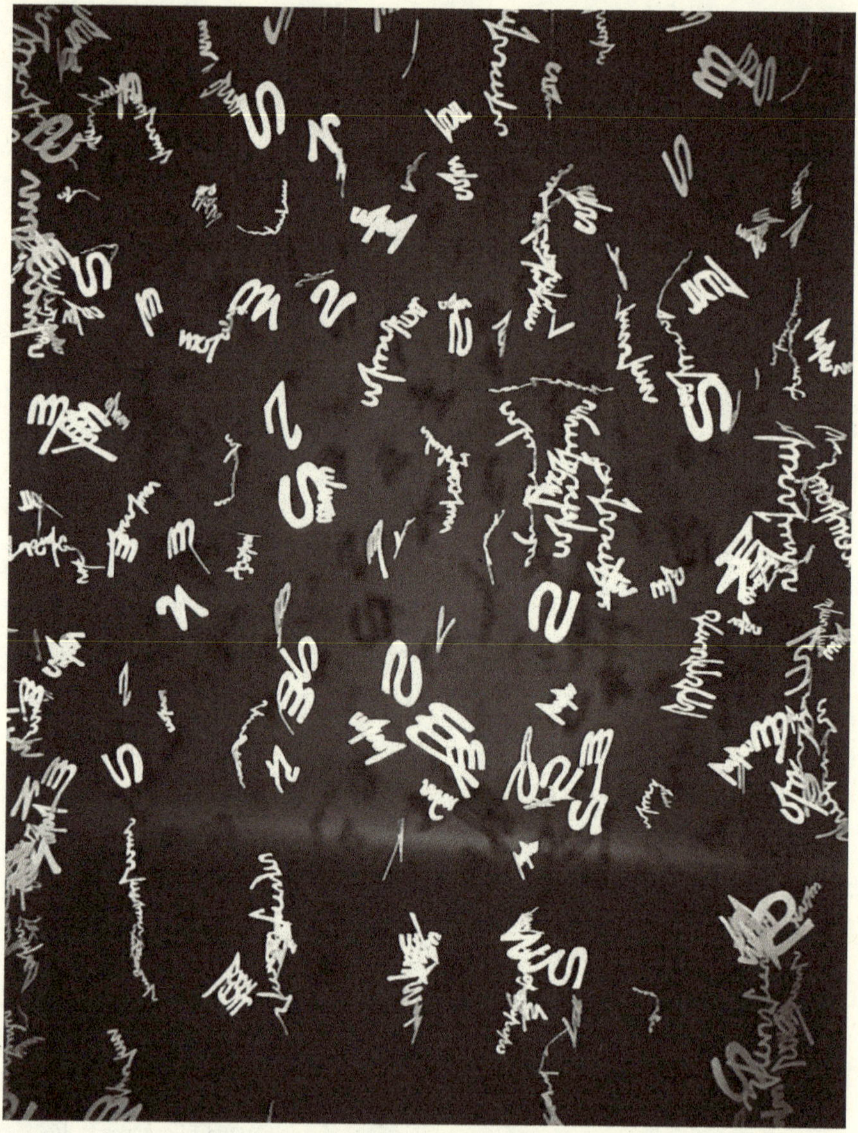

Word Fall

Kate Fitzpatrick

Cut paper and thread on a black backdrop

12 feet (height) 4 feet (width)

Reproduced with permission

INTRODUCTION

Invitation(s) To Change The World

Timothy C. Wells, Arizona State University
David Lee Carlson, Arizona State University
Mirka Koro, Arizona State University

> *There has never been a greater need for a critical qualitative inquiry that matters in the public sphere. We live in the audit cultures of global neoliberalism. The politics of evidence that define the audit culture marginalize critical inquiry. Our challenge is to push back, to resist, to redefine the place of the academy, indigenous epistemologies and the public intellectual in these public spaces.*
>
> —Denzin (2017, p. 8)

THE WRITINGS THAT CREATE *Intra-Public Intellectualism: Critical Qualitative Inquiry in the Academy* represent a diversity of perspectives and traditions yet come together in a distinct project, which has nonetheless refused to become singular and unifying in structure. We think it is best described as a project of proliferating explorations into the idea and practice of public intellectualism. No doubt an ambitious task.

The origins of this book can be found in a weekly reading group at the Mary Lou Fulton Teachers College at Arizona State University. The group, composed of qualitative researchers, doctoral students, and faculty from across the university, had been meeting consistently for more than 6 years (and continues meeting!) to read philosophy and collaborate on academic scholarship. Each of us as editors actively participated in and organized the group, as did many of the contributors to this book. In the fall of 2017, however, the group decided on a change of course. Instead of reading the laundry list of theory planned for the semester, we set our sights on a study of public intellectualism: what it does and has failed to do and how it might be refashioned and reanimated to address the predicaments of our contemporary moment.

Our study began with what we understood to be seminal texts on intellectualism from a critical perspective: Edward Said's (1994) *Representations of the Intellectual* and excerpts of Antonio Gramsci's (1971) *Selections From the Prison Notebooks*. In their texts, Said and Gramsci stage critical challenges to the tradition of intellectualism, exposing its ties to Eurocentric hegemony (Said) and bourgeois elitism, that is, the intelligentsia (Gramsci). In following these challenges, we explored notions of intellectualism through the critical writings of Michel Foucault, Gilles Deleuze, Henry Giroux, Judith Butler, and Luce Irigaray. Each of these texts provided openings for us to think about intellectualism differently, away from the singular, normative, gendered, and common sensible tradition that often accompanies academia. Perhaps more than anything, these texts invited a reconsideration of how our own scholarship committed to ethically transformative work in the public sphere, beyond the halls of academia, toward more equitable, compassionate, and lively worlds. We found ourselves within the field of critical qualitative inquiry.

Critical qualitative scholars maintain the importance of inquiry committed to social change. They reject the detached and disinterested role of traditional inquiry, that of the 20th-century ethnographer who studies the "natives" at a distance and equally reject the myth of the objective observer often necessitated in positivist and postpositivist research paradigms (Denzin et al., 2017). Instead, critical scholars understand inquiry as first and foremost an *intervention*, an act that is never neutral and always directed toward a particular end, foregrounding questions of social responsibility and ethics (Koro-Ljungberg & Cannella, 2017). For Norman Denzin (2017), critical qualitative scholars unite in a "commitment to expose and critique the forms of inequality and discrimination that operate in daily life" and "are called to *change* the world and to change it in ways that resist injustice while celebrating freedom and full, inclusive, participatory democracy" (p. 9). It is perhaps this call, this invitation to transform the world, that best characterizes critical scholarship of our kind, and it equally reflects what came to be our interest in public intellectualism. We soon realized, however, that not only would this study take us well beyond the fall semester but we also needed others to think, research, and intervene with us, which marked the formal beginnings and persistent middles of this book and collaborative writing project.

It is in this critical light that this book is not simply about public intellectualism, a survey of a field from above, but more so a series of interventions from within the study of public intellectualism. For the call of intellectuals "to speak the truth and to expose lies" (Chomsky, 1967, para. 4) seems somehow insufficient in light of contemporary predicaments surrounding knowledge, existence, and the public (see the Entanglement sections). This book works not on or around but entangled within these predicaments. The prefix *intra–* in the title, *Intra-Public Intellectualism*, alludes to this task. The term *intra* signals to the productive in-between of relation, the vitality of tension. The productivity of the in-between is what Karen Barad (2014) affirms as *intra-action*, the ontological entanglement of matter and agency, and describes as a process of "cutting together-apart (one move)" (p. 168). Our use of the term *intra* is not altogether different. In fact, a cutting together–apart can be thought of as the conceptual task of this book. It is an invitation to begin in the middle, to think not only diffractively but also differentially and unconventionally about 21st-century challenges to the public, to the university, and to the practice of public intellectualism.

Therefore, working in the field of critical scholarship with considerations of public intellectualism, the contributions to this book reside within a series of entanglements as a way to invite critical conversations about the role of the public intellectual in our current sociopolitical, academic, global, and environmental climate. Following these entanglements, we outline the book, introduce the interludes, and preview the chapters.

Entanglement 1: Knowledge(s)

What becomes of public intellectualism in light of the theoretical challenges of the 20th century? More specifically, how can the act of public intellectualism, so often conceived of as speaking truth to power, reconcile the lack of a capital *T* Truth? And how might conceptions of intellectualism address the displacement of the singular and unified speaking subject? These questions may seem tired and old. But in our current moment, which has witnessed the proliferation of "post-truth" and "alternative fact" discourses (Illing, 2019), such questions warrant reconsideration. As editors of this book, we hope to unearth the entanglement that the current sociopolitical challenges to knowledge have on the practice of public intellectualism.

The challenges set forward regard the very notions of foundational truth, law, and morality, central concerns in the practice of public intellectualism.

For example, the "abandonment of universals" (Ross, 1988), "incredulity towards metanarratives" (Lyotard, 1984), and the death of subjectivity (Derrida, 1993) put forward alternative functions of knowledges, thus shaping alternative practices of intellectualism and contesting taken for granted academic traditions (see also Lather, 1991). The issue is not simply the impossibility of a singular point of reference—knowledge, experience—but also the necessity of negation in any point of reference, that is, the idea that the presence of one thing requires the absence of another. Perhaps most important, we would like to create spaces to explore the spectral function of negation in the making of meaning and truth, the idea that the absent lurks within the present, as Foucault (1988) maintained, degrees of madness accompany the conditions of reason (also see Descombes, 1980; Derrida, 1993). Thus, it is in setting aside the search for universal truths, grand narratives, and essentialized selves that many authors in this book find productive spaces at the limits and incompleteness of truth discourses for the enactments of alternative knowledges and practices.

Yet questions remain as to how alternative worlds can be enacted through the absence of normative knowledges and how to focus on differences while paying attention to the particularities. Certainly, these are questions that have been explored and are broached in some of the chapters (see Chapters 1, 6, and 8). What is worth noting is the productivity of critique as it is conceptualized in an antifoundational approach. When understood less a *condemnation* than a *contestation*, as a "contestation without truths," critique withholds the moral judgment that tends to accompany universalizing approaches and instead engages "the ideological surface of popular discourses without automatically reaching out for the comfortable political 'truth' that lie[s] behind the often-reactionary force of the popular" (Ross, 1988, p. ix). It is in this light that scholars might prefer alternative notions of critique—*problematize*, *deconstruct*, *trouble*, and *queer*—suggesting a critique as something neither for nor against (Koopman, 2013). Often this means moving away from signification and toward performance, with the willful embrace of absurdism, parody, and irony as tactics that take the logics of truth to their extreme. No need to venture into the hallowed halls of academia; just turn on network television in the evening to find the pervasiveness of parody as critique in our contemporary moment.

All of this places the tradition of the intellectual and public intellectualism in a rather peculiar position and raises important questions, namely, Who exactly is privileged in critique as contestation without truth? and What does a critique neither for nor against offer? Our hope in this book is less to provide a resolution than to sit within the knots and engage entanglements productively around the question of the public intellectual and transformative scholarship.

Entanglement 2: Existence(s)

The second entanglement is found in the various turns toward ontology in the social sciences and humanities. For much of the 20th century, questions of existence, being, and reality took a back seat to those of knowledge, meaning, and value. The influence of contemporary theories posed serious doubts around the existence of texts outside of culture and society, language and meaning. Included in this skepticism were claims of materiality and materialism. The idea that matter existed "out there" in the world, separate and distinct from language and culture, garnered the charge of "naive realism." But by the end of the century, interest in materiality and ontology gained new traction, aligning less with the materialism of the critical Marxist tradition than with the materiality, embodiment, and place-based knowledges of feminist and Indigenous traditions (Truman, 2019; Watts, 2013), reviving skepticism to the very division of ontology and epistemology, existence, and knowledge.

Numerous labels make up the contemporary turn toward ontology, including that of new materialism, new empiricism, posthumanism, object-oriented ontology, and affect theory, to name a few. In the field of qualitative inquiry, this work is most present in what is referred to as *postqualitative inquiry* (Koro-Ljungberg, 2015; St. Pierre, 2011). It is research that typically makes the following claims: (a) Reality is enacted in relation and through practice, (b) different relations and different practices enact reality differently, and (c) different enactments of reality result in ontological multiplicity (Law, 2004; Lenz Taguchi, 2013; MacLure, 2015; Truman, 2019). Several correlates follow: First, in returning to questions of reality—ontology and metaphysics—there is a rejection of the reflexive division between nature and culture found in social constructionist as well as postmodern approaches (Truman, 2019). Second, because material worlds are emergent and not preexistent, agency might better be thought of as distributed, networked, and relational rather than individualized, intentional, and willed (Lenz Taguchi, 2013). Third, it becomes important to think about research beyond language and representation toward invention and creative experimentation (MacLure, 2015).

All of this poses significant questions to the tradition of public intellectualism: If practices enact realities, then what reality does the practice of "truth telling" and "speaking truth to power" enact? If reality itself is emergent, then certainly truths are as well. Can public intellectuals think of and/or do their practice beyond truth? Alternatively, how might the practice of public intellectualism learn from the place-based and embodied worlds of Indigenous and feminist traditions? and Can public intellectuals think beyond representation toward the enactment of different realities and the enactment of reality differently?

Such questions nod to the speculative interests of many working within the ontological turn. Speculative scholars take seriously the notion of "ontological multiplicity" and work toward different realities through experimentation with different practices and new relations, reaching toward the "out-there" without fully knowing what is to come (Shaviro, 2014). Deleuze and Guattari's (1994) nonrepresentational philosophy finds an ally here, as representation takes a back seat to "the creation of concepts and the laying out of a plane" (p. 36). It is in this light that critique becomes immanent, affirmative, and event-ful, less a matter of debunking than of assembling or modulating:

> This modulation can be augmenting (taking a certain tendency to the limit), diverting (deflecting it into a different tendency), transmutational (interacting with other tendencies in a way that invents a whole new direction as a kind of surplus-value of interaction)—or, it can lead to a clash that stops the process. And furtherance, convergence, becoming or blockage that happens, actually happens: it's an event. This kind of event-ful, affirmative critique is very different from criticism, or . . . negative critique. (Massumi, 2010, p. 338)

Although many others take up the ontological turn with different concepts—that is, networks, relationality, affect, process, assemblage, nonrepresentation—these affirmative and modulatory interests remain present throughout those working in the field. Certainly, this is work that is not without risk. The goal of this scholarship cannot be new for the sake of new or provocation for the sake of provocation but perhaps the multiplication of modes of life. And it is here in this speculative and experimental space, a space of uncertainty and contingency, that public intellectualism might find productive grounds for not only social but also existential transformation. The task would involve reviving the legacy of ontology as a cause worth fighting for in the realm of public discourse (see Chapters 3 and 9). Yet what this project will look like, we can only speculate.

Entanglement 3: Public(s)

The onset of the internet and global connectivity has redefined the public domain. Digital spaces are now part of everyday life. Blogs, podcasts, forums, video conferencing, and a bevy of social media platforms channel communication on global scales. Personal devices, including cell phones and wearable electronics, mediate the full extent of our waking as well as sleeping hours. The public is no longer simply found in the coffee shop, dinner party, or salon of Habermas's theorizing, but is now increasingly found in virtual environments. All of this suggests the need to reconceptualize understandings of the public, "our understanding of what 'civic' and 'political' actually mean now" (Candon, 2016, p. 2133). For the digitizing of the public is hardly without controversy and, in fact, represents what many consider an extension of the neoliberalization of society (Giroux, 2019). Nowhere is this more evident than in debates over freedom of speech in online environments.

Consider the case of YouTube, which has found itself caught in a flurry of protests over its decisions, or lack thereof, to regulate the content of its videos. Those on the right have cried foul over what they perceive as the liberal bias of YouTube's censoring practices, while those on the left have long felt that YouTube has served as a breeding ground for bigoted and hateful ideas (Roose & Conger, 2019). Since the 2016 U.S. presidential election, YouTube has been ground zero for disinformation campaigns, those seeking to undermine societal confidence and democratic processes through misleading, false, and "deepfake" videos (Metz, 2019). Recently, YouTube has attempted to "bring more authoritative sources and fact checks" to its videos (Pichai, 2019, 1:42). In doing so, YouTube, a subsidiary of Google, one of the richest companies in the world, positions itself as *the* curator of truth. Rightfully, questions are now being raised as to whether YouTube and other social media giants, such as Facebook, should, in fact, be considered public, regulated, and/or taken over for government control (Glaser, 2019). It is just one example of how digital and social media sites are reconstituting the ground of the public sphere, reigniting questions as to who and what constitutes the public and whether a singular, all-encompassing public sphere can or should exist.

The implication of these shifting grounds for the work of public intellectualism and more broadly critical qualitative inquiry remain uncertain. As we continue to enfold our lives into digital devices, what becomes of humanities research? How do digital spaces affect research directed toward the public sphere? In thinking about social justice and social change, are these digital environments enabling a more inclusive form of Habermas's (1993) "communicative action," or are they edifying the postmodern critique of rationalist discourse? Perhaps most foundationally, questions are needed about how digital devices, with the proliferation of data that they produce, reconstitute notions of the self. And what the proliferation of digital environments means for the practice of public intellectualism.

We do not attempt to provide answers to these important and provocative questions but surface these as entanglements that might become newly productive. In fact, the entanglements present in the reworking of the public sphere are another way to think about our use of the term *intra-public*. *Intra-public* emphasizes the multiplicity of publics that remain not only neglected and subjugated but also in between and in potential (see Chapters 5, 7, and 10). In short, it emphasizes the public sphere that remains virtual. The work of critical qualitative inquiry, and, more specifically, the study and practice of public intellectualism, might do well to consider the many sides of this equation, that which is present, subjugated, and *in potentia*. If digital environments increasingly channel the work of public intellectuals, then the role, function, and meaning made within these spaces demand their attention (see Chapters 2 and 4). Equally demanding of attention is how digital spaces might shape critical qualitative scholarship and whether—better, how—these spaces can be leveraged toward social transformation. Furthermore, if the public has become actualized in new ways, so, too, has the political. What the use of the *intra*– prefix also alludes to is the way that critical qualitative scholarship might work beyond representational truths to create new publics and new politics within digital environments. This is the explorative, experimental, and, as outlined earlier, speculative side of this book (see the Interludes).

The Chapters

Intra-Public Intellectualism: Critical Qualitative Inquiry in the Academy is situated within the tensions outlined previously. The authors of this book take up debates over critical qualitative inquiry, posthumanism, new materialism, decolonization, public scholarship, youth activism, affect theory, neurodiversity, gender, sexuality, and spirituality, as well as many others. Collectively, they engage in debates about the place and function of academic inquiry and how this inquiry might reconstitute the boundaries of the public in a more ethical and socially just direction. The book is composed of 10 chapters and a series of interludes dispersed throughout.

The Interludes

The interludes (collaboratively created by Mirka Koro, Marina Basu, Jorge Sandoval, Anani Vasquez, and Brian Grant) serve as creative reflections and extensions to the concepts and ideas encountered in the chapters. A mix of drawings, photographs, poetry, and reproduced art, the interludes build off of the notion of the intra in *Intra-Public* and appear between and sometimes within the chapters. It is through the interludes that readers experience the tensions, movements, and textures that undergird the thoughts, practices, and texts embedded within the workings of public intellectualism. The interludes can be read along with chapters or on their own. See "Map to the Interludes" at the front of the book for a page-by-page guide.

The chapters begin with M. Francyne Huckaby and Jonathan W. Crocker's chapter, "Intellectual Publics | Public Intellectuals," in which they explore the horizontal, spatial, and collective notion of *intellectual publics* as an alternative to the linear, hierarchical, and individualist framing of the *public intellectual*. Through the use of "exposition, poetry, images, and digital media" and a range of critical, postmodern, and posthuman theories, the authors "spark a (re)vision of the relationship between *publics* and *intellectuals*," opening space for alternative explorations, different knowledges, and the unfinished productivity of the agonic for the domains of the public and the practice of intellectualism.

In Chapter 2, "An Ecology of Truth(s) Telling Amid the Post-Truth Turn," Joseph D. Sweet and Taylor M. Kessner investigate public intellectualism in a post-truth world through interviews of four prominent public intellectuals. Situated within critical qualitative inquiry and drawing on Manuel De Landa's (1997) ecological theory, Sweet and Kessner explore intellectualism as a dynamic, malleable, and collective ecology. They suggest the term *meshwork* as a way to think through the collective production of not just intellectualism but also truth, a framework that extends the terrain and boundaries of critical qualitative inquiry.

In Chapter 3, "Guiding Public Engagement With Science Through a Branching Narrative of Qualitative Perspectives," Mathew D. Evans takes an experimental approach to sustainability, public engagement, and qualitative methodology in a "choose your own adventure" take on a fictionalized account of data collected from an interactive art installation seeking to engage participants in the science and future of plastics pollution. For Evans, the engagement sought in the art installation is reenacted in the text, as readers plot their way through various methodological decisions. Notions of public intellectualism center on effective engagement and the production of different realities through different methodologies.

In Chapter 4, "Whiteness and the Natural Order: Shame, Race and Public Intellectualism According to Jordan Peterson," Lauren Mark and Timothy C. Wells explore the practice of public intellectualism through the discourse of famed YouTube figure Jordan Peterson. In drawing on Sara Ahmed's (2004) theory of affective economies, they argue that Peterson's influence is as much about the resonance of his affect as it is about the ideas he puts forward. In doing so, Mark and Wells suggest that understandings of public intellectualism, as well as of gender and race, need to account for the deployment of as affect as much as for ideology and rhetoric.

In Chapter 5, "Is That a Ladybird on the Leaf? Public Intellectualism and Resistance With Very Young Children," Marek Tesar explores how children embody forms of intellectualism and resistance in everyday and often taken-for-granted situations. The question in the title, "Is that a ladybird on the leaf?" was posed by a child in what appeared to be an inopportune moment but, in fact, prompted his teacher to reconsider her role as an authority figure in the school. The child not only demonstrated intellectualism but also challenged the developmentalist idea of children as an intellectuals-in-the-making rather than intellectuals par excellence.

In Chapter 6, "Intellectual Undesirables: An Autoethnographic Reflection on Intellectual Contributions of the Neurologically Othered," Joshua Cruz explores the boundaries of intellectualism and neurodiversity. In an autoethnographic retelling of an experience tutoring a Vietnam veteran, described as "neurologically different," Cruz argues for neurologically different modes and practices of intellectualism, suggesting that "neurodivergence and intellectualism are not mutually exclusive." One of the implicit yet valuable lessons of the chapter is how qualitative methodological work might be rethought as neurodivergence poses challenges to notions like narrative authorship, ownership, and voice, central features of both critical qualitative inquiry and public intellectualism.

In Chapter 7, "Intellectual Gatekeepers: Reclaiming Black Queer Youth as the Public," Boni Wozolek explores the relationship between "intra-public" and the "colonized intellectual" in an arts-based education project with queer youth of color. Wozolek finds that schools and, more generally, public spaces serve as "intellectual gatekeepers," often denying space for the identities and values of marginalized youth, specifically those involved in her research. Thus, Wozolek urges a redefinition of intellectualism, one that functions to "recall the colonized ideals under which the status quote continues, as well as the entanglements of the intra-public within colonized norms."

In Chapter 8, "The (Un)Common Intellectual: Possibilities for New Relational Bonds," David Lee Carlson explores public intellectualism outside the traditional boundaries of academia and through matters outside traditional boundaries of intellectual discourse, namely, that of relationships and marriage. In reviewing three contemporary intellectual figures—Esther Perel, Dan Savage, and Michel Foucault—Carlson puts forward the notion of the common intellectual, someone who reconsiders conventional practices of relating and provides an alternative. It is these alternative modes of relation that Carlson sees as the potential for enacting not just new forms of pleasure but also new social orders.

In Chapter 9, "Soil Storying of Public Intellectualism: Ideas Mattering Through Care and Collectivity," Nicole Bowers and Adam T. Clark explore public intellectualism alongside notions of materiality, care, and community. They examine how community organizations and events and their own participation in these spaces function toward intellectual ends. They analogize the public intellectual to that of soil, suggesting that the intellectual needs to cultivate collective care for ideas and values to matter. Ultimately, they argue that collective engagement and care, not just knowledge production, should be the aim of public intellectualism.

The book comes to a close with Chapter 10, "Enacting Anzaldúan Spiritual Activism: Intersecting Personal and Collective Shadows in Public Intellectualism," in which Kakali Bhattacharya and Mildred Boveda draw on autobiographical experience, shadow work, and Gloria Anzaldúa's (2015) notion of *conocimiento* to investigate the "personal and collective shadows" of Western academia. In two separate accounts, Bhattacharya and Boveda demonstrate the wisdom that can accompany experiences of pain and healing connected to the lives and resistance of women of color in hostile, colonial spaces. In doing so, they make space for an intellectualism that embraces the personal and the spiritual in sustained activist work within academia.

Intra-Public Intellectualism represents a single step in a much larger project aimed at rethinking the role and practice of the intellectual in our current and future socio-material-political moments. It is our hope that this book serves as an invitation to others to continue the project of proliferating explorations in public intellectualism; refusing the conventional, the singular, and the resolved; and embracing the entanglement, the multiplicity, and the liveliness of the in-between. It is a project to not only critically but also creatively and experimentally reanimate the entanglements of knowledge, relational existence, responsibilities of academics, and the public domain. In short, this is an invitation to create and re-create *Intra-Public Intellectualism(s)* and their different forms.

References

Ahmed, S. (2004). Affective economies. *Social Text, 22*(2), 117–139.

Anzaldúa, G. E. (2015). now let us shift . . . conocimiento . . . inner work, public acts. In A. Keating (Ed.), *Light in the dark/Luz en lo oscuro: Rewriting identity, spirituality, reality* (pp. 117–160). Duke University Press.

Barad, K. (2014). Diffracting diffraction: Cutting together-apart. *Parallax, 20*(3), 168–187.

Candon, P. (2016). Digital publics: Re-defining 'the civic' and re-locating 'the political.' *New Media and Society, 18*(9), 2133–2138.

Chomsky, N. (1967). The responsibility of intellectuals. *New York Times Review of Books*. https://www.nybooks.com/articles/1967/02/23/a-special-supplement-the-responsibility-of-intelle/

De Landa, M. (1997). *A thousand years of nonlinear history*. Zone Books.

Deleuze, G., & Guattari, F. (1994). *What is philosophy?* (H. Tomlinson & G. Burchell, Trans.). Columbia University Press.

Denzin, N. K. (2017). Critical qualitative inquiry. *Qualitative Inquiry, 23*(1), 8–16.

Denzin, N. K., Lincoln, Y. S., MacLure, M., Otterstad, A. M., Torrance, H., Cannella, G. S., Koro-Ljungberg, M., & McTier, T. (2017). Critical qualitative methodologies: Reconceptualizations and emergent construction. *International Review of Qualitative Research, 10*(4), 482–498.

Derrida, J. (1993). Structure, sign, and play in the discourse of the human sciences. In J. Natoli & L. Hutcheon (Eds.), *A postmodern reader* (pp. 223–242). State University of New York Press.

Descombes, V. (1980). *Modern French philosophy* (L. Scott-Fox & J. M. Harding, Trans.). Cambridge University Press.

Foucault, M. (1988). *Madness and civilization: A history of insanity in the age of reason* (R. Howard, Trans.). Vintage.

Giroux, H. A. (2019). Neoliberalism and the weaponising of language and education. *Race & Class, 61*(1), 26–45.

Glaser, A. (2019, June 6). Bring back the golden age of broadcast regulation. *Slate*. https://slate.com/technology/2019/06/youtube-facebook-hate-speech-regulation-how.html

Gramsci, A. (1971). *Selections from the prison notebooks* (Q. Hoare & G. N. Smith, Trans.). Lawrence and Wishart.

Habermas, J. (1993). Modernity—an incomplete project. In T. Docherty (Ed.), *Postmodernism: A reader* (pp. 98–109). Columbia University Press.

Illing, S. (2019, November 16). The post-truth prophets. *Vox*. https://www.vox.com/features/2019/11/11/18273141/postmodernism-donald-trump-lyotard-baudrillard

Koopman, C. (2013). *Genealogy as critique: Foucault and the problems of modernity*. Indiana University Press.

Koro-Ljungberg, M. (2015). *Reconceptualizing qualitative research: Methodologies without methodology*. Sage Publications.

Koro-Ljungberg, M., & Cannella, G. S. (2017). Critical qualitative inquiry: History, methodologies, possibilities. *International Review of Qualitative Research, 10*(4), 327–339.

Lather, P. (1991). *Getting smart: Feminist research and pedagogy within the postmodern*. Routledge.

Law, J. (2004). *After method: Mess in social science research*. Routledge.

Lenz Taguchi, H. (2013). Images of thinking in feminist materialisms: Ontological divergences and the production of researcher subjectivities. *International Journal of Qualitative Studies in Education, 26*(6), 706–716.

Lyotard, J.-F. (1984). *The postmodern condition: A report on knowledge* (G. Bennington & B. Massumi, Trans.). University of Minnesota Press.

MacLure, M. (2015). The new materialism: The thorn in the flesh of critical qualitative inquiry. In G. Cannella, M. S. Perez, & P. A. Pasque (Eds.), *Critical qualitative inquiry: Foundations and futures* (pp. 93–112). Routledge.

Massumi, B. (2010, November). On critique. *Inflections: A Journal of Research Creation, 4*, 337–340.

Metz, C. (2019, November 24). Internet companies prepare to fight the 'deepfake' future. *New*

York Times. https://www.nytimes.com/2019/11/24/technology/tech-companies-deepfakes.html

Pichai, S. (2019, June 10). *Exclusive interview: Google CEO Sundar Pichai defends YouTube practices* [Video]. YouTube. https://www.youtube.com/watch?v=igYXPKctRyw&feature=emb_title

Roose, K., & Conger, K. (2019, June 5). YouTube to remove thousands of videos pushing extreme views. *New York Times*. https://www.nytimes.com/2019/06/05/business/youtube-remove-extremist-videos.html

Ross, A. (Ed.). (1988). *Universal abandon?: The politics of postmodernism*. University of Minnesota Press.

Said, E. (1994). *Representations of the intellectual: The 1993 Reith Lectures*. Vintage Books.

Shaviro, S. (2014). *The universe of things: On speculative realism*. University of Minnesota Press.

St. Pierre, E. A. (2011). Post qualitative research: The critique and the coming after. In N. K. Denzin & Y. S. Lincoln (Eds.), *The SAGE handbook of qualitative research* (pp. 611–625). Sage Publications.

Truman, S. E. (2019). Feminist new materialisms. In P. A. Atkinson, S. Delamont, M. A. Hardy, M. Williams (Eds.), *The SAGE encyclopedia of research methods*. SAGE. doi: 10.4135/9781526421036808740

Watts, V. (2013). Indigenous place-thought and agency amongst humans and non humans (first woman and sky woman go on a European world tour!). *Decolonization: Indigeneity, Education & Society, 2*(1), 20–34.

Speeding Up

Looking back
Full speed ahead
A Sankofa bird in mid-morning flight
Soaring between
truth
and
fiction

ONE

Intellectual Publics | Public Intellectuals

M. Francyne Huckaby, Texas Christian University
Jonathan W. Crocker, Texas Christian University

(Re)setting

IN THIS CHAPTER, WE EXPLORE public(s) and intellectual(s) through iterative (re)workings. Like Barad (2010), we question the presumed continuity of political thought and wonder, "What if it were otherwise?" (p. 240); what spaces open if we reject binaries that offer polarized opposites and the strong illusion that the choice is one or the other, us or them, here or there, deliberation or antagonism? We refuse the singular, linear argument about public intellectuals for intellectual publics. (Re)setting over multiple iterations and imagining in multiplicity, we offer "fragments constituting shifting relationality" (Koro-Ljungberg, 2018, p. 16).

Mathematically, iterations (Bloom & Ésik, 1993) are algebraic operations that create sequences of all morphisms by repeatedly applying the solution of the equation to the same computation that produced it. Iteration theory is essential for computer programming and is the convention for naming new and assuringly improved versions of computer programs (1.0, 1.1, 2.0, 2.1, 2.2, . . .). For Barad (2010), iterations are not linear or sequential but heterogeneous, differentiating, entangling, unending reconfiguration, enfolding, materialization. They are (re)openings more "akin to how electrons experience the world" (Barad, 2010, p. 244). We are in agreement with Barad that "[o]ne is too few, two is too many" (2010, p. 251). In this space between one and two, we consider the repetend "in decimal arithmetic repeated incidences" that "continue the generation of numbers through all time, you have these repetends forever occurring" (Clarke, 1872, loc 165).

We are opening possibilities for spaces, for other ways of being with(in) publics and intellectual(s). Instead of insisting on political engagement as it has been assumed to be, we resist given political strategies, critique, direction, and conclusion. We sidestep the simplistic and casual. What is herein, then, is relational, multiple, overlapping, and shifting. In essence, we deal other hands as offerings for other plays (Foucault, 1997) and imaginings that relinquish rules and strategies as they have been. As we face the impossibility of consensus and spurn antagonism, we seek spaces for intellectual publics to better understand our political opponents through discursive conflict and further our political goals based on this knowledge. In this regard, we strive toward agonic politics to critique the existing order and to work toward the construction of "new articulations and new institutions" (Mouffe, 2013, p. 11).

1.1 Intellectuals

We are in agreement with Gramsci (1989) that "all men are intellectuals" (p. 115)—provided a transformation of *men* into categories inclusive of all known and yet-to-come genders along with their infinite intersectionality (Crenshaw, 1991). We also caution against limiting intellectual capacities to *Homo sapiens*. Indeed, too many of us (humans) have become numb to the wisdom, knowledge, and pleas from the more-than-human that constitute this world. Thus, the distinctions of intellectual, public intellectual, and anti-intellectual are about social function(s) and role(s), more so than capacity, ability, or even species. As Gramsci (1989) noted, "nonintellectuals do not exist" (p. 115). We all have much to offer about how we conceive the world(s) we inhabit and are implicated in sustaining it (them), modifying it (them), or bringing forth new ways of thinking and being (Kurtz, 2019). Intellectuals, in function and relation, are especially crucial during crises that demand deep insight. Gramsci differentiated the traditional from the organic intellectual, Foucault (2000) the universal and specific, and here we (Huckaby and Crocker) do so with public intellectuals and intellectual publics.

Gramsci's (1989) traditional intellectual "given by the man [*sic*] of letters, the philosopher, the artist" and "journalists, who claim to be" such (p. 116) is similar to Foucault's (2000) universal intellectual as spokesperson and writer for the collective consciousness, master narrative, and truth. For Bauman (cited in Kurtz, 2019), they are interpreters for the public. These forms—traditional, universal, and interpreter—are consistent with "historically masculinist understanding[s] of the public intellectual as a lone figure looming large in the public eye" (Kurtz, 2019, p. 180), are more common in Europe than the

United States (Moseley, 2019), and are a more typical form of intellectual in the United States.

Created with every social group, Gramsci's organic intellectual offers a group "homogeneity and an awareness of its own function" economically, socially, and politically (Kurtz, 2019, p. 113). Struggles over ideology are key, especially in efforts to obtain dominance. When a social group successfully elaborates its own organic intellectuals, it is more efficacious in ideologically assimilating and conquering traditional intellectuals. Political parties, for example, are such mechanisms for "welding together" political intellectuals from a particular group's organic and traditional intellectuals (Gramsci, cited in Forgacs, 2000, p. 310). Political intellectuals may come to believe "they are the state," which is consequential for the state in actuality (Gramsci, cited in Forgacs, p. 310). Repetition is key for political intellectuals, tirelessly repeating their message is instrumental in "working on popular mentality" to replace "common sense and old conceptions of the world" with their own (Gramsci, cited in Forgacs, p. 340). While this approach is efficacious, we advocate for a different way.

A 20th-century transformation of Foucault's (2000) universal intellectual, the specific intellectual is immediately and concretely situated within struggles and concerned with the status, economic role, and political function of truth. They appropriate local knowledge(s) in political struggles. Black women thinkers serve as a model here—Audre Lorde, Ida B. Wells, Anna Julia Cooper, Barbara Jordan, Toni Morrison, Maya Angelou—as they produce "forms of knowledge for and with communities involved in the Black freedom struggle" while addressing the "struggles and brilliance of black womanhood and black life" (Wright, 2019, p. 173). As Huckaby (2007) has noted elsewhere, "the specific intellectual brings other forms and ways of knowing . . . and can expose knowledge unavailable to universal intellectuals" (p. 514), whereas the organic intellectual brings unity and economic, social, and political clarity to a group. Like the organic intellectual, specific intellectuals face dangers, fail to garner sufficient support, or risk manipulation for political purposes. Specific intellectuals work against the state or serve it, benefit or harm local communities, create or destroy. In these times of effective political intellectuals, an understanding of intellectuals and publics in conceptual and practical ways is required.

1.9999999999
repetend
    a number
replicated
    a decimal
recurring
    a word
restated
    an image
repeated
    an idea
recapped
    a form
recapitulated
    into infinity
reiterated
    irregular, unlike a refrain
rehashed
    anywhere and often
redone

1.2 Doxa

Doxa (δόξα) is a form of undisclosed common knowledge both distinct from *episteme* (ἐπιστήμη) or scientific knowledge and in contrast to *aletheia* (ἀλήθεια) or unconcealed knowledge. Often defined as common opinion, doxa is the foundation of actionable social knowledge. Doxa is what is taken for granted, described by Bourdieu (1984) as "the ordinary acceptance of the usual order which goes without saying and therefore usually goes unsaid" (p. 424). Along these lines, doxa restricts dominated publics to either "silence or a borrowed language" that is manufactured, bought, sold, and traded within the space of symbolic exchange (Bourdieu, 1984, p. 462). Doxa, for Bourdieu (1990, pp. 66–68), is a mechanism of symbolic power, a framework of common sense that (re)constructs a seemingly objective language game in which publics develop symbolic capital. A frequent critique of Bourdieu's deterministic formulation of doxa revolves around its devaluation of agency in that it does not leave much room for conscious resistance (Bourdieu & Eagleton, 1992; Myles, 2004; Smith, 2001). For instance, Eagleton (Bourdieu & Eagleton, 1992, p. 114) asks, "Is *doxa* not itself a more contradictory affair?" Even if doxa is concealed, Eagleton's question implies the possibility of evolving, multiple doxas operating side by side, functioning as interconnected *para-doxas* that converge and diverge in a shared space of conflict.

As a term, *intellectual publics* signifies a relationship between discursive activity and this doxic knowledge production. For Warner (2002), publics "do not exist apart from the discourse that addresses them" and are "understood to be an ongoing space of encounter for discourse" (p. 62). It is what takes place in these fluid spaces of encounter that constitute the social imaginary, an ongoing re-clarification of what is—or presumably should be—held *in common*. As these pre-reflexive knowledges circulate through networked publics (Asen, 2017), they "emphasize different relationships and construct alternative connections among people, advancing potentially competing visions of a public good" (p. 334). It should be noted that this competition is not antagonistic—in which publics seek the destruction of an enemy—but agonistic in which space for counterhegemonic plurality is maintained (Mouffe, 2013). In short, what constitutes publics is not their respective group commonality but the variable, undisclosed knowledges that move among them.

Therefore, doxic knowledge is not expressed through public exposure but through a shared (un)acceptance of the social imaginary that exerts a prevailing influence on inter- and intra-public discourse. This influence is necessarily multiple insofar as publics are always multiple. Common sense as a space of doxic conflict is also a space of potential consensual dissent or dissensual consent, and therefore a para-doxic space of exchange.

1.99999999

Intellectual publics are not objective Truth holding conglomerates. Instead, their public-intellectual character stems from a para-doxic truth-deciding function wherein decisions about truth(s) go (un)resolved in the frictive space of discourse.

1.3 Paradoxa and Aporia

Janus (see Figure 1.1), the Roman god of beginnings and endings, openings and closings, and thresholds, is not limited by binary oppositions. Depicted with two faces looking in opposite directions, Janus sees behind and before, the past–present–future within spacetimemattering. Janus offers alternatives to the traps of binaries and paradoxes, as does the Taoist Yin–Yang and West African Sankofa bird (see Figure 1.2). The Sankofa bird is a West African mythical creature. Its name, translated from Akan (a Ghanaian language) to English, instructs us to go back and get what was left behind. The Sankofa bird uses its head to look back and its beak to pick up what was left as it returns to the present.

Paradox is the seemingly illogical coexistence of contradictions that do simultaneously exist. From the ancient Greek παράδοξου (*paradoxa*), it is a received opinion or expectation that is contrary to belief (Baggini & Fosl, 2003). The features of paradoxes include a set of mutually inconsistent propositions, each of which seems true; an argument with good assumptions and reasoning but false conclusion; and an unacceptable conclusion born of seemingly good premises and reasoning (Cuonzo, 2014). Aporia (ἄπορῐᾰ) is also about contradiction, perplexity, the impassable, rhetorical doubt, and philosophical puzzlement. Paradoxa and aporia are not simply inescapable; they also

Figure 1.1. Janus Coin (2007).
Retrieved from https://commons.wikimedia.org/wiki/File:Janus_coin.png.

require other ways of thinking and being than those of casual habituation. They force us to examine premises and arguments in the effort to resolve—or not—the contradiction(s) posed, "to scrutinize what seems so obviously right" (Baggini & Fosl, 2003, p. 110).

Paradoxes are only (re)solved after identification and rejection of the mistaken reasoning or erroneous assumption and aporia in doing and (un)making amid knowing and unknowing. For Koro-Ljungberg (2010), this is about validity becoming "possible in doing the impossible" (p. 609). We enter such possible profundities every day simply because we are as we are, for we ourselves are paradoxes that breathe. Indeed, breathing is a paradox, requiring inhaling and exhaling to be whole (Palmer, 1997). Out of biological necessity, we innately resolve the opposition of the exhale and the inhale with autonomic shifting between the two to breathe. Our existence is dependent on a paradox. Walking is similarly paradoxical. Young new to walking struggle between standing against gravity and succumbing to it as they move with unsure feet and legs. Walking requires both standing and falling, shifting weight and balance from one leg to the other to overcome falling. Eventually the rhythm and balance are found. The para-doxa is selected, and the ideology is reflected as a result.

Figure 1.2. Brooklyn Museum 45.11.5 Gold Weight in Form of Sankofa Bird. Retrieved from https://commons.wikimedia.org/wiki/File:Brooklyn_Museum_45.11.5_Gold_Weight_in_Form_of_Sankofa_Bird.jpg.

1.9999999

> *Intellectual publics* stay within para-doxa and aporia, suspended "between too many good answers" (Sorenson, 2003, p. xii), allowing for "possibilities to develop . . . at the times of theoretical confusion, loss of power, privilege, and logic" (Koro-Ljungberg, 2010, p. 609). These conditions open space for intellectual publics to develop—much like falling between balancing makes for walking—means for moving and taking on more complex, multifaceted work.

1.4 Demagoguery

Intellectual publics are susceptible to demagogic influences—perhaps even more so than the individuals who compose them. Roberts-Miller (2019b, p. 173) defines demagoguery as the polarizing discourse that promises stability, certainty, and escape from the responsibilities of rhetoric by framing public policy in terms of the degree to which and the means by which (not whether) the out-group should be punished/scapegoated for the current problems of the in-group. Publics, then, by virtue of their discursive networks, are not immune to the extremes of in-group thinking. It seems that a plurality of truths and the recognition of this multiplicity necessitates a multipolarization and an acceptance of the conflictual positions that are inherent in politics. Problems arise, however, when this recognition breeds a sense of instability, uncertainty, and entrapment that too often results in an antagonistic retreat to the perceived safety of one's in-group. A reluctance to engage rhetorically in a multipolar political environment tends to lead to simplification via affiliation, a reduction of myriad perspectives into onto-epistemic binaries—*us* and what *we believe* versus *them* and what *they believe*—to avoid argument altogether.

This reduction to binaries is often coupled with *naïve realism* or the "belief that our beliefs are unmediated representations of the world," whereas others' beliefs are open to distortion, bias, and manipulation (Roberts-Miller, 2019b, p. 19). Simply put, this is an epistemic view that (a) *I/we have the right evidence and have drawn the proper conclusions* and (b) *they have it all wrong.* It would appear that *intellectual publics* should find ways to actively resist binarization of their own group and their perceived allies and a group defined as a union of their political enemies. But a para-doxic framework emerges out of the demagogic discourse of political publics whose beliefs run counter to one's own—demagoguery seems to beget more demagoguery, more in-group (re)location, and a reduction in productive democratic discourse across and within networked publics. Too often, however, critics of demagogic rhetoric point to charismatic leaders as the source of a given public's demagoguery when it is the obsession with charismatic leaders that supports the ongoing cycle of demagoguery (Roberts-Miller, 2019). While it is true that demagogues seek to "distort reality, meaning, and public sentiment" through the use of "weaponized communication" (Mercieca, 2019, p. 272), always looking for the demagogue masks the underlying rhetorical mechanisms through which a charismatic leader maintains political power (Roberts-Miller, 2019a, p. 243).

1.999999

Intellectual publics engage in multipolar policy discussions without resorting to demagoguery, onto-epistemic binaries, or *naïve realism*. More important, these publics can work to embrace multiplicity, reject out-group violence, and adopt a position of epistemic humility even—and especially—when confronting their own susceptibility to demagogic tactics.

1.5 Agonism

While intellectual publics may develop within group deliberative practices, they are keenly aware of the potentiality for antagonism (Roberts-Miller, 2019) with entities and groups positioned against them. They resist the overpowering, eradication, or annihilation of their opponents via discursive, material, or violent means as a strategy to forward their own political goals. Instead, they engage in the work to acknowledge the oppositional stance, and yet forward their own political goals. Taking heed of Arendt's (1954) warning, intellectual publics avoid educating political opponents to their own worldview. Instead, they see their opponents as already educated adults for "the word 'education' has an evil sound in politics; there is the pretense of education, when the real purpose is coercion without the use of force" (Arendt, 1954, pp. 173–174). As they steel themselves against demagoguery, they also reject using it as an oppositional tactic.

Agonism opens up spaces for coexisting and clarifying political positions through conflict without having to seek a forestalled consensus or resort to obliterating opponents. Dave Chappelle, in his Mark Twain Prize for American Humor acceptance speech (Robinson et al., 2020), explained agonism by first noting the ways comics are organic and specific intellectuals: "I don't think there's an opinion that exists in this country that is not represented in a comedy club by somebody. Each and every one of you has a champion in the room" (see timestamps 01:16:37–01:16:49). He continued by offering an example that distinguished antagonism from agonism:

> We watch you guys fight, but when we're together, we talk it out. I know comics that are very racist and I watch them on stage, and everyone's laughing, and I'm like, "Mmmm that motherfucker means that shit." Don't get mad at them, don't hate them. We go upstairs and have a beer. And sometimes I even appreciate the artistry that they paint their racist opinions with. (01:16:49—01:17:20)

Chappelle then set up his punch line to clarify agonism, "Man, it's not that serious. The First Amendment is first for reason" (01:17:20—1:17:25), and delivers it via antagonism: "The second amendment is just in case the first one doesn't work out. We've got to let some air out of the ball, man, the country's getting a little tight" (1:17:25—1:17:38).

Agonism exists at the in-between, agreement–antagonism, and consensus–dissensus. Agreement is a consensual realm, while antagonism is one of dissent. Agonism, therefore, is born on a plane between consensual dissent and dissensual consent (alf874, 2013). Agonism requires of us a developing comfort *with* and understanding *of* those things incommensurable.

1.99999

This shift from individual work of public intellectuals who interpret, engage, and share within public forums to that of intellectual publics repositions authorship and authority from the individual to the public. Such opening of shared thinking and acting removes the expert from the pedestal and asks us to identify and recognize a multitude of ways, spaces, and styles for public intellectualism (Alderman & Inwood, 2019). It offers spaces where roles, say, that of academics, fall away in favor of a space where publics are academic. We call for a rethinking and expanding of academic freedom, not just for faculty in institutions of higher education but also for "academic freedoms in a larger cultural field and social environment" (Göle, 2017, p. 879).

1.6 Danger and Truth

ideas notions
that make the world
are made by it, within it

some prefer to keep them hidden
unseen denied unknown
muted unheard forgotten
turned down
extinguish
silenced

risky when
spoken drawn
written down, preserved
exile obliteration exterminate annihilation
never certain which way it may go
for teller or the status quo

1.9999

Intellectual publics ask us to make allowances in spaces with others that counter what has come to seem natural. The work of crafting an argument that can be heard and of attuning ourselves to a variety of modes of expression becomes (un) easy communal work. It requires learning to trust and respect, to hear people out, and to speak not just to share but to allow for coauthorship. As authors and audience, words and ideas mix as means to move towards action. (Kurtz, 2019)

1.7 Civility

When *intellectual publics* take up contested issues and work to foreground complex and multipolar perspectives, the way in which they approach the task is often regulated by social conventions and a given set of rules of civic engagement. Often these rules adhere to some version of *civility*—a term that connotes good discipline, character, and decorum as civilized and their paired opposites as uncivilized. Along these lines, civility points to an imperialist history in which settler colonialists mark civil society as white and marginalized bodies and their dominated societies as uncivil, savage, or barbarous (Thiranagama et al., 2018, pp. 164–165). As Itagaki (2016) argues, the "politics of civility" in the post–civil rights era often appears as a "discourse of racial civility," which she defines as "the behaviors or practices expected of racialized subjects in order to assimilate into Whiteness or achieve the status and protections of U.S. citizenship" (p. 6). As one element of the neoliberal structure, a myopic approach to civility enacts a color-blind, gender-neutral, and heteronormative paradigm for political intervention. As others (Alexander & Hammers, 2019; Lozano-Reich & Cloud, 2009; Stuckey & O'Rourke, 2014) have suggested, these calls for civility often function as silencing mechanisms that work to discount activist movements and publics who represent a threat to the status quo.

Intellectual publics have learned from the legacy of the civil rights movement of the 1950s and 1960s, a period frequently sterilized of its "radical, militant nonviolence" and its commitment to disruptions of the political and legal order (Newkirk, 2018). Along these lines, *intellectual publics* continue this legacy by rejecting the "false peace of dominance" (Serwer, 2019) and instead chart experimental paths that upend regulation and amend convention in the name of justice.

1.999

Intellectual publics are aware of ever-shifting contexts that demand (un)civil approaches to political (dis)order. *Intellectual publics* take up civility itself as a site of resistance and critique with the understanding that calls to be civil are often mechanisms to comport publics to forms of external-bureaucratic and internal-rhetorical exclusion (Young, 2000). *Intellectual publics* continually (re) test the boundaries of civility through protest—a collective assertion that they will no longer remain silent and obedient.

1.8 Style and Practice

Public intellectuals invoke and address their audience(s) in ways that facilitate being heard and understood. Organic and specific intellectuals, given their relations to segments of the public, have more intimate understandings of their audiences than intellectuals of the universal, traditional, or translation varieties. This intimacy facilitates the understanding of beliefs, expectations, and attitudes between audience and intellectual and may be used for the benefit or to the detriment of the public the intellectual intends. The universal and traditional intellectual is less likely to have such organic connections to contexts, worldviews, and histories and therefore is more likely to invoke audiences. As "created fiction[s]" (Long, cited in Ede & Lunsford, 1984), invoked audiences require intellectuals to offer cues that define expected audience role(s). For public intellectuals who are writers, "the audience is not *there* in the sense that the speaker's audience is present" (Ede & Lunsford, 1984, p. 161).

Intellectual publics, by contrast, are simultaneously speakers, writers, and audience. At times, they may speak to broader audiences, which they will need to address and/or invoke. Dr. King's (1964) *Letter from Birmingham Jail* serves as an example of writing for an outside audience:

> While confined here in the Birmingham city jail, I came across your recent statement calling my activities "unwise and untimely." . . . since I feel that you are men [*sic*] of genuine good will and that your criticisms are sincerely set forth, I want to try to answer your statement in what I hope will be patient and reasonable terms. . . . The purpose of our direct-action programs to create a situation so crisis-packed that it will inevitably open the door to negotiation. I therefore concur with you in your call for negotiation. (p. 80)

This excerpt serves as just one example, and in no way do we claim it as an example of what all intellectual publics should do. Audiences and authors require different ways and methods of speaking, writing, and expressing—words, performances, protests, petitions, marches, silence, boycotts, direct action, sit-ins, occupying, refusals, conferences, publications, and so on. Audiences are not monolithic or unitary and have subgroups that respond differently to modes of expression. We do suggest that intellectual publics avoid antagonistic styles of engagement by treating "argument as a form of sport . . . delighting like puppies in tugging and tearing at anyone who comes near them" (Plato, 1973, p. 309). Again, we prefer the openings agonism allows.

With intellectual publics, the functions and actions of authoring exist among the group. Speaking, listening, and respect are equally important, especially when members are likely to misunderstand each other. Such a form of engagement is less common in contemporary society with our large populations, mediated technological existence, neoliberal individuality, and hypervigilant competition.

1.99

Figure 1.3. QR Code: Audio Selection from Critical Qualitative Inquiry: Partnerships, Obligations, and Activism in the Politics of Resistance panel discussion at the *2019 International Congress of Qualitative Inquiry.*

1.9 Too Few and Too Many

We understand this project as one contribution in an ongoing attempt to open space for solutions rather than solutions themselves. Along these lines, we believe these theoretical, conceptual, practical, imagery, wordplay, poetic, and media fragments direct us toward open spaces for exploration.

0.99 References

Alderman, D. H., & Inwood, J. F. J. (2019). The need for public intellectuals in the Trump era and beyond: Strategies for communication, engagement, and advocacy. *The Professional Geographer, 7*(1), 145–151.

Alexander, B. K., & Hammers, M. (2019). An invitation to rhetoric: A generative dialogue on performance, possibility, and feminist potentialities in invitational rhetoric. *Cultural Studies↔Critical Methodologies, 19*(1), 5–14.

alf874. (2013, March 13). Activist strategies: Agreement, agonism, antagonism. https://window874.wordpress.com/2013/03/13/activist-strategies-agreement-agonism-antagonism-2/

Arendt, H. (1954). *Between past and future: Eight exercises in political thought*. Penguin.

Asen, R. (2017). Neoliberalism, the public sphere, and a public good. *Quarterly Journal of Speech, 103*(4), 329–349.

Baggini, J., & Fosl, P. S. (2003). *The philosopher's toolkit: A compendium of philosophical concepts and methods*. Blackwell Publishing.

Barad, K. (2010). Quantum entanglements and hauntological relations of inheritance: Dis/continuities, spacetime enfoldings, and justice-to-come. *Derrida Today, 3*(2), 240–268.

Bloom, S. L., & Ésik, Z. (1993). *Iteration theories: The equational logic of interactive processes*. Springer-Verlag.

Bourdieu, P. (1984). *Distinction* (R. Nice, Trans.). Harvard University Press.

Bourdieu, P. (1990). *The logic of practice*. Stanford University Press.

Bourdieu, P., & Eagleton, T. (1992). Doxa and common life. *New Left Review, 191*(1), 111–121.

Clarke, M. (1872). *Human repetend*. Amazon Kindle: A Public Domain Book.

Crenshaw, K. (1991). Mapping the margins: Intersectionality, identity politics, and violence against women of color. *Stanford Law Review, 43*(6), 1241–1299.

Cuonzo, M. (2014). *Paradox*. MIT Press.

Ede, L., & Lunsford, A. (1984). Audience addressed/audience invoked: The role of audience in composition theory and pedagogy. *College Composition and Communication, 35*(2), 155–171.

Forgacs, D. (2000). *The Gramsci reader: Selected writings 1916–1935*. New York University Press.

Foucault, M. (1997). The ethics of the concern for the self as practice of freedom. In P. Rabinow (Ed.), *Michel Foucault: Ethics: Subjectivity and truth* (Vol. 1, pp. 281–302). The New Press.

Foucault, M. (2000). Truth and power. In J. D. Faubion (Ed.), *Michel Foucault: Power* (Vol. 3, pp. 111–133). The New Press.

Göle, N. (2017). Undesirable public intellectuals. *Globalizations, 14*(6), 877–883.

Gramsci, A. (1989). Prison notebooks: The intellectuals: The formation of the intellectuals. In R. S. Gottlied (Ed.), *An anthology of Western Marxism: From Lukács and Gramsci to socialist-feminism* (pp. 113–119). Oxford University Press.

Huckaby, M. F. (2007). A conversation on practices of the self within relations of power: For scholars who speak dangerous truths. *International Journal of Qualitative Studies in Education, 20*(5), 513–529.

Itagaki, L. M. (2016). *Civil racism: The 1992 Los Angeles rebellion and the crisis of racial burnout*. University of Minnesota Press.

King, M. L., Jr. (1964). *Why we can't wait*. Signet.

Koro-Ljungberg, M. (2010). Validity, responsibility, and aporia. *Qualitative Inquiry, 16*(8), 603–610.

Koro-Ljungberg, M. (2018). Thinking, willing and judging in (post)qualitative research: A series of re-settings. In M. F. Huckaby (Ed.), *Making research public in troubled times* (pp. 15–30). Myers Education Press.

Kurtz, H. E. (2019). Public intellectualism as assemblage. *The Professional Geographer, 71*(1), 179–183.

Lozano-Reich, N. M., & Cloud, D. L. (2009). The uncivil tongue: Invitational rhetoric and the problem of inequality. *Western Journal of Communication, 73*(2), 220–226.

Mercieca, J. R. (2019). Dangerous demagogues and weaponized communication. *Rhetoric Society Quarterly, 49*(3), 264–279.

Moseley, W. G. (2019). Trump's America or the people's America? A view from the periphery. *The Professional Geographer, 71*(1), 152–156.

Mouffe, C. (2013). *Agonistics: Thinking the world politically*. Verso Books.

Myles, J. F. (2004). From doxa to experience: Issues in Bourdieu's adoption of Husserlian phenomenology. *Theory, Culture & Society, 21*(2), 91–107.

Newkirk, V. R., II. (2018, June 28). Protest isn't civil. *The Atlantic*. https://www.theatlantic.com/ideas/archive/2018/06/the-civility-instinct/563978/

Palmer, P. (1997). *The courage to teach: Exploring the inner landscape of a teacher's life*. Wiley.

Plato. (1973). *The republic*. Penguin.

Roberts-Miller, P. (2019a). Demagoguery, charismatic leadership, and the force of habit. *Rhetoric Society Quarterly, 49*(3), 233–247.

Roberts-Miller, P. (2019b). *Rhetoric and demagoguery*. SIU Press.

Robinson, C., Matuza, M. B., & Winer, M. (Producers). (2020, January 7). Dave Chappelle [Episode 1]. In *The Kennedy Center Mark Twain Prize*. https://www.pbs.org/video/dave-chappelle-the-kennedy-center-mark-twain-prize-qbmxgn/

Serwer, A. (2019, December). Civility is overrated. *The Atlantic*. https://www.theatlantic.com/magazine/archive/2019/12/adam-serwer-civility/600784/

Smith, A. T. (2001). The limitations of doxa: Agency and subjectivity from an archaeological point of view. *Journal of Social Archaeology, 1*(2), 155–171.

Sorenson, R. (2003). *A brief history of the paradox: Philosophy and the labyrinths of the mind*. Oxford University Press.

Stuckey, M. E., & O'Rourke, S. P. (2014). Civility, democracy, and national politics. *Rhetoric & Public Affairs, 17*(4), 711–736.

Thiranagama, S., Kelly, T., & Forment, C. (2018). Introduction: Whose civility? *Anthropological Theory, 18*(2–3), 154–174.

Warner, M. (2002). Publics and counterpublics. *Public Culture, 14*(1), 49–90.

Wright, W. J. (2019). The public is intellectual. *The Professional Geographer, 7*(1), 172–178.

Young, I. M. (2000). *Inclusion and democracy*. Oxford University Press.

Looking Forward, Looking Back

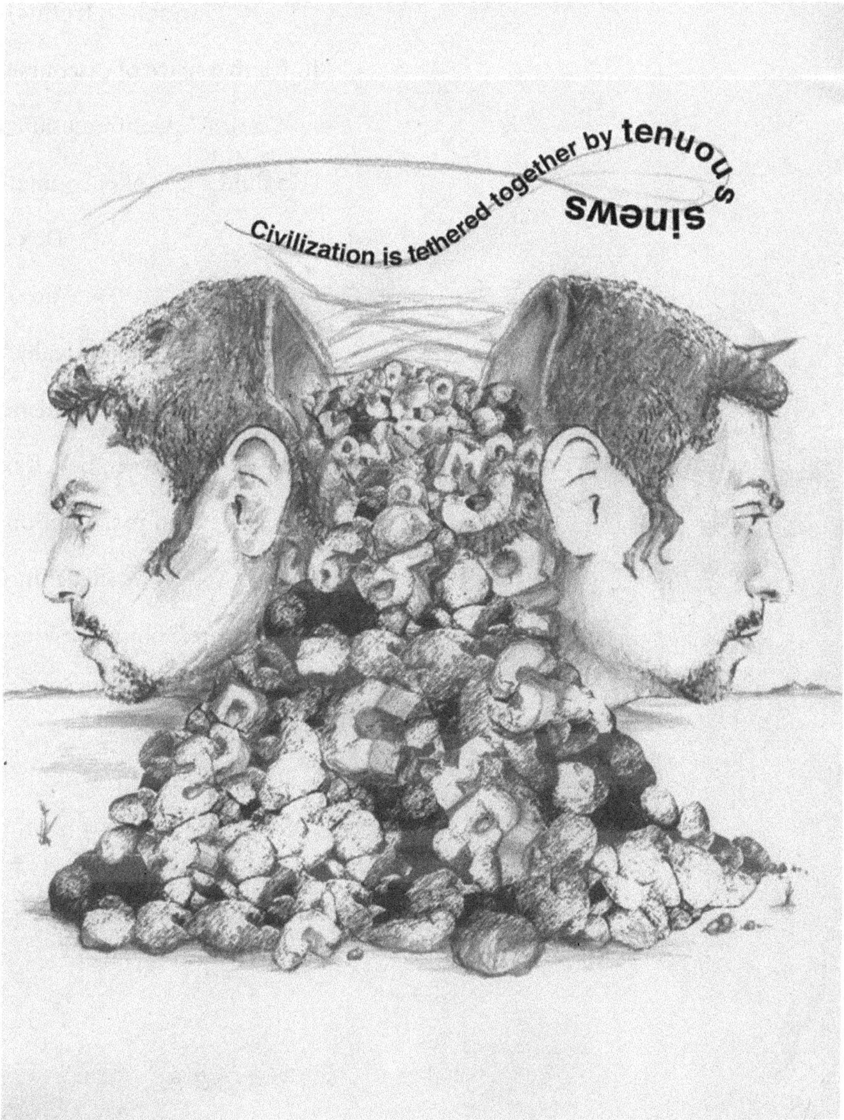

Unresolved Truth(s)

Unresolved truth(s)

In frictive space of discourse

Contradictions

In fluid space of encounter

Doxa

Para-doxa

My common reality

Uncommon agonism

Between belief(s)

Beyond presumption

Reaching

ahead/before/behind/besides.

Differing in Discourse

Iterations
At once
There
Not there
Repeated
With a difference
Differed
Deferred
Refracted
Reflected
Expanded
Enlarged
Recurring
Put into circulation
Endlessly
Relentlessly
Fractals
Fragmenting
Reality
Polarized

Announced
Uttered
Spoken
Not spoken
Cannot be spoken
Anything can be spoken
Spokes
Of the wheel
Turning
Endlessly
Saturated
With meaning
Therefore
Rendered
Meaningless
Toxic
Doxic
Paradoxic
Discourse

TWO

An Ecology of Truth(s) Telling Amid the Post-Truth Turn

Joseph D. Sweet, University of North Carolina at Pembroke
Taylor M. Kessner, Arizona State University

Environmental Threats

EVERY DAY ACROSS THE UNITED States, graduate students meet in cramped study spaces and banter over ordinary things: class assignments inviting them into their fields, research reports illuminating new ways of working problems, and techniques for workshopping intriguing questions. But, in 2017, fears replaced these and other typical watercooler conversations: A Republican tax bill sat on congresspeople's desks, and the future of graduate education appeared in peril. Although members of Congress eventually shouted down the section of the bill that reclassified tuition waivers as taxable income—a move that could have made postgraduate study all but impossible for all but the deeply privileged—its significance was not lost on students. Nor was it lost on their mentors. Larry Lyon, vice provost and dean of Baylor University's graduate school, described the plan as "probably the most serious threat to doctoral education we have ever experienced" (Sullivan, 2017, para. 6). The conservative faction of politics in the United States sent a clear message: We will repopulate the academe with ideologues, and funding will be our weapon of choice. As such, the project of public intellectualism under the auspices of academia changes dramatically as funding sources become scarce. The lack of funding remains among many concurrent shifts in the environment that create how academics go about doing public work.

Among these forces, the 2016 presidential election highlighted broad concerns regarding the place of knowledge and informed action in the United States. Some view the defeat of established political and social decency at the hands of "fake news," "alternative facts," and White supremacy as a watershed moment for public intellectualism. We wonder how the events of November 2016 intersect with larger onto-epistemological shifts regarding truths and the place of intellectual work. Specifically, we wonder how the project of public intellectualism shifts as "truth" is becoming ever more subjective, competitive, and conflicted.

Although this remains, we maintain that the project of public intellectualism can represent a unique contribution for and within pluralist democracy. As detailed in the following, Said (1996) and Foucault (Deleuze & Foucault, 1977) championed a traditional view of public intellectuals as those willing and able to identify the ways in which people dismissed to the margins suffer at the hands of the privileged. The privileged, then, reinforce their positions at the table where contradictions are supposedly taken up (but more likely ignored) and social goods distributed (Gee, 2018; Marx, 1867/1992; Zinn, 1998). Today, the project of critical qualitative inquiry (Denzin, 2017) is also predicated on the recognition that power is structured and institutionalized in ways that seemingly inevitably privilege some at the expense of others. Those engaged in this project understand scholarship as activism. But such activist scholarship—at least at the level of higher education—can thrive only if it meets certain criteria. Namely, public funding—the same funding on the chopping block in the 2017 Republican tax bill—remains necessary for this work because such scholarship works only if it remains unbeholden to outside interests.

Yet, the broader environment within which the ivory tower operates has shifted dramatically. As with the printing press, new communications technologies have dramatically altered how people find and access information. The industrialized written word shifted the locus of knowledge from the clergy and the bureaucracy to the printed word. Although this paved the way for the development of public intellectuals, a more recent shift from books to online platforms such as Twitter, YouTube, and Facebook has relocated knowledge away from traditionally valued knowledge and ways of knowing to anyone with a smartphone. These changes in media outlets correspond with concurrent shifts in how knowledge is produced and how truths are becoming ever more subjective. Thus, those engaging in the project of public intellectualism must consider these changes so that their work can reach beyond the ivory tower. We, therefore, propose reframing the project of public intellectualism through De Landa's (1997) framework of nonlinear history. In particular, we take up De Landa's ecological view of human history. We adapt De Landa's view to consider those who seek to do the work of public intellectualism as organisms within a broader ecology in which the public intellectual acts and is acted on. This view largely dismisses the notion of "fittest design," per se, as fitness is dynamic and constantly shifting just as the co-organisms likewise shift within their shared environment. Within such an ecological view, hierarchies and meshworks constantly form and unform, ossify and melt, in response to the shifting landscape in which they either persevere in one form or another or return to a world of spirit and energy. In such a view, the ecology in which people do their work is formed and reformed by bifurcations of energy, which produces possibilities for endless and multiple stable states. To be clear, we are not doing an ecological analysis. Instead, we use key concepts from De Landa to think about changes in the project of public intellectualism amid the post-truth turn.

To this end, we think with Denzin (2017) and leverage his "critical qualitative inquiry" (CQI) to frame our discussion. Denzin writes, "Our challenge is to push back, to resist, to redefine the place of the academy, indigenous epistemologies and the public intellectual in these public spaces" (p. 8). Though writing about methodology, he also indicates his hopes for what methodology might produce in a critical qualitative project. We believe much can be learned from thinking with his approach to CQI and how we engage what we call "The Project of Public Intellectualism."

As stated earlier, Denzin calls for a redefinition of public intellectualism, which is precisely what this project intends to do. Further, we think about the potential for how the project of public intellectualism can be re-envisioned as something more productive, more influential, and more meaningful in people's lives. We present the work through a critical qualitative lens in the hopes that through this work we honor CQI's charge to enact meaningful change and re-envision what it means to do the project of public intellectualism. As Denzin (2017) puts it,

> as global citizens, we are no longer called to just interpret the world, which was the mandate of traditional qualitative inquiry. Today, we are called to change the world and to change it in ways that resist injustice while celebrating freedom and full, inclusive, participatory democracy. (p. 9)

With this in mind, this chapter attempts to examine ways in which the tenets of CQI intersect with people whom we identify as doing this project and how De Landa's (1997) framing can deepen our understanding of this work. However, before we begin, we offer an outline to help guide the reader through the piece. Up to this point, we discussed some of the contexts regarding truth and external forces that have affected and continue to affect the project of public intellectualism. In the following section, we briefly review how previous scholars have theorized public intellectualism to lay the groundwork for putting these theories into conversation with De Landa and more contemporary scholars. Next, we detail the ways that we are taking up parts of De Landa's theory. Following this, we discuss how we are operationalizing philosophy as a method to think with De Landa and our participant events. After laying out this methodological framing, we present our understandings and consider them with how and what it might mean for the project of public intellectualism.

Public Intellectualism's Evolving Ecology

Many people have engaged with the idea of "public intellectualism," its manifestation, its product, its purpose, or have questioned its existence altogether. Throughout this chapter, we argue it does exist, though in ways that this book re-visions. Nevertheless, this work is vital to public engagement, and we also draw from previous scholars who thought deeply about public intellectualism in previous contexts. We draw from Gramsci (1989), Foucault (Deleuze & Foucault, 1977), and Said (1996) to contextualize and enrich how we frame the project within De Landa's ecology. Before we engage in this scholarship, however, we offer an accounting of "truths" and how they are operationalized and defined in our work and in previous scholarship. Though previous scholarship tethered public intellectualism to notions of (somewhat stable) truths, this breaks down amid the post-truth turn.

Evolving Truths Amid Public Turns

In his conversation with Deleuze entitled "Intellectuals and Power" (Deleuze & Foucault, 1977), Foucault argued that the traditional view of intellectuals held that they were those who spoke "in the name of those who were forbidden to speak the truth; [an intellectual] was conscience, consciousness, and eloquence" (p. 207). Though thinking with notions of truth proves difficult within current onto-epistemological trends, Foucault previously argued truths become (re)produced in particular spaces. Foucault (1997) writes, "I believe too much in truth not to suppose that there are different truths, and different ways of speaking the truth" (1997, p. 51). Thus, for Foucault, truths may exist but only in culturally specific sociohistorical contexts. However, Foucault argues that (under the traditional view) a public intellectual has the potential to function as "conscience, consciousness, and eloquence." Additionally, intellectuals accomplish this by speaking to and for those groups who are ignorant of these truths. Building from Foucault, and as we outlined in the introduction, we believe that the project of public intellectualism remains tasked with engaging competing and subjective truths that correspond with current iterations of how truths are being produced, who is producing them, and how they are consumed.

Nevertheless, any simplicity apparent in this work is misleading, for Foucault warns those doing intellectual work to be cautious of the power running through this type of public endeavor. He cautions wariness regarding both the power of censorship confronting this kind of work and the ways power permeates entire social groups to very real and often deleterious effects. Moreover, and most pertinent to the framing of the project of public intellectualism we take up here, he writes, "Intellectuals are themselves agents of this system of power—the idea of their responsibility for 'consciousness' and discourse forms part of the system" (Foucault, 1977, p. 207). That is, those doing the project of public intellectualism must be cognizant and sensitive to the forces affecting lives as these forces remain integral in the ecology within which public intellectuals are members. Foucault argues that intellectuals can act as both mouthpiece and actor for "conscience, consciousness, and eloquence," but at the same time, they must remain acutely aware that they are themselves agents within the system of power. Foucault's understanding of intellectuals and power provides important touchstones for thinking with what it means to do the project of public intellectualism amid recent onto-epistemological turns, and Said also brings important thinking to this project.

Said offers much regarding the conversation about what it means to do the project of public intellectualism. For instance, "real intellectuals," he says, are "those whose activity is essentially not the pursuit of practical aims" (1996, p. 5). As he implies here, "real" intellectuals push the practical aside to focus more on raising questions that confront "orthodoxy and dogma [and] to be someone who cannot easily be co-opted by governments or corporations, and whose *raison d'être* is to represent all those people and issues that are routinely forgotten" (1996, p. 11). Thus, he contends "real" intellectuals do the work of representing the under- or nonrepresented and, at the same time, do the work of this representation independent of what might be insidious actors such as governments or corporations. For Said, the "real" intellectual, then, acts independently and represents the marginalized, beholden to nothing and no one except those whom they represent.

Further, Said (1996) insists, "the intellectual is an individual with a specific public role in society that cannot be reduced simply to being a faceless professional" (p. 11). He attests intellectuals are something other than an average professional. However, while he champions intellectuals as influencing sociopolitical policy, he also rails against hubris and self-importance: "It is always easy and popular for intellectuals to fall into modes of vindication and self-righteousness that blind them to the evil done in the name of their own ethnic or national community" (p. 45). Different from Foucault's cautions regarding intellectual work within systems of power, Said warns that intellectuals risk becoming blind to the harm their cultural or national communities may inadvertently inflict. Though Said offers no remedy to the dangers that self-righteousness and vindication may carry, he insists that public intellectuals play profoundly important roles, including standing up and speaking out for the under- or nonrepresented.

Ultimately, Said (1996) asks "*the* basic question for the intellectual: how does one speak the truth? What truth? For whom and where?" (p. 88). In the work we engage with in this chapter, we wrestle with similar questions, and we take note that Said considers both how truth is created and whose truth is favored. While these questions become ever more vital as we round the post-truth turn, this chapter attempts to reconsider what it means to do the work of public intellectualism when the very nature of truth is continually up for (re)examination. Truths and notions of truths run through Said's understanding of public intellectualism, and we wonder how competing truths inform and influence the project of public intellectualism within the ever-shifting ecology that comprises cultures and communities. To think further about these ideas, we briefly consider the ways that Antonio Gramsci theorized public intellectualism.

Gramsci outlines two types of intellectuals. The first consists of a traditional or historically entrenched class of intellectuals that have been produced and reproduced for generations such as spiritual leaders, teachers, or politicians. He argues that these social groups emerge "into history out of the preceding economic structure, and as an expression of a development of this structure" (Gramsci, 1989, p. 114). That is, the materialities and economics of the system from which they come produce them in particular ways. Importantly, they also tend to exist as relatively ossified structures that exist in a "historical continuity uninterrupted even by the most complicated and radical changes in political and social forms" (1989, p. 114). Importantly, he asserts that "intellectual types" remain solid across history despite cultural, economic, and political upheaval. Though we will return to this idea later, it is important to note that this chapter uses De Landa to interrogate the notion of solidified intellectual types that persist despite cultural shifts.

Gramsci uses the term "organic intellectual" to describe intellectuals who are closely tethered to the masses and particularly to those who compose various social groups and classes. As he puts it, "every social group, coming into existence on the original terrain of an essential function in the world of economic production, creates together with itself, organically, one or more strata of intellectuals" (1989, p. 113). Thus, these intellectuals become through the needs of economic production within particular groups. He asserts that every new class creates organic intellectuals who "are for the most part 'specializations' of partial aspects of the primitive activity of the new social type which the new class has brought into prominence" (p. 113). That is, organic intellectuals occupy particular positions within the social group that those social groups created. With this framing in mind, this chapter considers how De Landa and the ecologies of particular social groups create different opportunities for the project of public intellectualism to thrive.

The legacies of Foucault's, Said's, and Gramsci's work provide opportunities to think about how the ecology in which they were working has changed; building from them creates an opportunity for re-thinking and re-doing. Further, not only do they represent an old hierarchy, but their theorization of public intellectualism also fits within an assumption of hierarchy. Thus, thinking the project of public intellectualism through a De Landian lens offers a substantive departure from previous theoretical explorations of public intellectualism.

Ecological Organisms

In his 1997 book *A Thousand Years of Nonlinear History*, De Landa argues that human experience can be conceptualized through a scientific lens. For our purposes, we take up De Landa's conception of ecologies, hierarchies, and meshworks to frame a new way of thinking about the project of public intellectualism. While we recognize the intricately and exceedingly complex nature of ecologies and the ways that De Landa theorizes them, we operationalize particular aspects of his theory to consider how the project of public intellectualism moves with ecological forces: namely, hierarchies and meshworks within an ecology.

We define ecology as the environment within which various and variable interconnected organisms exist with each other; the environment within which the public intellectuals traditionally operated has evolved. We argue the anti-intellectual tenor and increasingly multiple and subjective truths described above represent the tone of a broader ecology. Within this ecology, "public intellectualism" is but one organism among many, engaging in an ongoing give-and-take of ontological and axiological resources, moving from, to, within, among, and between traditional hierarchies and newly evolved and evolving meshworks.

The organisms within ecologies depend on their environment and the other organisms within it for cues regarding appropriate (re)actions, resulting in processes on top of processes (Gee, 2020). When we discuss cues and appropriate (re)actions, we allude to the ways in which those doing the project of public intellectualism make decisions about their roles within and in response to their evolving environment. By organisms, we mean the actors existing within the ecology, which reflexively shapes and is shaped by the actions of those actors. Rather than refer to individual "public intellectuals," per se, as is the tradition, we mean those individuals doing, either individually or collectively, the project of public intellectualism. Hierarchies and meshworks also require clear definitions.

De Landa (1997) spoke of the relationship between meshworks and hierarchies in two complex and interconnected ways. On one hand, he spoke of them as being in an ongoing dance between a fluid, organic process of becoming and unbecoming. On the other, he spoke of them in regards to a more static state of being. Meshworks are composed of loosely structured organisms connected to each other based on organic relationships of provision and need. Meshworks possess porous boundaries, with organisms coming and going with ease and frequency based on the needs and aspirations of the organisms, the meshwork(s), and the work each seeks to do in the world. Meshworks might collide with each other to form meshworks of meshworks, dynamic processes of dynamic processes. They are inherently amoebic, and they therefore easily change their shape in response to elements of the ecology.

In contrast, hierarchies take static shape when the boundaries of meshworks become rigid; hierarchies change their shape only with great difficulty. They form when meshworks calcify and lose their fluidity and flexibility. Organisms within hierarchies operate within and according to a much more rigid structure. This structure calcifies boundaries such that organisms face much greater difficulty moving into, out of, within, or between hierarchies. The calcified structure of hierarchies makes it difficult for the organisms within them to respond with agility to changes in the ecology. Most important, when the ecology changes and the calcified hierarchy is unable to change with equal speed, the ecology leaves the hierarchy behind. The hierarchy becomes ill equipped to thrive within the newly evolved ecology. When the hierarchy becomes ill suited to the new ecology, the organisms disperse again into fluid, adaptive meshworks. We argue that the project of public intellectualism is doing exactly this: dispersing from the hierarchical structure of old and into the meshworks with other ecological organisms.

As this framing implies, the world has changed dramatically in recent decades, and the organisms within the public intellectual ecology, such as media outlets and their producers and consumers, have likewise changed. New and emerging communication technologies have (re)shaped the communication habits of a global, interconnected community, and fading communication technologies like printed books symbolize a dynamic interplay between new and old. Learning institutions and their stakeholders, such as K–20 communities, educators, and administrators, remain the most affected by this shift. Indeed, that "regular" folks now produce media en masse, rather than consume it, highlights the tectonic shifts in the ecology of the project of public intellectualism. Thus, in this chapter, we wonder what these ecological shifts do regarding the project of public intellectualism.

Furthermore, humans are not "tropic to truth" (Gee, 2020); that is, humans orient not to truth but to comfort. They prefer instead the comforts of their personal networks (distributed in the 21st century among various internet tools) of trusted knowledge. Rather than a mantra of "In knowledge we trust," it may perhaps be more accurate to recognize "In trust we knowledge." With this in mind, the ecology of the public intellectual no longer supports a traditional static hierarchy in which knowledge creates trust in that knowledge. Rather, trust creates trust in one's subjective truth, and the project of public intellectualism is undergoing a concomitant shift. We argue that these changes in communication and media incapacitate the old hierarchy and that the project of public intellectualism is evolving with this ever-evolving ecology.

We believe that those who currently engage in the project of public intellectualism embrace the disintegration of hierarchies that traditionally housed the work. Some of those currently doing this work came of age amid this tectonic shift, whereas others were carried along with it. In our work, we explore how four individuals whom we identified as public intellectuals reflect the changes in their ecologies. We identified the four participants based on the following criteria: earning tenure at a major research university, having readership outside of academia, doing activism in the communities outside their universities, and having a Wikipedia page. We believe the last criterion provides a necessary marker for those engaging in the project of public intellectualism because Wikipedia exists as a public repository of collective knowledge. As detailed in the following, we create a meshwork of these participant events to think with how the project of public intellectualism evolves in congruence with ecological evolution.

Methodo-Philosophical Shifting

We recognize that De Landa (1997) offers very complex and nuanced ways of thinking, and our goal is not to capture these entirely. Rather, as stated earlier, our goal is to take some of his key concepts and explore what they produce as we consider the project of public intellectualism amid the post-truth turn. To do this, we draw from previous work in qualitative inquiry that thinks with theory to situate philosophy as a method (Jackson & Mazzei, 2012; Koro-Ljungberg et al., 2015; Lenz Taguchi & St. Pierre, 2017). As Koro-Ljungberg et al. (2015) point out, philosophy as method is a pivotal and recent turn in postqualitative inquiry that allows philosophy to open possibilities for thinking the not-yet thinkable. Additionally, Sweet et al. (2020)

Unworking

Beyond the ivory tower
A shifting landscape
A meshworks
Of multiplicities
Form
Unform
Reform

Outside the hallowed halls
Of the academy
Intellectuals
Meaningful
Productive
Influential

Achieving Wikipedia Status
Tethered to the masses
Organically
Speaking competing truths
Representing the marginalized
Called to change the world

The tower leans
The halls vacate
"Why doesn't this work matter more?"

problematize conventional notions of qualitative research and insist that methodologies "stay open to diverse and unseen possibilities" (p. 389). Thus, allowing philosophy to ground methodological explorations of actions and thought carries the potential to produce previously unimaginable insights. Further, "philosophy as method is an engagement, an ethical relationship with thought" (Koro-Ljungberg et al., 2015, p. 617). In the work we present here, we consider how De Landa's theorization of ecology and critical qualitative inquiry may resituate the ways we understand how people engage the project of public intellectualism.

Jackson and Mazzei (2012) challenge qualitative researchers to go beyond systematized notions of qualitative coding, which inevitably reduces the complexity of human experience into somewhat rigid, ossified, and persistent knowledge markers like themes. These kinds of reductions rely on static, decontextualized procedures that attempt to structure complicated human experiences. This type of qualitative research, they argue, seeks to uncomplicate that which is incredibly and profoundly complicated. "Good methodologists" conduct this work in the name of simplicity and interpretation without considering context and circumstance, and they do it all in the name of representation. Alternatively, Jackson and Mazzei (2012) attest that thinking with theory is not concerned with coding but rather allows researchers to think with, across, and through data to illustrate "how knowledge is opened up and proliferated rather than foreclosed and simplified" (p. vii). That is, using philosophy as method opens space to consider how qualitative work produces the previously unthought and acknowledges the complicatedness of human interactions. With this in mind, we consider the ways in which De Landa's (1997) ecological theories may enrich our understanding of the project of public intellectualism.

We lean on De Landa to guide our inquiry, and we acknowledge the potential that this onto-epistemological move may have regarding methodology. We see potential in bringing De Landa's theories to critical qualitative inquiry and to the project of public intellectualism due to the ways that ecological thinking might help us to consider how groups produce truths amid the post-truth turn. Philosophy as method carries the potential of "flexibility and plasticity of the research design within which what counts as research. Thinking with and about thought and conceptualizing philosophy as a method leads qualitative inquiry beyond the unthinkable" (Koro-Ljungberg et al., 2015,

p. 618). In a similar vein, we wonder how De Landa offers profound possibilities, and thus, we consider his theorization of ecology as foundational to the project we engage with here.

Ecological Meshworks

In Figures 2.1 through 2.5, we attempt to represent the project of public intellectualism as a De Landian meshwork: that is, as a nonlinear dynamic assembly of energies, collections, information, and materials. In these collections, we borrow from Cannon (2018, 2020) to think with how we create among and within the meshwork. These figures are our representation of this methodological thinking doing. To create the figures, we collaged, memoed, created lines of words, memoed, and memoed again. In this way, we put theory into the actions of transcription and analysis and mesh participants' statements with ours and De Landa's; in Figures 2.1 through 2.5, the computer-generated printed words are pieces of transcription from events we conducted with the four individuals whom we identified as active participants in the project of public intellectualism. We depict the words of each participant with a particular font, so while readers peruse the figures, they can differentiate participants by comparing fonts. We excerpted pieces of participant transcriptions that spoke to how the participants understood public intellectualism generally and their work for the broader public. The handwritten lines of words are quotations from *A Thousand Years of Nonlinear History* (De Landa, 1997; to clearly read all the quotations we wove through the meshwork, see the Appendix). The sticky notes written in cursive are Joe's memos, and those in block print belong to Taylor. By conducting our analysis in this way, we hoped to make connections between De Landa's theoretical frame and the work taking place within the current project of public intellectualism. We intended for the form of this analysis to take on aspects of its content. We hope that this speaks with an ecology of action that reconsiders previously held calcified and hierarchical notions of what it means to do the project of public intellectualism and what this doing may produce (see Figures 2.1–2.5). We recognize that we cannot make sweeping claims, but we also consider this a theoretical exploration regarding ecology, public intellectualism, and De Landa. We do not prescribe how to make sense of the meshworks. Rather, we invite the reader to experience them as they want.

Ecological Evolution

Through the methodological doings of this project, we consider how the project of public intellectualism exists within an ecology of shifting energies, materials, truths, and powers that compose local and global cultures. The meshwork in Figures 2.1 through 2.5 reveals that the work of public intellectualism is multiple and malleable. As we try to show throughout this chapter, and particularly in the figures, the project of public intellectualism exists in conjunction with its ecologies. This is not to say that they are organisms but rather that they (in a sense) behave as organisms would, organisms that ebb and flow amid the constant tiny bifurcations of an ever-evolving ecology. Unlike previously held conceptions of "The Public Intellectual," which positions individuals atop a highly structured hierarchy, the current project of public intellectualism has broken down into meshworks. At the same time, we recognize that meshworks have the potential to calcify into hierarchical constructions, but constantly evolving organisms resist the hierarchical crystallization that would occur if the meshwork becomes static. Moreover, we believe that "The Public Intellectual" was once part of an ossified hierarchy. However, time and ecological changes dismantle it, and it becomes part of one or multiple meshworks. In this way, the vestigial is always present.

De Landa (1997) reminds us that organisms can exist in multiple stable states simultaneously. An organism does not have to be in a hierarchy; it does not have to be in a meshwork. It can be in a meshwork of hierarchies or a hierarchy of meshworks. It can exist in liminal phases. In this chapter, we argue that the post-truth turn insists on new ways of doing the project of public intellectualism and that the previously regarded hierarchical and calcified iterations can no longer exist effectively. Thus, the project must remain fluid within the ecological meshworks that will carry with them endless possibilities for adaptation and change. Just as an anti-intellectual tenor, the post-truth turn, social media platforms, and the defunding of academic spaces create new opportunities for public engagement, academic environments must shift to consider and adapt to these opportunities.

Figure 2.1.

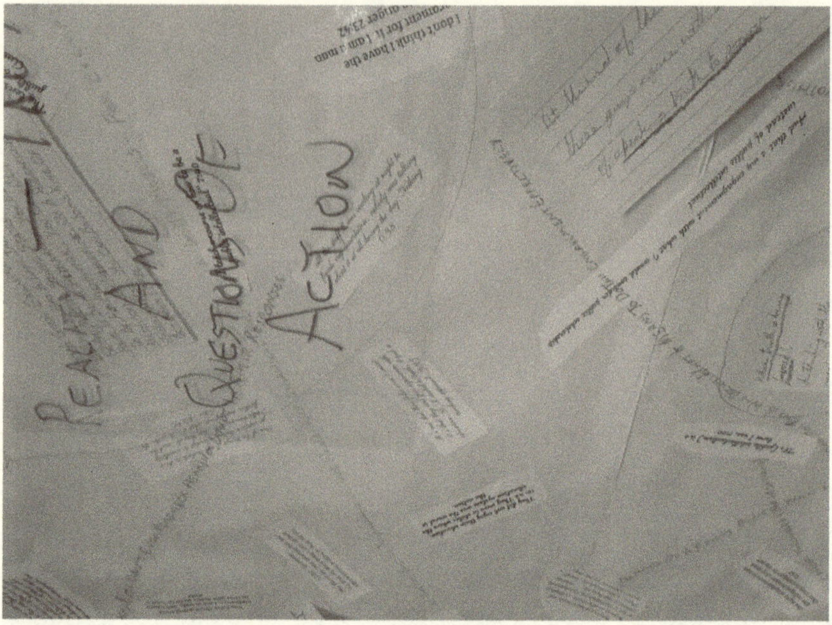

Figure 2.2.

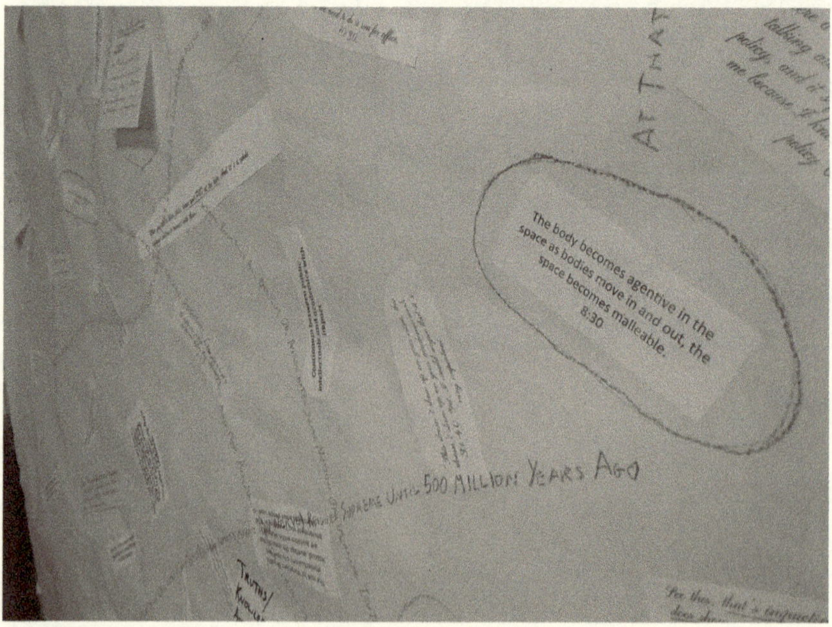

Figure 2.3.

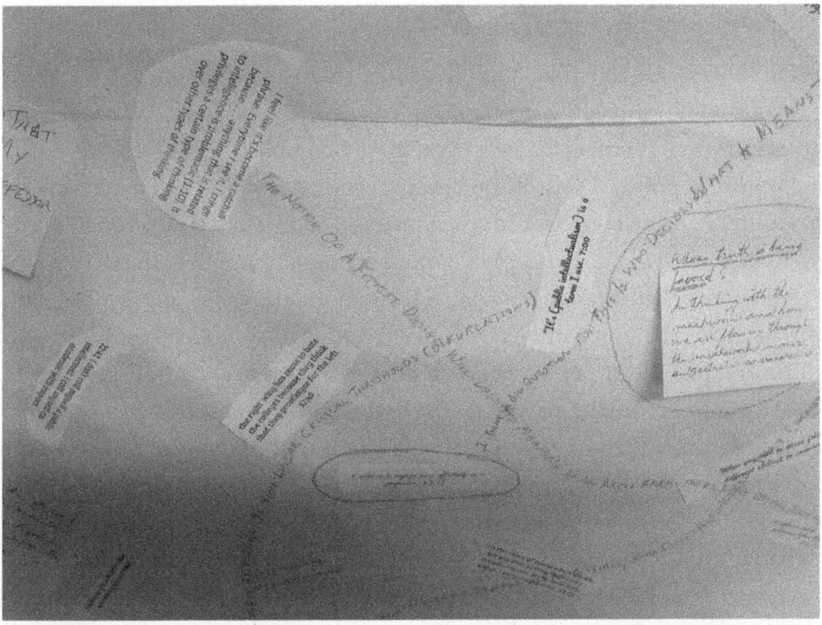

Figure 2.4.

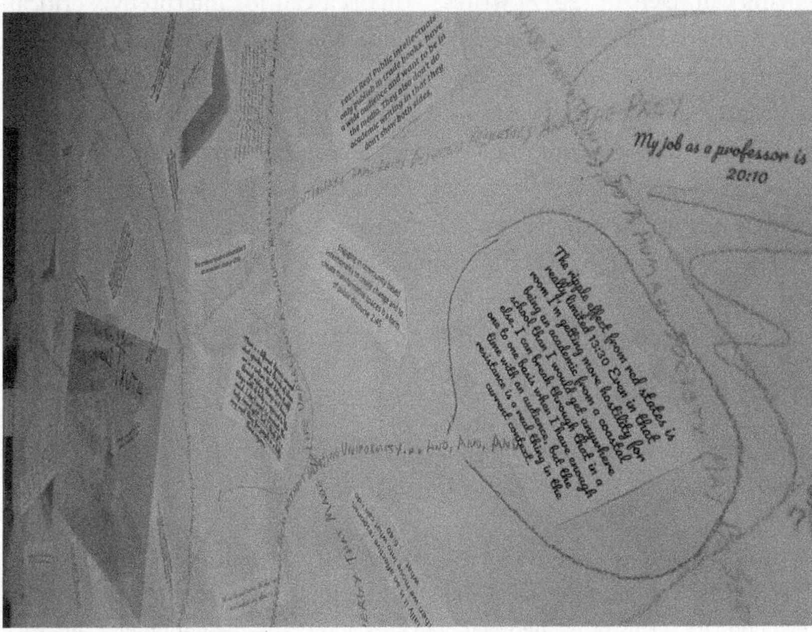

Figure 2.5.

Ecological Telling Truths

Latour (2019) argued that human beings share one reality, but we attest that competing, subjective, and multiple truths within that reality make the project of public intellectualism exceedingly complex. If, as Denzin (2017) implores, the point of critical qualitative inquiry is doing the hard work of community engagement to address injustices, competing truths remain central to how individuals conceptualize and act upon these injustices. Thus, we are still compelled to wonder whose truths matter, whose are favored, and who decides. The implications of multiple, competing, and subjective truths within the project of public intellectualism emerge as a central question to what the project might produce. That said, those doing this project must account for how their subjectivities flow through the ecology of meshworks and what predilections, blindspots, and axio-onto-epistemological underpinnings they always already carry.

Given the fact that we share a reality regardless of whose truths we favor, and Denzin's call for research that matters in the lives of people who endure injustice, we put the words of one of our participants into conversation with Denzin's call. Denzin (2017) writes, "This is a call for interpretive, critical, performative qualitative research that matters in the lives of those who daily experience social injustice" (p. 9). One of our participants ended our discussion regarding their work by stating, "You asked this question about why you do this work. The question that I always repose is, 'Why doesn't this work matter more?' instead of, 'Why are you doing this work?'" As we move toward a critical qualitative inquiry, we must move Denzin's and our participant's mandate forward: Do work that matters more, and make work that matters more central to conducting research.

Appendix

We included the following quotations from De Landa (1997) in the ecological meshwork:

> As biology begins to include these nonlinear dynamical phenomena in its models—for example, the mutual stimulation involved in the case of evolutionary "arms races" between predators and prey—the notion of a "fittest

> design" will lose its meaning. In an arms race there is no optimal solution fixed once and for all, since the criterion of "fitness" itself changes with the dynamics. (p. 14)

> Markets and bureaucracies, as well as unplanned and planned cities, are concrete instances of a more general distinction: self-organized *meshworks* of diverse elements, versus *hierarchies* of uniform elements. But again, meshworks and hierarchies not only coexist and intermingle, they constantly give rise to one another. (p. 32)

> Hierarchical constructions tend to undergo a homogenization before their materials harden into a pyramid, while meshworks articulate heterogeneous elements, interlocking them without imposing uniformity. (p. 40)

> Iberall was perhaps the first to visualize the major transitions in early human history (the transitions from hunter-gatherer to agriculturalist, and from agriculturalist to city dweller) *not* a linear advance up the ladder of progress but as the crossing of nonlinear critical thresholds (bifurcations). (p. 15)

> At each bifurcation alternative stable states were possible, and once actualized, they coexisted and interacted with one another. (p. 16)

> Much as a given chemical compound (water, for example) may exist in several distinct states (solid, liquid, or gas) and may switch from stable state to stable state at critical points in the intensity of temperature (called *phase transitions*), so a human society may be seen as a "material" capable of undergoing these changes of state as it reaches critical mass in terms of density of settlement, amount of energy consumed, or even intensity of interaction. (p. 15)

> In the organic world, for instance, soft tissue (gels and aerosols, muscle and nerve) reigned supreme until 500 million years ago. At that point, some of the conglomerations of fleshy matter-energy that made up life underwent a sudden *mineralization*, and a new material for constructing living creatures emerged: bone. (p. 26)

References

Cannon, S. O. (2018). Teasing transcription: Iterations in the liminal space between voice and text. *Qualitative Inquiry, 24*(8), 571–582. https://doi.org/10.1177/1077800417742412

Cannon, S. O. (2020). Making kin with comprehensive exams: Producing scholar in intra-action. *Qualitative Inquiry, 26*(1), 36–50. https://doi.org/10.1177/1077800419869962

De Landa, M. (1997). *A thousand years of nonlinear history*. MIT Press.

Deleuze, G., & Foucault, M. (1977). Intellectuals and power. In D. F. Bouchard (Ed.), *Language, counter-memory, practice* (pp. 205–217). Cornell University Press.

Denzin, N. K. (2017). Critical qualitative inquiry. *Qualitative Inquiry, 23*(1), 8–16. https://doi.org/10.1177/1077800416681864

Foucault, M. (1997). Friendship as a way of life (J. Johnston, Trans.). In *Ethics: Subjectivity and truth* (pp. 135–140). The New Press.

Gee, J. P. (2018). *Introducing discourse analysis*. Routledge.

Gee, J. P. (2020). *What is a human?: Language, mind, and culture*. Palgrave Macmillan.

Gramsci, A. (1989). Antonio Gramsci: Selections from the prison notebooks. In R. S. Gottlieb (Ed.), *Anthology of Western Marxism: From Lukacs to Gramsci to socialist-feminism* (pp. 112–144). Oxford University Press.

Jackson, A. Y., & Mazzei, L. A. (2012). *Thinking with theory in qualitative research: Viewing data across multiple perspectives*. Routledge.

Koro-Ljungberg, M., Carlson, D., Tesar, M., & Anderson, K. (2015). Methodology brut: Philosophy, ecstatic thinking, and some other (unfinished) things. *Qualitative Inquiry, 21*(7), 612–619.

Latour, B. (2019). *Down to earth: Politics in the new climate regime*. Polity Press.

Lenz Taguchi, H., & St. Pierre, E. A. (2017). Using concept as method in educational and social science inquiry. *Qualitative Inquiry, 23*(9), 643–648.

Marx, K. (1992). *Capital, vol. 1* (B. Fowkes, Trans.). Vintage. (Original work published 1867)

Said, E. (1996). *Representations of the intellectual*. Penguin-Random House.

Sullivan, E. (2017, December 18). *Grad students' tuition waivers will remain untaxed, after all*. NPR. https://www.npr.org/2017/12/18/570941259/grad-students-tuition-waivers-will-remain-untaxed-after-all

Sweet, J. D., Nurminen, E., & Koro-Ljungberg, M. (2020). Becoming research with shadow work: Combining artful inquiry with research-creation. *Qualitative Inquiry, 26*(3–4), 388–399. https://doi.org/10.1177/1077800419857764

Zinn, H. (1998). *A people's history of the United States*. The New Press.

Work-ing

Network
Artwork

Body work
Hard work
Road work
Public work
Code work
Thought work
Why work
Anti-work
Ante work
De-work
Un-work
Re-work

Post-work

Waiting Around

I've been standing around a long time

I've been waiting around
a long time

Good thing these shoes
Are comfortable
Because I forget what the line was for
And I don't see the end

All I see are more lines
What I thought was thick ground
Is masses of thin lines
In a weightless web

Good thing these shoes are comfortable
Because they are nothing else
Beneath my feet

THREE

Guiding Public Engagement With Science Through a Branching Narrative of Qualitative Perspectives

Mathew D. Evans, Arizona State University

Memo 1[1]

THE UNIVERSITY'S SCIENCE CARNIVAL COVERS the whole parking lot with its roller coasters and rows of games. A sopping wet professor of some kind perches above a dunk tank like a drowned cat. "Increase your velocity," he shouts to a little girl winding up a pitch to hit the bull's-eye and send him back into the water. The lighthearted fun makes you smile, but the audio recorder in your hand reminds you that you have a job to do tonight. If you don't collect data for research, then your career is going to be the next thing plunging into icy water.

You are a young scholar in the Environmental Sciences Department attached to a grant to help events, like the Science Carnival, do a better job of engaging the local community with science. At the last minute, your department head needed someone to collect data for an art exhibit. You jumped at the opportunity because your inbox is full of rejections, not even requests for resubmits. With your first review coming up in 4 months, you need something new in the works. The plan is simple enough—conduct interviews with people who visit an art exhibit called *Geodesic Radio*, whatever that is. You pass by a Photovoltaic Solar Cell Trivia booth, where players can win prizes for answering questions about solar cells. A tinge of skepticism hits you. Is testing the public on their knowledge of solar technology going to promote dialogue between science and the public? The whole point of the carnival is to support conversations between scientists and the local community through which both sides are contributing and benefiting (Davies, 2013; Trench & Bucchi, 2014). Personally, you prefer to think of public engagement with research writ large so that researchers, academics, and not just scientists are interacting with the public. You are particularly inspired by the Spanish philosopher Fernando Savater (2002), who suggested thinking *with* the public rather than for them. Some might say this is public intellectualism, a label you don't readily put on yourself because of the elitist connotations, but it could be a useful umbrella term.

After a few minutes of wandering, you come to what looks like a wooden shack without a door. Christmas lights strung around the eaves are at odds with its foreboding appearance, making it a curiosity. You keep walking, but a sign announces, "*Geodesic Radio*: a collaborative storytelling game," telling you that you've arrived.

You make sure that your audio recorder has full power and take a deep breath. "Here goes nothing." You walk faster, realizing that the sun is dropping down over the university tower and the carnival has already started without you.

Go to Memo 3.

Memo 2

"I'm curious how you see the Science Carnival and *Geodesic Radio* in conceptual terms, like as a researcher," you say to the tree.

"Look around us," he says, waving his branch at the booths displaying the marvels of science and technology. "The different elements that came together to form this event. This network, or, as John Law (2008) would call it, an actor network, is made up of you, the organizers, the grad students sharing their research. You all bring your own experiences, material being, and agendas and values that are relative to all sorts of things. You're all professionals using what you know to direct or influence the decisions that are made into how the event happens and how it was designed."

"That's very perceptive for a tree," you say.

"Please, call me Jorge," he says, shooing a bird from nesting in his branches.

"I see. So you're part of the event? Doing public intellectualism?"

"Arts-based research, but yeah, you could call it that."

"Nice. Okay, so if I'm using actor-network theory, I imagine I'm tracking down emails from the organizers, interviewing designers and contributors to the carnival. How am I approaching the data?"

"You could consider that from Foucault's (1980) power knowledge or system of governmentalities. It's about how different systems come together to work in terms of power through government functions or organizations."

"And then use grounded theory with the data?"

"Sure. What's fascinating is how the carnival is coming together to work as a body and produce something different."

"Like the player narratives from *Geodesic Radio*?"

"Sure, we're all producing new things, whether it's a story at *Geodesic Radio* or some arts and crafts at a booth."

You look at the crowds milling through the booths, children blowing up balloons, and grad students talking with the parents about photovoltaic solar cells. All that data send a shiver through you, it's so overwhelming.

"I better keep moving," says Jorge. "Take a flyer if you have more questions." He hands you a pink flyer. It says, "You win one free conversation starter at the Integrative Arts and Sciences Department. Drop by the basement for a chat."

"Thanks," you say to Jorge, who is waddling away.

It's well into the night, and the carnival is emptying as guests go home. When you get back to *Geodesic Radio*, you find Katherine taking down lights from the eaves.

With the flyer in hand, you decide to float the idea of using Foucault to approach your data. "I was thinking about our data. Have you thought about using a critical qualitative method, like Foucault?"

"Mmm . . . not so much, to be honest. But I'm open to whatever methods you're thinking about."

"I want to find something we're both excited about."

"I've wanted to try narrative analysis."

"Sure, me too!" You fold up the flyer and put it away for safekeeping.

You make plans with Katherine to get the player reflections transcribed for a data analysis session. A few days later, you arrive early at your favorite café, Lucky Star, near campus. On the table, you have the 17 narratives collected from *Geodesic Radio*. Katherine arrives sweating, helmet in hand from her bike ride over. You both decide that plot analysis (Daiute, 2014) is a good place to start analyzing the narratives. This method outlines the basic structure of a narrative and interprets what the events mean to the participant.

"Let's do this," says Katherine, and she begins reading one of the narratives. You both come to a narrative you like and compare how each of you plotted it until you agree on its structure. In your laptop, you cut up the participant's transcript into setting, initiating action, and so on.

"The coda is interesting," you say, and then read it aloud. "'The future can be saved. We'll try to do better. But we will fail. And we'll try again. And we'll do it.'"

"Really cool," says Katherine. "The player continues to use 'we' to include himself and a broader society in the actions of the story. It speaks to humanity not just prevailing and being hopeful but full of struggle and failure."

"Definitely," you say. "How about our research questions? We're interested in the values players express. It sounds like the character is fighting to restore the ocean; pollution is bad; collective effort seems to be necessary to overcome the conflict."

"I'd agree with that."

You nod, but something troubles you. You were *expecting* to find these kinds of values, maybe even hoped to find them too because that's how you feel about plastics pollution. You shift uneasily in your chair.

"Something the matter?" asks Katherine.

"It's the researcher in me looking for more."

"That's fair, but what we have is not bad."

"True," you admit.

Katherine congratulates you both on doing a good day's work. She takes off to another meeting, and you get ready to head back to your cubicle. But you can't shake the feeling that you need to dig deeper into the data. You remember Jorge's flyer. You unfold the pink paper and recall his invitation.

Do you:

1. Take up Jorge's invitation to talk to more researchers about your analysis. Go to Memo 9.
2. Decide that your analytical approach is good enough. Go to Memo 12.

Memo 3

Inside the shack, you find what could be a teenager's messy bedroom, except for utility lights trained on a crazy board that cries out conspiracy theories. It has photos pinned to the board and connected by yarn to other clues, like baggies of plastic, drawings, and newspaper printouts (see Figure 3.1). You do a double take when you see a hazy photo of a ramshackle village on a barge floating in the ocean. Your first impression of the crazy board is that you have entered a postapocalyptic water world of the future overrun with plastics and trash.

"Oh cool! Our first player," says a young woman with short-cropped black hair and wearing a tank top. "Welcome to *Geodesic Radio*!"

"Thank you," you reply. You scrunch your brow as you look about the room. "Isn't there supposed to be a radio?"

"The radio is part of the fiction we're telling. It's not here. You see, in our story there is a scientist named Xavier who has a machine at his lab called Geodesic Radio. It gives him glimpses of the future and clues of what may happen. He pinned them up here," she says, pointing to the crazy board. "We need your help to piece together the story. What's the future going to be like?"

"Cool," you say, nodding. "I'm the researcher brought in to help collect data."

"Terrific! Thanks for coming in last minute." You shake hands with Katherine Ball, a grad student who introduces herself as one of the designers of *Geodesic Radio* and a marine biologist.

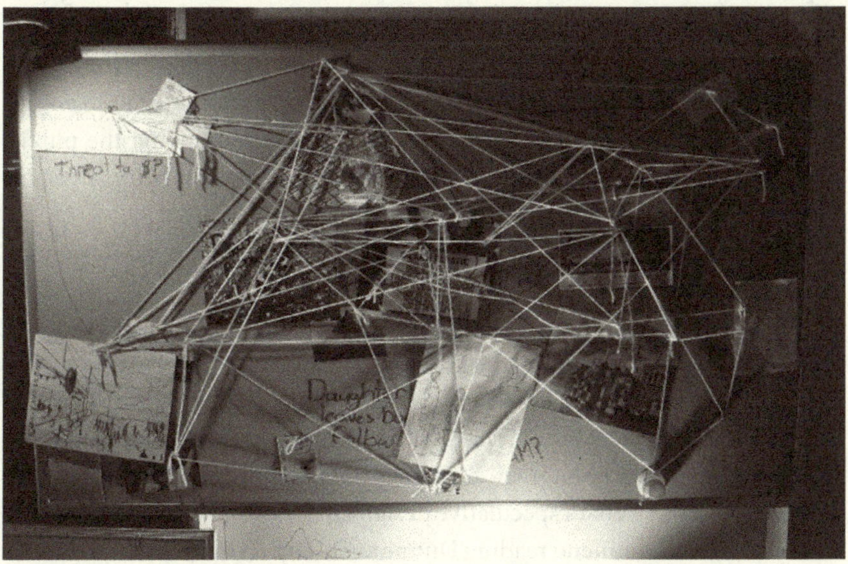

Figure 3.1. Geodesic Radio's Crazy Board With Yarn Connecting Clues.

"So what are people supposed to do with the board?" you ask.

Katherine hands you some yarn. "Look at the clues and choose the ones that speak to you, that tell you a story, and then connect them with the yarn."

"So that's the collaborative storytelling," you say.

"Yep! We give them the pieces of a story, and they put it together how they want. Our slogan is 'Crowdsourcing the Future' because players are helping us think about plastics pollution and what that means for us as a society."

"Instead of a scientist doing a lecture on the dangers of pollution, people get to imagine a world where it's already a reality."

"Exactly," says an older man with glasses, stepping into the shack. He wears a bowling shirt and cargo pants, looking every bit the artist. He introduces himself as Ken Eklund, another designer of *Geodesic Radio* and a visiting artist at the university. "Mathew Evans, the third designer, would be here collecting data for us, but he's working on his dissertation, sadly. So we're fortunate to have you, a living, breathing qualitative researcher to help us out with the research."

"No, thank *you* for bringing me on board. There's some real potential here to engage the public with plastics pollution. Or at least, we will see," you say as your skeptical side kicks in. "Tell me about the research side of your game."

"Roughly speaking," says Katherine, "we want to see if a collaborative story telling game, such as *Geodesic Radio*, reproduces the same dissemination model of science communication, or if it is an opportunity for locals to engage with science. We're also hoping to take the next step in giving the public, players to us, a chance to engage with the ideas rather than being a passive audience."

"So we're *not* interviewing the players to make claims about public opinion on plastics pollution."

"Right. Here is our study design," she says, handing you the papers.

"Thanks," you say, scanning the Methods section. Your mind makes a mental stutter where it says that analysis will consist of "coding" but no mention of a theoretical perspective. Perhaps this is where you can be most useful to the team, bring some ontological and epistemological clarity. A new term catches your eye. "What's speculative design all about?"

Ken says, "I recommend reading Dunne and Raby's (2013) book *Speculative Everything*. The idea is that a designer can create a futuristic artifact to invoke a fictional world. The artifact is tangible, feels real, so the player infers a whole reality based on the object. We use pictures and sketches on the crazy board to invoke a future reality overrun with plastics in the ocean. We want to lure players in and provoke a response."

"Sounds promising," you say. You glance at the lit review again, your eyes drawn to the potential of speculative design in public engagement with science:

> Dunne and Raby (2013) in *Speculative Everything* explain that such works have the power to "probe our beliefs and values, challenge our assumptions and encourage us to imagine how what we call nature could be different . . . [create] a place where the future can be debated and discussed before it happens so that, at least in theory, the most desirable futures can be aimed for and the least desirable avoided" (p. 66). Moreover, rather than simply trying to educate the public about an issue, *Geodesic Radio* attempts to create a "cultural [representation] of science as open-ended and also available for interpretation and critique" (Trench & Bucchi, 2014, p. 6) so that the public, once given a provocative prompt, can then speak their mind.

"All right," you say. "I'm so on board with this." You read on, noting that after players have connected clues to make a story, researchers do a semistructured interview by asking them, "What story did you make?" and "Do you see any connection between your story and what you see today in our world?"

You hand audio recorders to Katherine and Ken, ready to begin gathering data.

Dusk falls and the carnival comes to life with families, university students, and people from the neighborhood flooding the booths. One student brings his mother to *Geodesic Radio*. You show them the crazy board, let them make a story, and then record the semistructured interview. The hideout's small space gets crowded as Katherine brings in two frat guys and Ken finishes up another player. You are amazed at the players' creativity and how each story is so different. After recording your eighth story, you notice your voice is tired and your feet are sore. Needing a break, you spot a tree by a bench not far away.

As you walk over to the bench, you think about how to approach *Geodesic Radio* from a research perspective. The crazy board certainly inspired participants to talk about a world ruined by plastics pollution in the ocean. You sigh at the thought of just analyzing the stories through "coding," which always

Figures 3.2–3.4. Clues on *Geodesic Radio*'s Crazy Board.

feels like codeword for grounded theory without much theory. You are the resident "qualitative analyst" for the group. You should be able to contribute a bit more than that. Another thing bothers you. One player, an older gentleman in a tie who seemed to be an administrator at the university, grumbled that there were no clues to "take real action." All the clues, he complained, are negative.

"I guess you can't please everyone," you say, and let out a heavy sigh as you sit on the bench.

"No, you cannot," says the tree.

You are startled to find a man's bearded face in the hollow of the tree. Dark brown paint hides his face except for his blinking blue eyes.

"I thought you were a tree!"

"It's okay. I get that a lot," he says, and chuckles. He nods toward a sign hanging from his branch that says, "What's on your mind?"

"I should have expected talking trees at a science carnival."

"So what's bothering you?"

"It's very, uh . . . academic."

"Try me," insists the tree. "That's what I'm here for."

You decide to take a chance on this talking tree.

Do you:

1. Ask the tree for advice on how he would methodologically approach *Geodesic Radio*. Go to Memo 2.
2. Tell the tree you want *Geodesic Radio* to start a conversation on plastics pollution with the public but not limit their gameplay. Go to Memo 4.

Memo 4

You clear your throat and address the man in the tree. You explain what happened with the disgruntled player feeling like the clues he had to work with on the crazy board are "too negative."

"That's a real dilemma," he says, looking at his branchy hands. "That could tie into subjectivity, right? When people come together and participate in a collaborative effort to either generate a product or an art piece. If you look at it from an arts-based research perspective, it's about them bringing in their own subjective being. Dewey's (2005) *Art as Experience* has got some really interesting writings about aesthetics. And when you're talking about how players connect clues with yarn, Dewey talks about aesthetics as making intelligent connections, like, for example, when you look at art, not everybody has a similar aesthetic experience because, of course, everybody has their own subjectivity. According to Dewey, some people don't even have an aesthetic experience, because when you're interacting, you're making connections that are intelligent because you're identifying aspects and components that are meaningful to you, and that establishes a connection. If they don't make that meaningful connection, then they're not really having an aesthetic experience."

"So maybe that's why that disgruntled guy didn't like *Geodesic Radio*."

"Sure, here's an analogy for aesthetic experience. I'm a car guy. When I drive a car, for me, it's an aesthetic experience. I get in the car and connect with the feel of this machine, how it drives, the tactical experience on the road, whereas for somebody else who's not a car guy, they just get in a car and want to get from Point A to Point B. So it's all about the individual making intelligent connections."

"What *they're* bringing to the table."

"Right, it's the art, but also their previous experiences, the ethics that they bring with them. Also, like Erin Manning (2016) says, the shiny objects that draw us into the experience have some significance for us."

"Yeah, the crazy board and the sci-fi part bring people to the game."

"Exactly. And because it's very subjective, everybody has a different connection to it, right?"

"You're pretty smart for a tree," you say.

"Please call me Jorge."

"Okay, Jorge the Wise Tree. So not everyone is going to have an aesthetic experience with *Geodesic Radio*." You let out a heavy sigh. You still wonder how to design *Geodesic Radio* so that it is more open-ended for players to make stories. Then again, you question if you really have time to fiddle with an art exhibit when you should be working on a proposal for the data you already have.

Do you:

1. Thank Jorge for his suggestions and call it a night. Go to Memo 5.
2. Ask Jorge how to change *Geodesic Radio* to be more open-ended. Go to Memo 6.

Memo 5

The next morning, you are sitting at your favorite café by campus, Lucky Star. You are working on your laptop going over a few rough transcripts from player stories. With coding software, you begin the coding process, noticing a lot of phrases referring to pollution and people living on boats. You ignore the voice in the back of your head asking for a more nuanced methodology.

You take a hard sip of black coffee, your third cup that day. Your eyes flutter as you fight to keep focused. It's going to be a long, long day in the salt mines.

The End

Memo 6

You make a mental note about what Jorge the Wise Tree said about Dewey and Erin Manning. You grin, thinking, "*Geodesic Radio* is not everyone's cup of tea. But people can still have more options in the collaborative storytelling."

"Well," says Jorge, straightening one of his branches. "From an arts-based methods perspective, and this ties in with Erin Manning's (2016) archivist experience; to have a genuine engagement of where you have data that's [*sic*] produced that isn't [*sic*] already predetermine, you engage in the middle when the participant is already in action. Then you leave it open to whatever is produced. It's about not having a predetermined outcome, right?"

"*Geodesic Radio* is predetermined by the topic, and that we want them to make a story."

"Yeah. And I don't think that that's a bad thing, getting them to create a story. I think it's how they get to the story that you want to open up so that maybe you're not directing them toward a certain story or a certain interpretation. I would look at what is expected of them in terms of their involvement. You could give them the option of using different mediums to generate a product or to engage in an activity that elicits some sort of response. Maybe open what they can do with the yarn. For example, give two simple prompts: 'Use the yarn and make connections.' See what they do with it. You can have a look at *Method Meets Art* by Leavy (2015) if you're interested in these ideas."

"Maybe the players make curlicues with the yarn or connect different parts of the *Geodesic Radio* hideout together, like the walls and books."

"Sure," says the tree. "I better keep moving. Take a flyer if you have more questions." He hands you a pink flyer. It says, "You win one free conversation starter at the Integrative Arts and Sciences Department. Drop in on the 2nd floor for a chat."

"Thanks," you say to the tree as it waddles away. You stash the flyer in your back pocket. Before making any suggestions to your newfound collaborators, you decide to do a bit more investigating.

The next morning you find Integrative Arts and Sciences, a stark postmodern glass-and-steel building that makes you wonder where the funding comes from. With the flyer in hand, you climb concrete stairs to the second floor and hear punk music coming from an open door. With nothing else to go on, you follow the raucous drumming to the office of Professor Doddly. You find a spindly man with a long beard standing over piles of slips of paper spread over the floor. He picks up a slip and puts it into a pile.

"Professor Doddly?" you shout above the music.

"Yes?" shouts back the spindly man. He isn't nearly as old as he looks. "Am I being too loud?"

"Not at all." You show him the pink flyer that Jorge gave you. "Have a minute to chat?"

"Certainly!" He turns off the music and points to a chair for you.

"Are you assembling data?"

He sits cross-legged on the floor. "Yes, in fact, I'm playing around with how aggressive affect influences coding."

"Sounds interesting." You show him pictures of *Geodesic Radio* on your cell phone and mention that the design was originally guided by speculative design.

Doddly lifts his hands in caution. "I don't know much about public engagement. I mostly think in terms of academic audiences, but it reminds me of public intellectualism—"

"Of course, me too."

"—which is more about opening spaces. Did you ever read *Representation of the Intellectual* by Edward Said (1994)?"

"Vaguely," you recall.

"Said did a series of lectures over BBC Radio. Basically, he set out to speak as simply as he could because his audience weren't scholars. So you could certainly look at *Geodesic Radio* in a similar way, opening up a space to talk about—"

"Plastics pollution in the ocean, right. Where I'm getting stuck is keeping that space open as in the players can interact with the crazy board without feeling like we're pushing our perspective on them."

"Reminds me of when I was a teacher," says Doddly, straightening his beard. "I was doing public pedagogy, teaching civil rights to immigrants and migrant workers. I tried to talk about civil rights. I felt like I was . . .

indoctrinating them. I realized quickly nobody came to learn their rights. They wanted to learn English or hang out. So I can see your point."

"My inclination now is to make *Geodesic Radio* more open-ended."

"Right. When you said, 'speculative,' I thought of something, but it's not speculative design."

"Okay, I'm open to anything."

"Affect theory calls itself speculative, but it's not speculative in the sense that it's predictive or prophetic."

"That's similar to speculative design," you explain. "The designer is making an artifact that suggests a future reality that is possible but not necessarily plausible. It's not trying to predict the future either."

"But affect theory is speculative as might we alternatively exist in the current moment? What other potentiality might we work with to rewrite a future? Your player in *Geodesic Radio* is on a direction or a certain path. In order to divert that path, you need to divert things in the present. What could the player actualize in their current environment?"

"Oh, so speculative theories would give players agency at the start, in the present. In other words, what could the player do now to change the future?"

"Right. That kind of gets out of a humanist framework. So much of who we are is narrating about all of our experiences since we're extracting so much of that consciously and subconsciously, nonconsciously. It's kind of always theorizing on some level about alternatives there might be."

"I think I follow you."

"You should check out Brian Massumi (2002), by the way. Affect theory would say that people have potential, forces that exist before they work with the clues. *Geodesic Radio* is a trigger."

"Exactly," you say, thinking about how the tree mentioned Dewey's intelligent connections.

"You can design the game so that the player remains suspended for a little longer in the present rather than giving them direction."

"Right!"

"That makes me think of academic articles in general, not just *Geodesic Radio*'s design."

"I don't follow," you say.

"Intellectuals, researchers, all of us should find ways to say we're not just riding the ship. How do you set up a research project that can effectively suspend determinism for a moment and just help people recognize on some level that we're heading toward an ocean filled with trash is *not* inevitable? Then taking agency in that process and make it clear like 'Oh, now I have to make decisions about which direction to go.'"

You slump back in your chair—mind blown. Adding more agency in the design for *Geodesic Radio* is one thing? Changing from writing a traditional academic article is another. But the possibility is intriguing.

Do you:

1. Embark on a redesign of *Geodesic Radio* with your new theories. Go to Memo 7.
2. Ask Professor Doddly more about writing a different kind of article. Go to Memo 8.

Memo 7

You say to Doddly, "You've given me a lot to work with for a redesign." After thanking him, you take your leave and head to your favorite café by campus, Lucky Star.

With your laptop out and a spicy chai, you type out what you've learned about Dewey's intelligent connections and what Doddly said about affect theory's speculative aspects, noticing a fair bit of overlap. Both argue that the player brings some combination of inclinations in how they will interact with the game in terms of past experiences, what will make sense to them in the moment, and what clues connect to them on a conscious or unconscious level. Thinking about this idea of potential and triggering potential, you sketch out on a pad a mock-up of how the crazy board can look. Instead of putting all of the clues on the board for players to connect, you also put a stack of clues to the side to let them find pictures that speak to them. The *players* can add pictures to the crazy board, which might suspend the directionality of the game and let them have more agency in shaping how their story unfolds. Give the player yarn with the simple prompt of "Make creative connections" too, like Jorge suggested.

You grin madly at the new version of *Geodesic Radio*. Maybe Ken, Katherine, and Mathew would want to collaborate on this. The possibilities seem endless!

The End

Memo 8

"I want to hear more about turning whatever it is I am writing into a nontraditional academic article," you tell Professor Doddly, taking out your laptop.

"Whatever article you end up writing . . ." He frowns, seemingly not sure if he should say what he is about to say. "Do you remember reading those *Choose Your Own Adventure* stories as a kid?"

"I loved them."

"The reader gets options. It isn't so prescriptive. What if an academic article could convey what the researchers took away from the data or took away from this project?"

You nod in agreement. Working on *Geodesic Radio* has felt like an adventure. "Nothing about this project has been anything like I've done before."

"There you go. Make reading the article a little more active. But I'm only saying that partly because I want to think of a way for what you did here that isn't just abstracted. How can an article embody the agency that your participants experience too?"

You love it. That part of you that wants to break from the same old way of doing academic work is scratching at your mental door. "I'm really excited about this. Could this be for the public?"

"I envision it differently," says Doddly. The young academic leaps up excitedly to rearrange his legs. "An unconventional article needs to be within academia. That's part of how I think about critical qualitative inquiry. I think of it as a little bit like activism, and it's not just protest activism but making your work not just sit on the shelf to be read. Like activating people in different ways."

"Like a dynamo or a catalyst?"

"Precisely! We shouldn't predetermine what direction readers go off to."

"Honestly, I've never been comfortable standing up on a soapbox and dictating my ideas to people as if they are the be-all and end-all of ideas," you confess.

Doddly nods. "I think maybe that's partly why we're in research too. It's figuring out more answers."

You agree, more inspired than you've been in a long time. Suddenly, you imagine the opening paragraph of a branching narrative based on this research: "On your way to a Young Qualitative Researchers' Happy Hour, a sudden storm sends you running for cover toward the Integrative Arts and Sciences building . . ."

You snort with laughter. It's way over the top, but at least it can be engaging in a different way—and fun to write.

The End

Memo 9

The next morning you find Integrative Arts and Sciences, a stark postmodern glass-and-steel building that makes you wonder where the funding comes from. With Jorge's flyer in hand, you descend a stairwell into a hallway with a door at the end. You poke your head inside, discovering a large workout room with a mat in the middle and mirrors on the walls, only it is stuffy and humid like a jungle dojo. A burly man in a white T-shirt and loose cotton pants held up by a golden cord with blue tassels is doing leg stretches.

"Good afternoon," you say. "Is this a good time?" you ask, showing the pink flyer.

"Sure, Are you here for the capoeira class?"

"No," you admit. "I've come to ask your advice about a research project."

"I have a little time before my students arrive," says Professor Lux, who introduces himself as a qualitative methodologist. "What's it about?"

Realizing you have just a moment of Lux's time, you give a quick breakdown of *Geodesic Radio* as a public engagement with science research project. You show him pictures on your cell phone of the crazy board.

"Fascinating," says Lux.

"I'm stuck on the analysis, though," you confess. You show him your plot analysis of the player narratives.

Lux suddenly does a wheelhouse kick that turns into a series of cartwheels around you. "I'm thinking," he says, as if to reassure you that kicking can be good for thinking. Once he finishes, he says, "So in the clues, an albatross represents activists? And there is something about growing orange trees?"

"Right, that particular participant connected those clues."

"Is there a way to interpret that with literary analysis or symbolically?"

"How so?"

"An albatross, at least in literature, is a common symbol to represent a bad omen and hardship. Remember the poem 'The Rime of the Ancient Mariner'? If you have an 'albatross around your neck,' it comes from that poem. But it's a phrase that's used now to represent a really heavy weight or something."

"I never thought of that."

"The orange trees. Do they represent life? Do they represent sweetness?"

"From having talked with the designers, I don't think they intentionally created these clues as symbols."

"They could be Jungian archetypes, right, which suggest that some of those things are unconscious for us—our associations with things like the ocean, for instance."

"The game is about plastics pollution, but I never thought of the ocean as a symbol."

"There are a lot of stories and meanings for the ocean. It's seen as a destroyer or a life giver. But Jung would tell us that there is a collective unconscious that uses those things with meaning. In cognitive linguistics, Lakoff and Johnson (2008) and Turner (1987) suggest that cognitively, humans are drawn to make metaphors out of certain symbols and ideas, or conceptual metaphors. We can all get on board with a metaphor and just understand the meaning of it without ever having to have it described to us to the point where it doesn't even strike us as a metaphor anymore when we use it."

"I see. It's taken for granted."

"Yeah. If I described someone as being in the springtime of their youth, we don't go, 'Oh, how literary of you.'"

"Right. So for my analysis, would I try to understand the objects or the persons or their actions metaphorically?"

"Metaphorically or symbolically. That's kind of a more linear way of trying to understand the symbolism."

You laugh. "Okay, how would you approach it?"

"We can parse out a story into plots, or you could try structural analysis, right?"

"Another kind of narrative analysis?"

"Right. But another interesting thing to do is to look at what's going on rhetorically within those plot points. So, first off, why is this the plot point here? Why did they decide to structure it that way, and what kind of information are they giving us in this plot point? And that might be where you start to get into symbolic or metaphorical analysis too. What makes this plot point stand out as opposed to this next plot point? Then what makes that next plot point unique? What does it rhetorically do to create or build the story in this way?"

"Oh that's interesting. And would you be looking for patterns between these different stories?"

"You could. I think you absolutely could, and that might be a kind of like paradigmatic analysis à la Polkinghorne (1995). You could make some generalizations if you wanted to. You could let the stories stand on their own. Each one has a unique way of being told. I think it could be telling." Lux waves to a student dressed in an identical white T-shirt, cotton pants, and cord as him. "Looks like I need to go."

"Sorry," you say. "I don't want to get in the way. Thanks so much."

"One more thing. You should check at Meow Wolf."

You laugh. "That sounds like a furry convention."

"It does, but it's not. Meow Wolf is a huge interactive art exhibit in Santa Fe. *Geodesic Radio* reminds me of it, the immersive, alternate-reality stuff."

"Cool!" You promise to check it out and bow before leaving the dojo.

In the stairwell, you sit down and search Meow Wolf on YouTube. A slew of videos show up on your phone. You check out one video blogger who does a tour of it. You are blown away by what looks like an entire building of far-out, trippy rooms and clues everywhere. It's like *Geodesic Radio* with a million-dollar budget!

You feel an itch to jump in your car and see it yourself.

Then again, you need to get working on the analysis if you want to have a proposal ready.

Do you:

1. Hightail it to Santa Fe to check out Meow Wolf for yourself. Go to Memo 10.
2. Try out analyzing the narrative symbolically. Go to Memo 11.

Memo 10

The drive through northern New Mexico is spectacular. The blue sky and forest mountains are refreshing compared with your stifling office back at the university. You drop into the valley that is Santa Fe, instantly falling in love with the adobe buildings and little streets that make the city feel like a small town. Following the directions from your map app on your cell phone, you pull into Meow Wolf's parking lot, which has a giant red robot smelling a flower. The sculpture doesn't move, but you feel in your heart that Meow Wolf is bursting with creativity. Who needs to write proposals and do the academic rat race anyway? You enter the white adobe building barely able to contain your excitement. At the front counter, you ask a girl at the cash register selling tickets, "Are you guys hiring right now?"

"You know what? We are."

"Excellent!" you say, leaving behind your old life for good.

The End

Memo 11

You leave the Integrative Arts and Sciences building inspired to dig into your data again. You plop down in your favorite nook by the fireplace at the café, Lucky Star. With an eye out for conceptual metaphors as Lux had mentioned, you notice how the boats appear in the narratives that players of *Geodesic Radio* made:

> **Resolution strategy:** "And we end up living on boats."
> **Resolution final ending:** "But like they eventually get off the boats."
> **Coda:** "The future can be saved."

What strikes you is how the boats are a refuge from disaster and a transitional time in the story. When the crisis is over, the people, presumably humanity, is able to return to land. Looking at the transcripts of some of the other narratives, you notice a similar metaphor of boat as a transitional period. Sometimes "people" manage to return to land, and sometimes they don't. With pollution being the cause of the conflict in most cases and the main character attempting to overcome the pollution somehow, you get the sense that the players express the feeling of humanity being adrift, in a transitional space that they may not be able to recover from.

Using conceptual metaphor as a guiding concept for analyzing the data feels like it provides a more interesting, nuanced analysis. You take a sip of spicy chai, feeling inspired and hopeful.

The End

Memo 12

Using narrative analysis on the data feels like a promising direction. You meet Katherine again at Lucky Star, finish the analysis, and put together a proposal for National Collaborative on Science Communication (NCSC). You cross your fingers and hope for the best.

A few months later, the time on your appointment at the university runs out. You are at your office packing up your cactus and goats-in-trees calendar. Just then you get an inkling to check your email one more time. You take out your laptop and see in your inbox that the NCSC conference emailed the results of your proposal. You read:

> "We are pleased to inform you . . ."

Your mind swoons as you read the rest of the acceptance letter for your group's proposal. It came a little too slowly, but at least you have landed a promising new direction for your research.

The End

Note

1. Katherine Ball, Ken Eklund, and Mathew D. Evans displayed *Geodesic Radio*, an interactive art installation, at EMERGE 2019 at Arizona State University. *Geodesic Radio* was originally conceived as a platform to talk with the public about plastics pollution as an example of public engagement with science (Trench & Bucchi, 2014). In terms of research, narratives generated from the interactions were analyzed using narrative analysis (Daiute, 2014). However, this text is meant to offer readers an opportunity to apply other theoretical perspectives to the project, or not, depending on the reader's choices. This is accomplished through a branching narrative (Crawford, 2012), whereby readers make choices as the protagonist (an

early-career researcher) of the story, choosing between which "memo" to advance the plot. The reader is referred to directly by "you" and called on to determine where the story goes. As such, inquiry becomes a portable, interdisciplinary work in progress that is examined through various theoretical lenses. Contributing authors provide critical, arts-based research and other perspectives by way of being characters in the narrative. With a little curiosity and the right choices, you will get to meet them.

As such, this text is a literary representation of inquiry that cannot be passively consumed or gleaned for an objective Truth (Gergen & Gergen, 2000). Readers are "producers rather than merely consumers of knowledge" (Petersen, 2013, p. 293) as they make choices and interpret their own progress in relation to how the text conceptualizes success. Gergen and Gergen (2000) also argue that literary representation can perhaps reach audiences outside of academia. Although this is ideal, the goal is to show how qualitative research and science communication can be in dialogue with one another. Why qualitative researchers should tinker in science communication, and vice versa, is answered best by Said (1994), who argues that public intellectuals must be willing to wander into other fields. Researchers should not always feel the need to be the expert who represents a single perspective or their discipline's interests to others. Rather, as public intellectuals, both sides should recognize they have much to offer and much to gain by leaving their silos and risk collaboration and the cross-pollination of ideas..

References

Crawford, C. (2012). *Chris Crawford on interactive storytelling*. New Riders.

Daiute, C. (2014). *Narrative inquiry: A dynamic approach*. Sage Publications.

Davies, S. R. (2013). Constituting public engagement: Meanings and genealogies of PEST in two UK studies. *Science Communication, 35*(6), 687–707.

Dewey, J. (2005). *Art as experience*. Penguin.

Dunne, A., & Raby, F. (2013). *Speculative everything: Design, fiction, and social dreaming*. MIT Press.

Foucault, M. (1980). *Power/knowledge: Selected interviews and other writings, 1972-1977*. Vintage.

Gergen, M. M., & Gergen, K. J. (2000). Qualitative inquiry: Tensions and transformations. In N. K. Denzin & Y. S. Lincoln (Eds.), *Handbook of qualitative research* (2nd ed., pp. 1025–1046). Sage Publications.

Lakoff, G., & Johnson, M. (2008). *Metaphors we live by*. University of Chicago Press.

Law, J. (2008). Actor network theory and material semiotics. In B. S. Turner (Ed.), *Blackwell companions to sociology: The new Blackwell companion to social theory* (pp. 141–158). Blackwell publishers.

Leavy, P. (2015). *Method meets art: Arts-based research practice*. Guilford Press.

Manning, E. (2016). *The minor gesture*. Duke University Press.

Massumi, B. (2002). *Parables for the virtual: Movement, affect, sensation*. Duke University Press.

Petersen, E. B. (2013). Cutting edge(s): An ethnographic drama in three acts. *Cultural Studies↔Critical Methodologies, 13*(4), 293–298.

Polkinghorne, D. E. (1995). Narrative configuration in qualitative analysis. *International Journal of Qualitative Studies in Education, 8*(1), 5–23. https://doi.org/10.1080/0951839950080103

Said, E. W. (1994). *Representations of the intellectual*. Vintage.

Savater, F. (2002). *The questions of life: An invitation to philosophy*. Polity Press.

Trench, B., & Bucchi, M. (2014). Science communication research: Themes and challenges. In Massimiano Bucchi & Brian Trench (Eds.), *Routledge handbook of public communication of science and technology* (pp. 17–30). Routledge.

Turner, M. (1987). *Death is the mother of beauty: Mind, metaphor, criticism*. University of Chicago Press.

Reaches End in the Middle

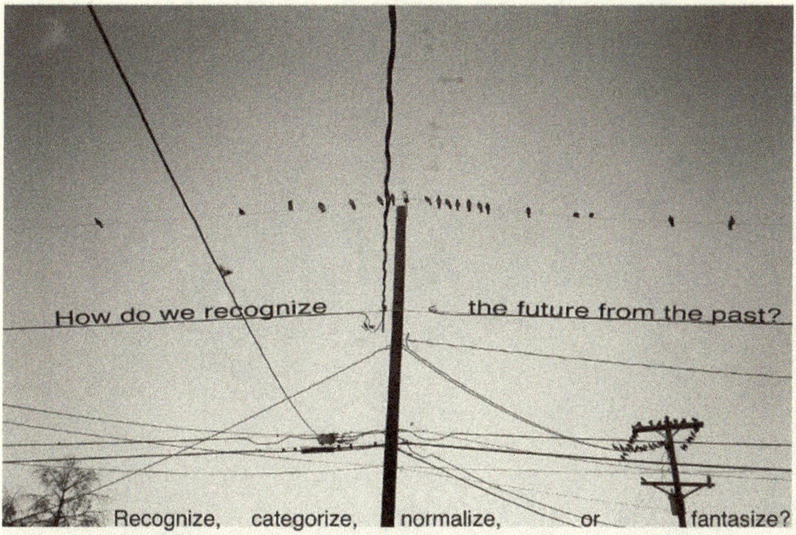

How do we recognize the inert from the living?
Or perhaps the once lived?
The leaf – did it leave? What is left?

Leaf litter. Left to die a death.
Or left to nourish possibilities?

Litter in the ocean of plastic.
Strings to connect the geodesic.
Shortest path that stretches.
Reaches end in the middle.
Breaches conventions.
Communication o v e r f l o w s.
Radioed, transmitted, broadcast, codified
Ideas set a
d
On an ocean of speculation r
Generative futures. i
f
Scientist public. Public scientist.

Narrator is narrated. Reader writes. t.
Albatross. Drop your weight. Take flight.

Jigsaw

Purvaj Aranya

Lazar cut of digital artwork

12 inches by 10 inches

Reproduced with permission

FOUR

Whiteness and the Natural Order: Shame, Race and Public Intellectualism According to Jordan Peterson

Lauren Mark, Arizona State University
Timothy C. Wells, Arizona State University

In their respective, varying realms of politics and public intellectualism, both Donald Trump and Jordan Peterson work to empower groups who have struggled with affective burdens of racialized shame in recent years. Their motivations may be different, but their messages appear to reach similar demographics: white heterosexual U.S. males. Although prominent scholars and journalists have dedicated articles and books to unpacking the meaning behind Trump's popularity (Berlant, 2016; Grossberg, 2018; Schaefer, 2019), few scholars have addressed Peterson's impact, which is experiencing growth in the relatively more specialized public spheres of university campuses, conference stages, and YouTube.

Jordan Peterson has been considered the most influential public intellectual of the Western Hemisphere (Brooks, 2018). A professor of psychology at the University of Toronto, Peterson gained popularity on YouTube for his lecture-format videos on culture, religion, and politics, which regularly receive thousands and sometimes millions of views. He is a fierce defender of Western cultural values, the freedom of speech, and Christian morality and an equally fierce critic of the academic left, identity politics, and political correctness. His audience is overwhelmingly young and male who, as David Brooks (2018) writes, "feel fatherless, solitary, floating in a chaotic moral vacuum, constantly outperformed and humiliated by women, haunted by pain and self-contempt" (para. 4). And most recently, his self-help book, *12 Rules for Life: An Antidote to Chaos* (Peterson, 2018), has gained international recognition, selling more than 3 million copies. Put simply, Peterson's influence and audience rival that of any other academic, at least in the West.

Unsurprisingly, critiques in his direction abound. In prominent profiles, he has been labeled a "custodian of the patriarchy" (Bowles, 2018) and has been accused of relying on "tired old myths" endorsed by scholars who were once fascist sympathizers (Heer, 2018). Other YouTube personalities (ContraPoints, 2018) have similarly challenged his defense of biological gender, intelligence, and racial disparities. Only recently has he been taken to task in academic journals for his "superficial" treatment of Freud (Burston, 2019) and "mischaracterizations" of postmodernism (Klein, 2018) and Marxism (McLaughlin, 2018). To his credit, Peterson has engaged in a series of debates and discussions with prominent intellectual and academic figures. Yet Peterson's critics have largely confined themselves to the validity and efficacy of his ideas, leaving unexplored the specific practices that constitute his widely influential discourses.

In our response to the call for the present book, we explore the practice of public intellectualism through the discourse of Jordan Peterson. Specifically, in drawing on affect theory, we examine the affective dimensions of Peterson's persona as a way to understand his influence and appeal. Lawrence Grossberg (2018) writes that affect "encompasses a variety of ways in which we 'feel' the world in our experience, including moods, emotions, maps of what matters and of what one cares about, pleasures and desires, passions, [and] sentiments" (p. 11). As we argue, Peterson's deployment of affect is what makes his message effective and desirable. It is what garners him support and provides him the channel to relay his conservative, Westernized, and masculinist worldview. To make this case, we first review public intellectualism within the field of public pedagogy, outlining affect's role in the alignment of individual bodies with collective interests through Sara Ahmed's (2004a) concept of affective economies. We then analyze one of Peterson's (2017) most popular lecture-format videos, "Identity Politics and the Marxist Lie of White Privilege." We then conclude with a discussion of Jordan Peterson and advocate for the further uptake of affect within public intellectualism scholarship and practice.

Public Pedagogies and Affective Economies

The field of public pedagogy maintains the importance of studying learning that occurs beyond school walls. Many working within the public pedagogy field approach their work through the study of popular culture, focusing on films, television shows, and video games, while others study public spaces, exploring the learning that occurs in museums, libraries, and parks (Sandlin et al., 2010). Still others look toward political discourse and social activism as sources of knowledge and learning outside of traditional schools. Not far from this, and, in fact, embedded in much public pedagogy research, is the exploration of public intellectualism.

In their review of the public pedagogy field, Sandlin et al. (2011) identify early and later strands of research on public intellectualism. The early strands of public intellectualism research focused on individual actors and the communities for which they advocated. The intellectual was understood diversely as a "disseminator [of] expert knowledge," an "intervening authority," and a "counteract [to] the hegemony of popular culture" (Sandlin et al., 2011, p. 355). This early work centered the intellectual's influence in particular public spaces. However, more recent research into public intellectualism has problematized the narrow individualism of the field, suggesting instead that collective engagements, not individual actors, make up the work of the intellectual. In both early and later strands of this research, the focus has been on the formation and discussion of collective interests in public spaces. This focus directly aligns with the broader notion of a public sphere, initially popularized by Habermas (1962/1989) in his tracings of the emergence of a bourgeois European space that mediated between the state and society in the late 17th and early 18th centuries. He described how the growth of a market mentality transformed public discourse into a commodity (1962/1989, p. 161). Public intellectual scholars benefit from Hauser's (1999) more recent extensions of Habermas's public sphere as a space where "strangers discuss issues they perceive to be of consequence for them," where discursive exchanges form the bases for a "shared awareness of common issues, shared interests . . . and self-constitution as a public whose opinions bear on the organization of society" (p. 64).

In this chapter, we similarly consider the public as a "set of activities" that emphasize collective rather than individual and private interests (Biesta, 2012). Traditionally, these have been thought of as languages, rules, and norms that mediate the interaction of the society and the state (Biesta, 2012). However, these interactions are increasingly occurring in digital and online environments, such as YouTube. As a set of activities, the public is less a physical *space* than a *domain* that holds the potential for a conversation about collective and political interests (Biesta, 2012). The study of the public in public intellectualism has largely confined itself to the function of language and ideas in public spaces, yet we maintain that the study of public intellectualism equally needs to consider the use and expression of affect.

Thus, our focus in the present chapter is how affect functions within the workings of public intellectualism. Following the recent affective turn (Clough, 2008), we maintain that values and interests move as much if not more so affectively as they do intellectually (i.e., reason and rationality). In our current era, affective alignments with political figures override a willingness to acknowledge instances in which favored politicians fail to adhere to the law or uphold the interests of a shared nation. Furthermore, political supporters transpose their own overreliance on affective alignments onto those in opposing parties or with perceived opposing loyalties, assuming that others allow their own affective biases to dictate their actions. For instance, earlier in 2020, a survey polling more than 1,000 Americans about President Trump's impeachment included responses such as the following affective dismissals: "They [Trump's persecutors] just don't like the man because he's not a politician" (Gerald Wilson, quoted in Mervosh et al., 2020, para. 18) and "You can tell that the Democrats are just out to get Trump. I feel like there's no grounds to impeach him" (Cherece Mendieta, quoted in Mervosh et al., 2020, para. 19). Respondents' appraisals of the situation are not rooted in facts or knowledge but in *feelings* of Trump's innocence or surmisings of who the other side *likes* or *doesn't like*. Although textual and video evidence of affectively led citizens is available to millions of consumers through news outlets such as the *New York Times* or *The Daily Show*, this is primarily produced for the amusement or bemoaning of largely liberal-minded audience members. Rather than viewing this as a foregone conclusion of an undereducated U.S. public, we would better serve the future of our collective political interests by more closely examining how affective connections predispose people to be receptive toward ideas that pose as reasonable or intellectual.

In short, the affective side of public intellectual research has been underexplored. Within the field of public pedagogy, affect has only been recently considered (e.g., jagodzinski, 2013; Springgay & Zaliwska, 2017), while the larger field of cultural studies has approached affect in a number of ways. For instance, Papacharissi (2016) has studied affect in the public sphere in what she terms affective publics, "networked [communities] that are mobilized and connected, identified, and potentially disconnected through expressions of sentiment" (p. 311). In studying affective publics, she looks at Twitter use and online versions of the Occupy movement as unifying, identifying, or dividing. She speaks to the power of hashtag malleability to be defined, redefined, and reappropriated through affect, exploring how mediated feelings of connectedness impact networked publics and the structures of storytelling. Papacharissi points to the underlying mechanisms of affective publics, "powered by affective statements of opinion, fact, or a blend of both, which in turn produce . . . connecting . . . expression" (p. 316) with the ability to "produce disruptions of dominant political narratives by presencing underrepresented viewpoints" (p. 318). Similarly, we explore the functioning of affect in digital environments, focusing on Jordan Peterson's YouTube channel, yet we rely on the affective theories of Sara Ahmed and specifically her notion of affective economies.

Ahmed (2004a, 2004b) explores how affects, like emotion, function to align the bodies of individuals with collective interests, values, and beliefs. In doing so, she argues against the idea that emotions reside within or even outside of the body, instead suggesting that emotions work to form the very inside/outside distinction: in effect, defining, orienting, and intensifying the boundary of bodies (2004a). Ahmed provides the example of stubbing one's toe on a table. For her, it is not simply that the table and the toe collide but that the intensity of the pain makes the surfaces of the toe and table determinant. Ahmed (2004b) states:

> I become aware of my body as having a surface only in the event of feeling discomfort (prickly sensations, cramps) that becomes transformed into pain through an act of reading and recognition ('It hurts!') which is also a judgement ('It is bad!'). This transformation of sensations into an emotion might also lead to moving my body away from what I feel has caused the pain. (p. 29)

It is not simply the sensation of pain that demarcates the self but also the transformation of that pain into emotion, which relies on an interpretive judgment. The more a feeling is judged through an emotion, the more defined the boundary of the self becomes. The feeling of pain becomes an orienting device, directing individuals away from what they perceive as harmful.

Yet this process for distinguishing oneself in the world can equally function on the level of the group. To explain this, Ahmed deploys (2004a) the term *affective economies*.

Affective economies describe how emotions operate and intensify within social and political discourse. Similar to capital, the circulation of affect creates an intensifying effect, whereby the greater the circulation, the greater felt the affect. Much like on the individual level, on the collective level, intensified affect intensifies boundaries. Spaces of heightened affect create stronger divides between us and them through affective hegemonies that constitute legitimized ways of feeling. Ahmed provides as an example the association of fear with the body of the refugee. For her, it is not simply that the circulation of affect labels refugees as fearful but more so that the circulation of fear defines and surfaces the body of the refugee. What this suggests is that affect, along with discourse, not only communicates ideas about bodies but also actively shapes individual and collective bodies, in a sense, hardening the public sphere.

Therefore, in taking up Ahmed's positioning of emotion as formative in the shaping of social bodies, we study Peterson's (2017) talk titled *Identity Politics and the Marxist Lie of White Privilege*. The talk is one of his most popular videos and has been viewed more than 3.6 million times. The reach that he has in this talk alone warrants its consideration, as few other public figures, let alone academics, have access to an audience of this size. Like Ahmed, our interest lies in how Peterson marshals affect to surface the insides and outside of social grouping. Specifically, we ask how Peterson's deployment of affect affects the body of the public, which we explore in the following sections.

"The Lie of White Privilege"

Peterson's talk consists of over two hours of what he considers a "deconstruction" of postmodern, identitarian, and Marxist theories of culture and society, categories of knowledge that carry the impression of residing above the average nonscholarly fray. To render these intellectual genres accessible, he draws on familiar sources of knowledge such as biblical stories, historical anecdotes, and elemental forms of social research to challenge what he sees as interconnected and underlying theories of the left. His traditional, vested style of dress and inclusion of personal anecdotes give the viewer the impression of a trusted professor trying to convey the secrets of his vast ocean of knowledge in terms you will understand. Despite entering his YouTube channel with a fully formed skepticism of his intellectual stances, both of us as authors found ourselves being drawn into the affective layer of comfort created by Peterson's folksy yet articulate manner, where he spoke of interpersonal dynamics with children and pets and ventured into allegorical stories that began with a hint of the familiar yet developed with the intriguing promise of the new.

As we suggest, all of this is not enacted coincidentally. Peterson is less interested in the particularities of ideology and more interested in reaffirming a particular kind of affect that hinges on Western values and practices. As we argue, contrary to the title of his talk, "the lie of white privilege," the view Peterson advocates *does*, in fact, privilege whiteness but through affective means, which we unpack in the following section.

The talk begins with Peterson's defense of the status quo of Western society, which he sees as functioning rather well. He does this by pitting power and competence against one another in a mutually exclusive scenario, acknowledging that the current "system" (one that postmodernists, intersectionalists, and activists are trying to overturn) is "30% warped, something like that" (Peterson, 2017, 103:47). He dismisses any degree of systemic corruption or imbalance by prioritizing the traits of individuals. "It's not much more than [30% warped] because we can account for people's success across life by looking at their individual differences: intelligence, conscientiousness, emotional stability, creativity . . . we can do a pretty good job of predicting their trajectory" (2017, 104:03). Peterson's framing of the world via a natural order, whereby some will inevitably fall at different points in the bell curve through innate characteristics and abilities, at no greater fault of society, legitimizes the stratification of contemporary society.

This perspective allows his largely white audience to hone in on their own experiences in ways that support them at the expense of reflexivity to a broader social context and any advantages that context has granted them. As someone who grounds legitimacy in empiricism and numbers, even in his estimations, Peterson strives to distinguish his approach from that of feminist scholars engaging with qualitative, ethnographic methods, where they "pen a few notes about how [they] think the world is constructed, and then [they] can screw up the entire political system" (2017, 111:19). As part of his charge to uphold established orders, Peterson directs his affect of equality and fairness to reempower and unite those who find themselves "pushed to the margins" by identity politics (which he identifies as those that call attention to influences wrought by sex, sexual orientation, gender, race, etc.) and by individuals who claim that the system is more problematic than the nominal amount that Peterson asserts is "not so corrupted that the lights go off" (2017, 104:21).

It is here that Peterson establishes a foothold for his own goodwill by placing it in relation to opposing groups whose nature he claims to be wrong and violent. As such, he frames "Marxism [as] fundamentally based on hatred rather than sympathy and empathy" (2017, 105:27), supplying as evidence Ukrainian corpses that piled up once experienced farmers were exiled as a result of their relative privilege. He uses this reference to a massive loss of life under previous communist regimes to rationalize his projection of a current unflinching postmodernist propensity for spilled blood. Peterson creates this alignment by framing postmodernists as the next generation that emerged to take up the baton once Marxist theory had proved unsuccessful, who are probably still "fine with mass murder of those who stand in their way" (2017, 103:47). He attempts to foreground this presumption of inherent danger as a given were postmodernists to gain power. In doing so, he not only recenters the old white guard but also remarginalizes those attempting to gain a degree of foothold in the center.

This is something that is equally evident in the contrast that Peterson draws between Judeo-Christian and Marxist worldviews. The contrast hinges centrally on contrasting theories of suffering. For Peterson, the Marxists find suffering in class inequity, with the bourgeois ruling class oppressing the proletariat working class. It is material and found in factors external to oneself. The Judeo-Christians, on the other hand, understand suffering as a simple fact of life: "[It is] built into the structure of self-conscious being" (2017, 37:43). This brand of suffering is psychological, an essential aspect of living. In one perspective, suffering stems from material environments, and in the other, suffering stems from within the self. According to Peterson, the former, Marxist theory, is mistaken, as it fails to account for one's own faults in the experience of hardship.

The Marxist theory explains a repeated frustration that Peterson has with social activists. It is a frustration that is present throughout his talk. Social activists locate the sources of suffering and hardship on the level of the social instead of on the level of the individual. For Peterson, they neglect their own responsibility in their experience. Yet Peterson goes further to suggest that contemporary activists of the postmodern–Marxist–intersectional type hold not only misguided ideals but also misguided motives. They seek power, not justice. Their expressions of sympathy and goodwill only mask an underlying resentment. As Peterson explains, Marxists "don't like the poor, they just hate the rich" (2017, 60:23), and "if you paid the sociologist as much as the investment bankers, they'd be capitalists very rapidly" (2017, 76:48). Perhaps most frustrating for Peterson is that he feels like his emotions are being manipulated, lamenting that activists work through

> historical ignorance and philosophical sleight of hand to render us so god damn guilty about what our ancestors may or may not have done so that we allow our shame and our guilt to be used as tools to manipulate us into accepting a future that we do not want to have. (2017, 116:17)

For Peterson, this is not just locating problems external to oneself; it is also manipulating emotion to gain power. It involves a deception that corrupts the individualistic and merit-based values of Western society.

Lauren Berlant (2016) points out that interest groups involved with civil rights and feminism invoke manners and emotions in ways that "get right in there and reject what feels like people's spontaneous, ingrained responses" (p. 5). This rejection of conditioned ways of life is inextricably tied to individual positionality when faced with potential steps toward personal improvement. From the perspective of political continuums, Schaefer (2019) states that "leftists use shame to challenge not only the politics of others, but also themselves, grinding away their own sense of comfort in a relentless project to become more sensitive, more thoughtful, more moral" (p. 6). This approach assumes those who embrace this strategy have *something* to grind away and will *still* have something to stand on once the grinding away has begun. The approach assumes that those who chose this somewhat self-sacrificial strategy are in a relative position of strength or, at least, steadfastness. Conversely, those possessing certain advantages, such as white heterosexual males, who are told that their ingrained responses are wrong, are not actively choosing to grind away at their comfort. Tomkins proposed a definition of shame that carried similar debilitating effects as guilt, through mutual affects of "indignity, of defeat, of transgression, and of alienation" (cited in Sedgwick & Frank, 1995, p. 133). His definition includes the reignition of negative affects each time one reencounters the shame-invoking object, which simultaneously reduces one's experience of joy. For Tomkins, shame functions as an overarching meta-affect that affects all other emotional states (Sedgwick & Frank, 1995). Underneath this power of this pervasive affect, one may begin to feel that he is standing on shaky ground, regardless of the positionality he holds through his identity categories. In these instances, a person will need to be built up through a reinforcement of the familiar, and this is precisely the need that Peterson meets, which requires an affirmative stance.

Peterson deploys his filter of white nationalism with a softening tone of jovial mockery that functions on two levels. First, it solidifies the parameters around his enclave of inclusivity which begins to form around white patriarchal nationalism toward the end of his speech. He belittles that prospect of existent structural inequalities by conflating them with a projected dismissal of traditional research methods by feminists and activists: "There's no such thing as methodology anyways, that's all part of the oppressive white male European patriarchy, so we can just not bother with that" (2017, 111:10). Second, Peterson further capitalizes on existing grievances against a burgeoning global economy at the expense of North American prosperity. He references recent disappointments experienced by North America's white working class by blaming growing economies in China and India to explain the gap between what is desired and what is manifested, thereby forming an affective economy that includes passive video consumers and active commenters. Peterson then additionally associates North American culture with whiteness when he attempts to brush off intersectional critiques that he reframes as majority critiques:

> If you're Chinese this is a majority privilege, and if it's majority privileges, like isn't that just part of living within your culture? So let's say you live in your culture, you're privileged as a member of that culture, well, obviously, that's why [*sic*] the culture is for, why would you both [*sic*] building the damn thing if it didn't accrue benefits to you? (2017, 112:19–37)

By creating an analogy between North American societies and the presumption of a relatively racially homogenous culture such as China, Peterson effectively claims that the natural or original North American order is white. He builds on this affect of racial inclusivity by speaking to his audience's sensitivity toward negative attributions to whiteness, charging people with racism who dare to use the concept of white privilege:

> You might notice that to attribute to the individuals of a community the attributes of that community on the basis of their racial identity is called racism. That's what racism is, there's no other way of defining it. It's attributing to the individual the characteristics of the group as if the group was homogeneous. (2017, 113:27)

Peterson conflates racism with privilege in this dismissal of a structural advantage conferred on people who are read as members of North American culture. He ignores the system of symbolic representation embedded in specific North American cultures that allows certain people to experience themselves as kin (McKittrick, 2015) and other people as subjugated others (Sharma, 2015). Peterson's determined emphasis of the individual above all in society centers notions of self-determination and rugged individualism (Hsu, 1983), whereby an individual relies on oneself mentally and physically to singularly determine his fate at the exclusion of acknowledging impeding or aiding external factors. He links this myth of individual self-sufficiency to a narrative of the naturally ordered bell curve, where populations that find themselves in relatively more disadvantaged positions are there because of innate inferiorities.

It is in this manner that Peterson continues his attack on intersectional scholars by conflating structural inequities, such as marginalized racial categories or sex, with clear disadvantages of cultural capital, such as intelligence or attractiveness, using mockery as his continued weapon of choice.

> What if you're a Black woman? That's a problem, because, well now you've two dimensions of differentiation. What the hell are we gonna do about that? What if you're gay and Black and female? Well then, what if you're not very bright and gay and Black and female? And then what if you're ugly and not very bright and gay and Black and female? (2017, 108:09)

Through his diminishment of intersectionality, Peterson excludes everyone who he claims positions themselves or is positioned by nature as disadvantaged: Black, gay, female, ugly, dumb . . . using white, cisgender, heterosexual, intelligent, able-bodied maleness as the overarching barometer. He conflates qualities that occupy positions of power with those that carry innate measures of superiority.

Finally, Peterson cements an inclusivity to genetic inheritors of oppressive legacies from the past—framing the current "us" as those genuinely "oriented towards the good," as opposed to socialists, postmodernists, and social justice warriors who are merely pretending to empathize. According to him, they are merely in it for the exhilaration of being right. He maintains this affirmational affect as a tool for empowerment against any residual guilt and ensuing acquiescence that might arise from the "manipulations" of those benefiting from identity politics, as noted earlier.

In these ways, Peterson gathers a quelled potential among white males and marshals it into a collective body with the generation of public spheres through his public talks, in person and online. In essence, he creates affective economies that give rise to legitimate ways of thinking and feeling by reflecting immanent stirrings already present within this population. We can see the formation of these collective bodies through resonant comments on his YouTube talks. Comments posted to the video addressed in this chapter alone include the following examples by YouTube users:

> I am almost 60 yrs old and have been trying to articulate these thoughts with my kids and anyone who would listen for 40 of those years, This is the best 2 and 1/2 hours leaning [*sic*] I have had since I left the Marine Corps. (Timothy Richards, 2017)

> The guilty feeling that I never could put my finger on always perplexed me. Dr. Jordan has lifted the veil. I can see now. I was brainwashed to hate myself because I'm a white male. Because of Dr. Jordan I'm no longer ashamed of what I had no control over. (RobS ZZZ, 2017)

> I'm 51 yo and have been bombarded by BS guilt trips by the left my entire life for being a white male. From Phil Donahue to Oprah. From commie school teachers to sensitivity training in the Navy after Tailhook. I've never treated anyone badly or felt superior to others based on my "whiteness". However I do hold the right to judge! I judge people by their appearance and body language. I judge people by the "content of their character". I am not ashamed of this. And I am not ashamed of being WHITE. (Runs with Sharp Objects, 2017)

We see in these comments how empowerment manifests through the removal of shame or guilt for being white and male. The function of marshaling affective economies connects a population of white North American males, first, through the identification of residual feelings of shame or guilt and, second, through their subsequent overturning through spoon-fed assertions of academic capital that scaffold an advancement for the average layperson. Peterson's tone of mockery framing his oppositional stances gives the appearance of reducing them to straw-men arguments while simultaneously lending an air of credibility to his positions. It is a credibility that leverages what might be thought of as latent affect within his audiences. Although in Peterson's case, this affect is tied to racialized and gendered norms, public intellectualism with other interests might leverage affect differently, which is what we explore in our concluding section.

Conclusion

I went online for answers, and I found Peterson.

—Henderson (2019, para. 8)

An effective public intellectual does more than just offer the dissemination of knowledge outside formal social boundaries. With endless choices of expert knowledge holders on YouTube and other streaming channels, a public pedagogue must also convince potential audiences that she/he/they have their well-being and growth at heart and help them feel empowered. Earlier, we mentioned Papacharissi's (2016) work highlighting the mobilizing power of affective publics, joined through mediated feelings of connectedness powered by a variety of factual and opinionated affective statements. The power of these publics stems from their ability to disrupt prevalent political narratives by "presencing underrepresented viewpoints" (Papacharissi, 2016, p. 318). As Peterson's ideas gain traction across populations, the public sphere of Petersonian influence widens to find a voice through beneficiaries of his advice. Based on published accounts of several of Peterson's followers whose writing has appeared in the *New York Times*, *The Atlantic*, and *Medium*, he does this by "inform[ing] us about the world and impart[ing] guidance on how we should act within it . . . His lectures infuse ordinary activit[y] with new meaning" (Henderson, 2019, para. 10). "He helps listeners [from across the political spectrum] figure out what they want in life and pursue that . . . [and] get control of their lives and navigate the world" (Slayback, 2018, "A Few Notes to Peterson's Rise to Prominence," para. 12). Even one of Peterson's critics, Nellie Bowles (2018), analyzes his technique as one in which "he tells his audiences that they are smart. He is bringing them knowledge . . . [of what] they already know and feel in their bones . . . described through religious allegories" (para. 1). By drawing on familiar sources such as Christian allegories and culturally embedded myths, such as those that position women as the weaker sex, Peterson's lessons affirm in his listeners things that they feel that they already knew and give them a sense of knowing how to process those thoughts. In short, he increases his listeners' stock in a world of affective economies by elevating aspects for which they already feel an affinity.

In doing so, Peterson effectively mobilizes a population that feels it has been neglected and passed over, endorsing their empowerment in ways that run counter to seeming hegemonies of current popular culture (Sandlin et al., 2011). He acts as a savior connecting knowledge from earlier times, while clad in a three-piece suit, for those forced to share a once larger piece of the pie. He relegitimizes sentiments recently rendered taboo in the formation of new affective economies valuing male empowerment. Peterson's economy of affect enables his audience to feel as if they gain tools for rationalization and empowerment in ways that leave them blameless for reasserting that empowerment, as they have simply succumbed to the natural order of things. Just as Ahmed's (2004a) framework predicted, the rejection of racial and gendered shame and subsequent deployment of pride shape Peterson's audience and their opponents into respectively determinant bodies.

When one places the word *critical* before any title, it is assumed that one will investigate perspectives that involve surroundings structures and contexts of power (Halualani, 2019). As critical qualitative researchers, it behooves us to ask ourselves: How does our research speak to broader audiences? How will we frame our research so that it is relevant and pragmatic to them? Jordan Peterson's work demonstrates how affect can be marshaled to package intellectual ideas (or at least, their appearance) in ways that engender individual change. Rob Henderson, a former child of foster care, became the first person in his birth family to go to college, followed by graduate studies at Cambridge University, thanks to Peterson's online advice for how to get into graduate school for psychology. YouTube commenters spoke of being freed from hating themselves for being white and male, and from feelings of shame over "what [they] had no control over" (RobS ZZZ, 2017). Peterson's natural order framing, while erasing the existence of structural violence and marginalization, provides an antidote for some to the toxic affect of shame. Tomkins equates shame with a "sickness of the soul which leaves man naked, defeated, alienated, and lacking in dignity . . . strik[ing] deepest into the heart of man" (as cited in Sedgwick & Frank, 1995, p. 148). Peterson fills the need created by the "increasing saturated shame panopticon" (Schaefer, 2019, p. 7) within an increasingly interactive 21st-century social world, capitalizing on logics that place whiteness, masculinity, and heterosexuality at the center. He uses affective economies to mobilize individual success in their daily and professional lives while also convening masses of people who endorse his philosophies within a broader public sphere. In this respect, Peterson has been more successful than a significant portion of academic scholars. As critical qualitative scholars and as individuals invested in the transformation of society to benefit those who are most in need, Peterson is someone worth studying for his ability to create continuity between social needs and intellectual ideas, however distorted his presentations are of those ideas. It is time for us, as scholars, to look beyond the mental gymnastics of isolated theorizing to find connections with affective undercurrents in the broader world and to strive to do work that reaches to meet needs circulating within those currents.

References

Ahmed, S. (2004a). Affective economies. *Social Text, 22*(2), 117–139.

Ahmed, S. (2004b). Collective feelings: Or, the impressions left by others. *Theory, Culture & Society, 21*(2), 25–42.

Berlant, L. (2016, August 5). Trump, or political emotions. *The New Inquiry*. https://thenewinquiry.com/trump-or-political-emotions/

Biesta, G. (2012). Becoming public: Public pedagogy, citizenship and the public sphere. *Social & Cultural Geography, 13*(7), 683–697.

Bowles, N. (2018, May 18). Jordan Peterson, custodian of the patriarchy. *New York Times*. https://www.nytimes.com/2018/05/18/style/jordan-peterson-12-rules-for-life.html

Brooks, D. (2018, January 25). The Jordan Peterson moment. *New York Times*. https://www.nytimes.com/2018/01/25/opinion/jordan-peterson-moment.html

Burston, D. (2019). It's hip to be square! The myths of Jordan Peterson. *Psychotherapy and Politics International, 17*(1), e1475.

Barrowed Tunes

Mockingbird sing
Pull on my heartstrings
Illuminate
Dreary overcast
With the silver linings
Of your dotted
Treble clef
Perform your ventriloquism
Speak your might
Audience whispers
Under cover of night
Mockingbird sing
Stolen lines
And borrowed tunes
Ring true

Clough, P. T. (2008). The affective turn: Political economy, biomedia and bodies. *Theory, Culture & Society, 25*(1), 1–22.

ContraPoints. (2018, May 2). *Jordan Peterson* [Video]. YouTube. https://www.youtube.com/watch?v=4LqZdkkBDas

Grossberg, L. (2018). *Under the cover of chaos: Trump and the battle for the American right*. Pluto Press.

Habermas, J. (1989). *The structural transformation of the public sphere* (T. Burger, Trans.). MIT Press. (Original work published 1962)

Halualani, R. (2019). *Intercultural communication: A critical perspective*. Cognella.

Hauser, G. A. (1999). *Vernacular voices: The rhetoric of publics and public spheres*. University of South Carolina Press.

Heer, J. (2018, May 21). Jordan Peterson's tired old myths. *The New Republic*. https://newrepublic.com/article/148473/jordan-petersons-tired-old-myths

Henderson, R. (2019, April 22). What Jordan Peterson did for me. *New York Times*. https://www.nytimes.com/2019/04/22/opinion/jordan-peterson-cambridge.html

Hsu, F. L. (1983). *Rugged individualism reconsidered: Essays in psychological anthropology*. University of Tennessee Press.

jagodzinski, j. (2013). Pedagogy in the public realm: Affective diagrams of thinking feeling in the X-Men and beyond. In J. Sandlin, M. O'Malley, & J. Burdick (Eds.), *Problematizing public pedagogy* (pp. 89–100). Routledge.

Klein, D. B. (2018). On Jordan Peterson, postmodernism, and pomo-bashing. *Society, 55*(6), 477–481.

McKittrick, K. (Ed.). (2015). *Sylvia Wynter: On being human as praxis*. Duke University Press.

McLaughlin, N. (2018). The two Jacobys: Contradiction, ironies and challenges in new left critical social psychology after Jordan Peterson. *Free Associations, 72*(1), 1–26.

Mervosh, S., Bogel-Burroughs, N., Swales, V., Smith, M, Hassan, A., Rojas, R., Taylor, K., & Del Real, J. A. (2020, January 22). We asked 81 Americans about impeachment. Here's what they had to say. *New York Times*. https://www.nytimes.com/interactive/2020/01/22/us/impeachment-voters.html

Papacharissi, Z. (2016). Affective publics and structures of storytelling: Sentiment, events and mediality. *Information, Communication & Society, 19*(3), 307–324.

Peterson, J. [Jordan B. Peterson]. (2017, November 13). *Identity politics and the Marxist lie of White privilege* [Video]. YouTube. https://youtu.be/PfH8IG7Awk0

Peterson, J. B. (2018). 12 rules for life: An antidote to chaos. Penguin Random House.

Peterson, J. P. [Jordan B. Peterson]. (2019, January 1). Q & A 2019 01 January [Video]. YouTube. https://www.youtube.com/watch?v=mXPmLZRAPSo

RobS ZZZ. (2017, November 13). Re: *Identity Politics and the Marxist Lie of White Privilege* [Video file]. Retrieved from https://youtu.be/PfH8IG7Awk0

Runs with Sharp Objects. (2017, November 13). Re: Identity Politics and the Marxist Lie of White Privilege [Video file]. Retrieved from https://youtu.be/PfH8IG7Awk0

Sandlin, J. A., O'Malley, M. P., & Burdick, J. (2011). Mapping the complexity of public pedagogy scholarship: 1894–2010. *Review of Educational Research, 81*(3), 338–375.

Sandlin, J. A., Schultz, B. D., & Burdick, J. (Eds.). (2010). *Handbook of public pedagogy: Education and learning beyond schooling.* Routledge.

Schaefer, D. O. (2019). *The evolution of affect theory: The humanities, the sciences, and the study of power.* Cambridge University Press.

Sedgwick, E. K., & Frank, A. (Eds.) (1995). *Shame and its sisters: A Silvan Tomkins reader.* Duke University Press.

Sharma, N. (2015). Strategic anti-essentialism: Decolonizing decolonization. In K. McKittrick (Ed.), *Sylvia Wynter: On being human as praxis* (pp. 164–182). Duke University Press.

Slayback, Z. (2018, January 25). Why do intellectuals oppose Jordan B. Peterson? *Medium.* https://medium.com/age-of-awareness/why-do-intellectuals-oppose-dr-jordan-b-peterson-f8b4e6dbe04c

Springgay, S., & Zaliwska, Z. (2017). Learning to be affected: Matters of pedagogy in the artists' soup kitchen. *Educational Philosophy and Theory, 49*(3), 273–283.

Timothy Richards. (2017, November 13). *Re: Identity Politics and the Marxist Lie of White Privilege* [Video file]. Retrieved from https://youtu.be/PfH8IG7Awk0

Legitimized

Power

Standing **on SHAKY GROUND**

Mock and minimize

Defeat shame

Collective bodies gasp,

Sigh

Dialoguing with Frank

Frank: How might one go about developing ideas and educating the public? Might this be one task of a (public) intellectual?

Meena: Does the (public) intellectual bear responsibility for educating the public? Or is there a call for the public to be, first and foremost, public intellectuals, or intellectual publics? The responsibility of the public intellectual has to be borne by the public. To depend on someone – to guide, to be guided by – then loses the intellectual and only the public remains.

Sara: I think this is a complicated question. We always live in the past in some ways and many past ideas of education and educating also live in us, shape our current actions, and visions of the future. At the same time, living completely in the past or allowing the past to solely shape our future can also be problematic. The entire dichotomy of past and present, education then and now is highly limiting the ways in which one might constitute herself as a public intellectual and relational/community-driven scholar. It could be argued that if a scholar constitutes oneself as an intellectual within binary structures, all actions and concepts form a relation to and become only possible within the existing boundary. Moving outside the boundary and its limits would introduce a new scale and completely different conceptual space where intellectualism might not be even recognized or it would appear as unthinkable while it still would be operating. Furthermore, we cannot answer this question about the tasks of the public intellectual without asking questions about the subject, power, discourses, relationality, more than human activities and thinking, virtuality, and more.

Derrida (1993): "By itself, the expression 'limits of truth' can certainly be understood – and this would be an indication – as the fact that the truth is precisely limited, *finite*, and confined within its borders. In sum, the truth is not everything, one would then say, for there is more, something else or something better: truth is finite [*finie*]. Or worse: truth, it's finished [*c'est fini*]. However, by itself, the same expression can signify – and this time it would not be an indication but the *law* of a negative *prescription* – that the limits of truth are borders that must not be exceeded." (p. 1)

Frank: Intellectuals play a crucial role in initiating dialogue, curiosity, and engaging public. However, in the current political climate stimulating creativity and dialogue of difference is increasingly challenging to do. It could also be argued that we have come to expect too little from the public. "The political elites have drawn the conclusion that the way to re-engage is to be less demanding and less challenging. What is often called the *politics of inclusion* is a project that is designed to bypass the problem, by demanding very little of people, and seeking a technical quick-fix for the political malaise" (Furedi, 2006, p. 84).

Sara: Are you proposing that desirable discourse is no longer about how the public needs to know more about the world and scientific advancements but it is about the lack of substance and concrete ideas? It is also possible that the lack of substance can offer an efficient shelter for all forms of political and scholarly propaganda and selectivism. This lack of substance and content presents quite a shift in thinking about the capabilities and interests of public, I think.

Frank: Yes. Public, not as an independent unit but public as driven by many politicians and fake news, seems to like it better when the solutions are provided to them in the simplest form possible and they might generally be pleased that no decision needs to made by them. Rather decisions have been made. In addition, I propose that society does not protect what it does not value. Therefore, intellectuals need to address and generate initiatives of public and society value. Does this imply more effective marketing of ideas which align more clearly with the interests of the public?

Sara: I am not sure. I wonder whether intellectuals will survive without the society's support. What might make intellectuals and their thoughts (ir)relevant?

Frank: The survival of (public) intellectuals might be even an irrelevant question. Maybe they no longer exist as we have come to know them. "Through a variety of devices—life-long learning, certificates of competence, training and development—people's intellectual and cultural life becomes subject to institutional expectations. These trends stimulate a mood of conformism and passivity" (Furedi, 2006, p. 154). Conformism both feeds and starves intellectuals. Furthermore, the relevance of intellectualism and intellectual thought can never be proven without a form of political impact, transformational value, and socio-cultural significance. However, the more important question has to do with the subject-object of the impact, fields of transformation and privilege associated with socio-cultural significance. I argue that "In an era of the infantilization of culture, treating people as grown-ups has become one of the principal duties of the humanist intellectual" (p. 156).

> Arundhati: "What I wanted to know was: can a novel be a city? Can you stop it being baby food, which can be easily consumed? So the reader also has to deal with complexities that they are being trained not to deal with." (Roy, 2018)

Derrida, J. (1993). *Aporias*. Stanford, CA: Stanford University Press.

Furedi, F. (2006). *Where have all the intellectuals gone? Including a reply to Furedi's critics*. London: Continuum.

Roy, A. (2018, June 17). Arundhati Roy: "The point of the writer is to be unpopular." An interview with Tim Lewis. *The Guardian*. Retrieved https://www.theguardian.com/books/2018/jun/17/arundhati-roy-interview-you-ask-the-questions-the-point-of-the-writer-is-to-be-unpopular

Riding Waves

FIVE

Is That a Ladybird on the Leaf? Public Intellectualism and Resistance With Very Young Children

Marek Tesar, The University of Auckland

PUBLIC INTELLECTUALISM HAS BEEN SOMEWHAT in a crisis in the 21st century, at least until recently. Perhaps this can be best demonstrated by the current situation in global politics and the growing apathy that has been widely replacing revolutionary engagement. The leaders of many countries have been elected on unrealistic or disturbing promises (and premises), and their public engagement has been reduced to discourses that aim not only to divide, to challenge, to antagonize, and to impose chaos but also to pave the way to what we now are calling the post-truth world. The leaders of current times argue and aim to please the masses with statements that do not historicize or seek the truth or a higher purpose beyond the desires of our contemporary existence. Climate change has reached crisis point, and despite some countries already being affected, either by literally sinking or by being on fire, other major countries (and, indeed, in some cases, those countries that are on fire or sinking) and their leaders pursue an economic model that places the human subject on a pedestal. We see the idea of a "public intellectual" being attacked, the labels of discourses used in unprecedented ways, acting to disrupt and produce chaos and simplicity. There is a clear message to make everything that appears complex simple, to reduce the responsibility of the human subject, and for failed attempts to reduce the entrapment, guilt, and injustices of colonization: the increased military flexing of muscles, the lack of inspiration and imagination from the leaders of the human race, and the absence of a higher binding purpose in political statements. These are just some of the observations of the first two decades of the 21st century.

However, in this "doom and gloom" of the practices and scenarios being discussed around the world by families, friends, colleagues, and strangers during mealtimes, meetings, and breaks, there is also some unprecedented change that we have not had experienced for some time. The dominant discourse that has been pressuring all citizens, filling the public discourse with xenophobia, intolerance, and injustice, has been also in some, particularly smaller, countries challenged and turned into amazing examples of subversion against these disturbing dominant trends. Indeed, there is something to admire about a 34-year-old female Finnish prime minister being elected into government, and in New Zealand, Jacinda Ardern, who gave birth to her child while in office, managed to unite the country following the horrifying Christchurch massacre events. From Sweden, we have a 17-year-old, Greta Thunberg, who not only has managed to mobilize children in schools around the world but also has challenged world leaders, adults, in a way that few adult-run organizations could achieve.

As such, it is unjust to claim the 21st century, thus far, as a universal disappointment. And although public intellectualism has been devalued, if not removed, from the mainstream media and discourses, there are pockets of resistance and ideas of change that we are yet to fully unearth and follow. Most important, the death of traditional universities as places of intellectualism and knowledge and debate because of their transformation into neoliberal business machines has, on one hand, pushed intellectuals to the side while, on the other, prompted the emergence of extraordinary groupings of academics and scholars focused on resistance and theorizing the change. This has occurred while the roles of university presidents or vice-chancellors have become analogous to executives in large corporations.

Among this turmoil, this chapter explores how we have taken for granted the notion of the public intellectual and understand "public" and "intellectual" as something that is somewhat expected to emerge and occur naturally in our societies. The chapter further teases out understandings of ideology and intellectualism as detailed in the scholarship of Havel before then exploring the potential of expanding our traditional conceptualizations of who can become a public intellectual. To do this, we draw on the narrative and experiences of "Mary" (a pseudonym), an early childhood teacher in New Zealand who conceptualizes her role as teacher as one of intellectual and activist while positioning children not as innocent and helpless but rather as public intellectuals in their own right.

The Story of a Public Intellectual

It is not an easy task to define who is, or what it means to be, a public intellectual. Twentieth-century philosopher-turned-politician and country president Václav Havel pondered extensively over the role of an intellectual and public engagement in politics and everyday life. He referred to the notion of "responsibility" in his political philosophy as one of the critical narratives that accompanies the idea of the intellectual. In particular, Havel's (1985) writing and thinking, and the performance of his being, were concerned with what it means to be a thinker and intellectual and the fate of the human subject in politically and ideologically charged contexts. It is an important question to ponder and is the question that potentially goes to the core of what and who is the public intellectual. And although Havel based his philosophical framework on the modeling of experiences of living in a country that exercised an extreme ideological governance (Czechoslovakia), the idea of defining "ideological governance," and "extreme," has in today's global studies been an equivocal meaning-making endeavor. So does the term *intellectual* and its tenuous link to an academic. As Goodson (1999, p. 289) argues,

> Of course it would be wrong to equate intellectuals with academics. But, since the word "intellectual" first emerged in Russia to characterise the nihilistic university students, more and more intellectual life has been colonised by the massive expansion of universities. Edward Shils describes intellectuals as persons with unusual sensitivity to the sacred, an uncommon reflectiveness about the nature of their universe and the rules which govern society. . . . In the past, they have found patrons as disparate as royalty, the aristocracy, the church, the army, newspapers, the media, welfare and begging. But as Halsey notes . . . nowadays we are forced to the conclusion that institutions of higher education are their major institutional location.

It is interesting to return to Havel and to discuss how he has perceived what we could refer to as the public intellectual. Havel's talk at Victoria University of Wellington in New Zealand pondered the notions of "intellectual" and "responsibility" through a careful reading of Popper. In his talk, Havel (1997) went as far as attempting to define, who is an "intellectual":

> Let me try—just for the moment—to define an intellectual. To me, an intellectual is a person who has devoted his or her life to thinking in general terms about the affairs of this world and the broader context of things. Of course, intellectuals are not the only ones who do this. But they do it—if I may use the word—professionally. That is, their principal occupation is studying, reading, teaching, writing, publishing, addressing the public. Often—though certainly not always—this makes them more receptive to more general issues; often—though certainly not always—it leads them to embrace a broader sense of responsibility for the state of the world and its future. (p. 175)

As Havel has argued, an intellectual is by default carrying a public voice or is part of public engagement. Every human subject, every citizen in Havel's theoretical framework, constructs and creates aspects and parts of the society; everyone is part of it. Everyone contributes to it, everyone suffers in it, and in the end, everyone is responsible for its performance and becoming. In other words, the unifying factors of a "public system" within which the intellectualism takes place are the experiences of human subjects, as they link and relate to the public engagement under ideological governance.

As such, the role of a public intellectual is to comment on, to elevate private discourses, to expose, and to critique; it is to comment and to speak up; it is to refuse to become locked in within private life. It is a social contract that the public intellectual will accept. Although all human subjects and citizens in Havel's work are part of the system, and as such, there is no one who is outside of the system; we all share the same ideological concerns. There is no free subject for Havel, as all citizens in any ideological settings are part of a social contract within the system. All subjects are formed through complex power relations within the parameters of ideologies of the society. Rose (1993) addresses issues of these power relations and claims that there is "no simple distinction between those who have power and who are subject to it" (p. 287) in any ideological society. The ideology thus operates within a similar consumer value system and becomes a form of consumer society. This is the same for every academic and every citizen, as Havel (1985) sees it, and the challenge to the role of the public intellectual:

> In a democracy, human beings may enjoy many personal freedoms and securities that are unknown to us, but in the end they do them no good, for they too are ultimately victims of the same automatism, and are incapable of defending

> their concerns about their own identity or preventing their superficialization or transcending concerns about their own personal survival to become proud and responsible members of the polis, making a genuine contribution to the creation of its destiny. (p. 91)

One of the major contradictions of any ideological systems within which a public intellectual operates is the distinction between private and public life for its citizens. Havel's argument can be translated to the academic-intellectual, whose intellectual potential is accepted in writing, in thinking, in supervising and whose thesis utilizes critical theories and methodologies, mostly in the classroom, or in writing or at the conferences. However, if this intellectualism becomes public, and, thus, the intellectualism usually contained within the academic space becomes a public critique of a system, of the order of things, of the university, that becomes a concern of a system and its governance. As such, we have accepted that governing agencies tolerate intellectuals as long as their efforts have not crossed into the public domain, and public support is displayed and demonstrated. In Havel's theoretical framework, this leads to a potential intellectual double life and to thinking of how being public intellectual can be seen as a dangerous profession (see also Foucault's, 2001, work on parrhesia or Kuntz's, 2018, interpretation of Foucault's parrhesia).

These tensions between being a private and public intellectual are perhaps less noticeable in some ideological systems than in others. However, viewing of this private and public dichotomy can occur from multiple angles. It does not necessarily mean that we shall perceive them as opposites. From one angle, this may seem like a retreat from power pressure and ideological space, while from the other angle, it may be the victory of the ideological system for the public intellectual to be joining it and its impact on citizens in the form of an "inner immigration" as turning inward that produced an "intellectual form of [a] double life" (Ash, 1991, p. 9).

Havel's (1985) work on power relations and the notion of a public intellectual in the ideological space, similar to Foucault's work, analyzes the shift in the construction of power relations and, thus, the way power is exercised. Havel examines and teases out the shift toward more sophisticated, complex, and calculated forms of discipline and punishment that produce citizens (and public intellectuals) in any ideological context. There is a claim that ideology and the subject position of the public intellectual have transitioned from an idealistic toward a calculated construct, shaped by the shift from direct to complex, nonlinear power relations. Part of this complexity in relations of power is the role that desire plays in upholding certain subjective positions toward power. And although in a certain way the concept of "desire" is related to a market-based idea that keeps the system functioning and united, at the same time, the notion of "desire" is not an acceptable way of living a life for a public intellectual. The intellectual cannot accept living a life in private, or to accept public discourse without a critique, commentary, or other forms of intellectual activism. As such, it creates a concern, deal, or social contract that is not acceptable for any intellectual.

Being a public intellectual, following the preceding theoretical framing, is to be free and speak publicly, to critique subjects and structures that shape the institutions within which the intellectuals operate, to be outwardly true, and to challenge the post-truth discourses that have become the dominant discourses of our times. Public intellectuals speak of the past and present, understand texts and thoughts that came before, speak to protect others, and try to pave an intellectual pathway to the future. However, such tasks seem both daunting and dangerous and almost incapacitating given the ideological grounding and boundaries that intellectuals face. As such, the next section traces the origins and potentiality of this ideological narrative.

The narrative thus far was very adult-focused. We have accepted that public intellectuals exist, that they are part of the society, and that they experience a complex predicament. We are yet to address the histories of these possibilities of what resistance is, what is possible with very young children. Thinking with teachers of young children about public intellectualism and resistance can potentially be an important link to consider while discussing public intellectualism.

Resistance With Very Young Children

I've been spending a lot of time in early childhood centers, particularly with a teacher who for the purposes of this chapter I call Mary. Mary once asked me, "How do we confront and deconstruct the power relations associated with the theory/practice divide, to foster children's intellectualism, agency, and activism?" That is not an easy question to ask or to respond to, even if Mary is a parent-activist and a public intellectual in her own right. My discussion with Mary became focused on the rejection of the hegemonic discourse positioning power in "theory" over "practice," "teacher" over "learner," and, more specifically, "adult" over "child." It is in this space that public intellectualism with children diminishes, as it becomes a power relation in its own right; the interdependency and relationality linked together, Mary says. It also positions power and knowledge as a dynamic process and public intellectualism becomes a philosophical problem, not an ontological inadequacy of being a child.

Mary says that there are multiple ways in which the teaching team members view their role as public intellectuals and activists, whose role is to empower children as active agents who shape (present tense and not the future will shape) the world around them. There is a role that teachers as public intellectuals need to undertake, mostly within the context of something that has been historically a hierarchical relationship between the adult and the child. The philosophical inquiry implicates how teachers' view of children can be deconstructed and reconceptualized through the philosophical research of childhoods to dismantle the hierarchical constructions that serve to predetermine and govern relationship dynamics among people, places, and things. Mary says that while she is at work, she often feels that she is part of a system that promotes the silencing and oppression of children and does not allow the potentiality of public intellectualism to thrive. She finds this particularly challenging, although she is on the journey of recognizing her own bias and emotions and understanding that liberation is subjective.

Mary is very interested in philosophical thinking in relation to the children's agency, activism, and public intellectualism with young children. She brings fresh ideas and perspectives, which challenge the outlook of a child as too young or incompetent whose voice does not count and should not be taken seriously, and, in such a notion, challenges the established developmental hierarchy and norms that may silence our youngest citizens and reduce the potential public intellectuals growing up in our early childhood centers. She is embodying New Zealand's curriculum framework *Te Whāriki* (Ministry of Education, 2017), which conceptualizes children as already being "competent and confident learners and communicators, healthy in mind, body, and spirit, secure in their sense of belonging and in the knowledge that they make a valued contribution to society" (p. 9). Mary sees this as a potentially positive framework, within which the recognizing of young children's activism and public intellectualism can take place despite perhaps wanting to ask, for example, how the idea of "competence" is assessed or measured and who might benefit. Mary says that she is focused on fostering dialogue and action with children (and with other adults) to embody learning environments that prioritize the manifestation of mindfulness and respect in our interactions with each other and the world around us in the present moment rather than participating in a process for achieving social norms we cannot be certain will benefit all or any of us at a later time (Tesar & Arndt, 2020).

Being a public intellectual, and an activist who wishes to make a difference has, at times, been challenging. As Mary describes it, it has at times felt like being a cog in a factory. "It's lunchtime! Time to come inside!" she repeated so enthusiastically, thinking, as she has shared, that the appeal in her voice will trigger children's hunger and that they all can then toddle happily together to the lunch table. For Mary, so many moments like these are where she felt herself becoming annoyed at her role in shuffling children along to participate in structured routines (she used the word *shuffling* as a soft way of saying "creatively coercing," she says). Mary says that, of course, mealtimes are important, and a child will likely need to eat while at the center; however, a number of ethical considerations come into play in this simple interaction, particularly when communicating with a young child. This child, for example, might not be hungry right now at the center's time for lunch. This child might be peckish, however presently preoccupied with, for example, an important question, "Is that a ladybird on the leaf?" Mary notices. Suddenly, it seems Mary has this child's attention, and a few others gather around at the prompt of her proclamation. She has stepped out of the cog machine and into the present. Mary and the children together are awed by the beauty and fascination of this creature. Lunch inside resumes, and Mary figures there will likely be some for us even if we do not head in right now. Mary quickly informs her colleagues about what is happening out here, and they are free to continue watching the ladybird. After some time, the ladybird can no longer be seen, and the remaining children seem to notice lunch. In moments like this, Mary says that she, and the children, are reawakened. This child acted on their own behalf, resisting teacher's commands and showing adults what they could see. For Mary, the most fruitful learning for that child that came from the teacher in that interaction were the messages that connected them with our environment and one another.

It is in Mary's vignette that we see the role of axiology in teachers' intellectual work with very young children. The public intellectual cannot accept being locked away in an ideological space. Axiology is the philosophical study of value, which can be seen as a study of both ethics and aesthetics. Whereas ethics is concerned with the concept of what is correct, right or good (whether individual subject or ideology), aesthetics studies the idea of attraction, beauty, harmony, and coherence. Mary, with her children, has witnessed the tension between ethics and aesthetics, the ideas of right or wrong, the ladybird and the routine. It is the idea of the public intellectual in every citizen, in every teacher, in every child to speak up, to become a public intellectual in the most everyday, mundane spaces and experiences.

Childhoods and Adulthoods

One of the increasingly prevailing discourses of childhoods is its inherent antithesis to the qualities of adulthood. It holds this position in a dichotomy, which is dangerous for understanding the potentialities and boundaries of public intellectualism. The image of children and childhood is often portrayed as someone and something that does not have the capacity to be an intellectual, not even a public intellectual! The idea of childhood is typically associated with the idea of development, becoming, growing, learning, in-waiting, with ontological incompleteness (Tesar & Jukes, 2018). This developmental thinking ensures that we separate and segregate thinking between childhood and adulthood and children and adults. Instead, we are pushed to see them in the developmental sense, as an in-betweenness, as those who developed the competency to participate effectively in society as public intellectuals. To simplify, it positions children less as active and more as requiring guidance from adults to achieve competency or intellectual capacity or, at least, the responsibility to ensure the course of transition between childhood (sub-intellectualism) and adulthood (intellectualism) is followed with the desired outcome—the complete intellectual and thus productive contribution to the society and a public performance of intellectualism.

In early childhood centers, there seems to be a pattern of learning outcomes children need to follow in order to be considered to be "on the right track." A lot of these involve the establishment of certain habits of behavior, compliance, and modes of communication. Mary says that she hears people say things like "That child should be able to sit still by now, listen by now, count to *x* by now." And although Mary appreciates the convenience that can arise when children abide by our expectations, she is wary of any certainty around what children "should" be doing. At the university as a student, she felt constantly restless and fidgety. Mary says that she is still unsure of how to read an analog clock to tell the time. It remains a mystery to her how she came so far through education, and graduated with a degree, without meeting that standard. And we place such constructed expectations on children's learning and behavior, and sometimes in even more sophisticated ways than even adults could meet up to themselves, Mary says. She further wonders that it seems to be accepted that different adults have unique characteristics, that they are different people with different ways of life; however, children who don't meet the benchmarks of learning and behavior generally decided by adults—they are problematic, or, as I say, inconvenient, in the eyes of adults. Why is it that adults seem desperate to socialize children when, paradoxically, we place such high value on the characteristics we attribute to youthful exuberance in adults, for example, energy, lightheartedness, liberty?

Mary, the public intellectual, tells us about the state of a "child" and "childhood" in current society. This is related to Havel's (1985) concerns about what it means to be a "public" and "intellectual." It is the philosophical lens that may help us provoke our awareness of what we could argue is an inherent obligation that adults possess to set things "right" and "correct" for children, to pursue their public intellectual careers, and to fix and correct them when they are perceived as "in need" or "out of order." That is indeed invoking of the awareness of the socially constructed nature of the characteristics of "order" rather than philosophically what it means to be an adult and what it means to be a child. This philosophical positioning fosters adults' competence and capability to view children as public intellectuals as they negotiate their way through an unpredictable world alongside adults, as public intellectuals in their own right rather than intellectuals in the making. It makes sense to think of our children as intellectuals "here" and "right now" rather than intellectuals who will be and become.

Making of Public Intellectual

The story of Mary and her children is the story of the making of a public intellectual. It is the endless thinking and being with tension between childhood and adulthood, the prior knowledge and emerging experiences, desires, and even the ownership of knowledge. Adults seek to possess knowledge and strive to make decisions regarding children that are supposedly in the children's best interests. However, as children are often excluded from the decision making about their own childhoods, there is a potentially hidden intellectualism presented in the childhood undergrounds, hidden from the sight of adults. Havel (1985) tells us that all citizens, including children, are victims, supporters, and rebels at the very same time in their negotiations with the systematic ideologies in which they are growing up. As such, we can perceive children as participants and well-informed social actors who do struggle with resistance as a form of intellectualism while also contributing to the necessary sustainment of order within their contextual environments. This argument suggests that a child as a public intellectual is capable of participating in issues of justice, rights, fairness, nature, climate change, and others.

As such, how have we ended up with the young leader as Greta Thunberg? Her story seems to be removed from kindergartens but at the same time far away from the world of a rational man, of the university professor we started this chapter with. Greta Thunberg's activism and public intellectualism have challenged the established boundaries, the ideas about who should be the leader, and what direction and with what action we should proceed. Although the 21st century has been a disappointing century thus far indeed, we could not have imagined that it would be a teenager from Sweden who would showcase the leadership and power of young activists and public intellectuals. Greta is the link between Mary's young children in the kindergarten and the rational man who makes the decision for us all. And the rise of Greta (and other young people) challenging the hierarchy, forming the arguments and asking the right questions, is the most challenging and exciting anti-ontology of childhood we have witnessed and makes Mary confident that her children, if she will follow the ladybird instead of a routine, will thrive on activism and will be part of the public questioning and march of young children.

Mary says how adults are always around and children do not necessarily want her to know everything they are saying and doing, but she must supervise them at all times. How will children ever figure anything out on their own if Mary is always there to offer her experienced expertise as a rational, educated human being? This is not only Mary's challenge; this is a challenge for us all as well.

References

Ash, T. G. (1991). *The uses of adversity*. Granta Books.

Foucault, M. (2001). *Fearless speech*. MIT Press.

Goodson, I. F. (1999). The educational researcher as a public intellectual. *British Educational Research Journal, 25*(3), 277–297.

Havel, V. (1985). The power of the powerless. In J. Keane (Ed.), *The power of the powerless: Citizens against the state in Central-Eastern Europe* (pp. 23–96). Hutchinson.

Havel, V. (1997). *The art of the impossible: Politics as morality in practice*. Knopf.

Kuntz, A. M. (2018). *Qualitative inquiry, cartography, and the promise of material change*. Routledge Press.

Ministry of Education. (2017). *Te Whāriki he whāriki mātauranga mō ngā mokopuna o Aotearoa early childhood curriculum*. New Zealand Government.

Rose, N. (1993). Government, authority and expertise in advanced liberalism. *Economy and Society, 22*(3), 283–299. doi:10.1080/03085149300000019

Tesar, M., & Arndt, S. (2020). Problematising and activating Te Whāriki through the childhood studies lens. In A. Gunn & J. Nuttall (Eds.), *Weaving Te Whāriki: Aotearoa New Zealand's early childhood curriculum document in theory and practice* (pp. 181–194). NZCER Press.

Tesar, M., & Jukes, B. (2018). Childhoods in the Anthropocene: Re-thinking young children's agency and activism. In N. Yelland & D. Bentley (Eds.), *Found in translation: Connecting reconceptualist thinking with early childhood education practices* (pp. 76–90). Routledge.

Publish with Care

Study
Round, red coccinellidae
Read
Inked braille
Across its back
Teach
Of leaves
And light-winged departures
Write
Six-legged tracks
Across my palm
Publish
In excited voice
With animated hands
Rush of public
Dropped playground balls
Empty swings sway
Crowd gathers
Chubby, grubby
Little hands
Reach
Cupped
With care

In a Crisis

colonized expansion
There are pockets of resistance and ideas of change
ublic intellectualism in a crisis

Notice the Present

See that fine thread
Silken
Woven
From one side of the rotting bamboo to the other
Caressing the miniscule mushroom on its way
So fine
That you can barely see it
Yet to see
Really see something
Takes time
Like it takes time
To make a friend.*

Like it takes time
To notice the ladybird
Like it takes time
For the rotting bamboo
To nourish life
Like it takes time
To notice change
On a scale
That is beyond our
Human space-time-
Clock-mechanical-appendage.
Time - to stop
Break the routine
Break up time
To notice the present.

* "Nobody sees a flower – really – it is so small – we haven't time – and to see takes time like to have a friend takes time." – Georgia O'Keeffe. From "Georgia O'Keeffe: Exhibition of Oils and Pastels" Catalogue, Jan 22 – March 17, 1939, An American Place, New York City.

SIX

Intellectual Undesirables: An Autoethnographic Reflection on Intellectual Contributions of the Neurologically Othered

Joshua Cruz, Texas Tech University

> Just don't do anything to upset him. He doesn't like high-pitched noises. He really hates whistling, so be sure not to do that around him. He's not usually violent, but . . . well, it just didn't work out with his last tutor. And stick to talking about computers. He's going to try to tell you stories.

DS's CARETAKER TOLD ME THIS over the phone. I have worked as a tutor in some capacity for almost half my life—sometimes informally, as a volunteer in high school or university spaces, and sometimes more formally, as a salaried or contracted employee of different tutoring agencies. In this case, I had been hired as an independent contractor through a tutoring agency to make house calls to students in my area. But in my time tutoring, I had never been forewarned about a student who might have aggressive tendencies, posttraumatic stress disorder (PTSD), and/or dementia, and I had never before been briefed about how I should present myself to the student to assure my safety. What had I gotten myself into? DS, a Vietnam War veteran, had hired me—or, rather, his caretaker had hired me on his behalf—to help him with basic computer literacy skills. Computer literacy I could do, but I had not signed up for violent mood swings and eggshell walking. I was primed for the worst, but I had taken the contract.

DS was, in fact, an old hippie, a term that he did not personally identify with, but he was willing to accept it if someone else described him that way. And the characterization I received from his caretaker before our first meeting, while perhaps medically, pathologically, and technically accurate, could not have missed the mark more. He was soft-spoken and frail but not feeble. He tended the garden in his retirement community apartments, despite excessive heat and drought. He was a vegetarian. He collected artifacts from outside, like plant life and dead bugs, and would examine them through microscopes. His dog, a hairless terrier, loved him, and he loved his dog. And he was a fount of information. Tutoring sessions for computer literacy turned into ghostwriting his memoirs. What strikes me about my interactions with DS was how uneasy I felt when I was first told about him as compared with my actual experience. I wanted as little to do with him as I could, and I was ready to dismiss him entirely. Once I met him, I discovered a gentle soul with stories to tell.

My purpose for writing this short autoethnographic piece is twofold: It is first to trouble the ways that we think about those whom we call neurodivergent and to echo existing calls for neurodiversity (e.g., Dyck & Russell, 2019; Manning, 2016), recognizing contributions of the neurodivergent within the intellectual sphere. Second, I would like to share my experiences interacting with DS and use these as a way to think about how those who are categorized as neurodivergent might, in fact, be public intellectuals in their own right, making important contributions to our world. This is important when we think of calls to celebrate those who are neurologically othered (Manning, 2016) as well as calls to diversify what might count as intellectual activity (Collini, 2002). Specifically, I reflect on one of the memoirs that DS shared with me and consider how DS contributed to the public sphere intellectually. I also consider how my own assumptions about DS changed over the months that he and I interacted and describe how, as researchers, we might bracket our own assumptions about people and participants that we include in our studies. Choosing participants based on specific criteria is common, especially in qualitative research, but my experiences with DS remind me that we can learn from unexpected experiences, and this learning can shift our perceptions of the taken-for-granted, whatever that might be in our own research, in this case, public intellectualism.

Before I focus on DS, I begin by thinking through what it might mean to be a public intellectual. I argue that knowledge/intellectualism is a discursive construction, a move that I believe destabilizes the notion of what counts as intellectual, in an effort to make room for those whose intellectual contributions might be dismissed otherwise as empty madness.

Knowledge, Intellectuality, and Sanity: Discursive Constructions

In opening a discussion about who can be considered a public intellectual, we need to first consider what defines a public intellectual. The simple answer is that this kind of intellectual is one who produces knowledge for public consumption. The public intellectual exists "midway between the great minds and the people so as to serve the function of transmitting and popularizing philosophic knowledge" (Melzer, 2003, p. 7). This leads one to wonder: What exactly constitutes knowledge? As Foucault tells us, knowledge—knowledge of good and bad, right and wrong, value, the knowable, sayable, and doable (Gordon, 1991)—is a social construction, and thus, by extension, so is the public intellectual. Goodson (1999) notes that "public knowledge is itself an ideological position" (p. 279), that is, contingent on a broad set of social beliefs. Knowledge is knowledge by recognition by some public, and who is "knowledgable" is relative to the beliefs of a public, or at least a coalition of individuals, that recognizes information as knowledge.

In short, knowledge and those who are seen to dwell in the realm of knowledge (i.e., intellectuals) are discursive constructions. Studies on discursive constructions span a range of disciplines and topic areas, but most current studies focus on the construction of identities or kinds of people, groups, institutions, and nations (e.g., Banda & Mawadza, 2014; Stoegner & Wodak, 2016). Wodak et al. (2009) call the discursive construction "an imaginary complex of ideas containing at least the defining elements of collective unity and equality, of boundaries and autonomy" (p. 22). This complex of ideas is typically mediated and reified through various politically and socially discursive acts such as images and language in the media. Thus, "knowledge" is wrapped up in various propaganda. Beliefs about where knowledge resides, what knowledge should produce, what knowledge is about, and what it is directed at all construct a general sense of what knowledge is, largely the result of what a particular group chooses to identify as knowledge.

The public intellectual, that individual who possesses and metes out knowledge, can only be said to possess knowledge if the knowledge is recognized as such under various governments. Stoegner and Wodak (2016), as well as Glasson (2012), note that "intellectual" can be used to classify and construct certain kinds of individuals. Based on various propaganda, intellectuals may be either leader (reformist, trendsetter, mogul) or pariah (egghead, lazy, armchair communist). Important to remember, however, is that discursive constructions are not stable facts. Any singular conception discursively constructed is malleable, only "real to the extent that one [has] conceived of it, believes in it, and identifies with it emotionally" (Wodak et al., 2009, p. 22). This means that the identity of an intellectual does not exist beyond collective recognition of it as a "real" construct. As soon as recognition falters—as soon as what counts as knowledge changes—belief in who the public intellectual is also changes.

Tied to the idea of intellectualism and knowledge is the idea of what constitutes a sane agent, or one who is able to use knowledge in a rational, "normal" way. Who is rational—alternatively who is irrational or insane—is contextually motivated. Farrelly (2015) notes that "'mental health problems' can be understood as occupying a social space between the individual experience of mental distress and the shifting and conflicting social constructions of what is considered normal and abnormal human behavior, emotion and cognition" (p. 2). In short, mental health "problems" do not exist beyond our ability to recognize them, and a look at our history of insanity tells us this: For instance, that the criteria for insanity have changed several times over the course of the last four centuries (Dreyfus & Rabinow, 1983; Foucault, 1965/1988, 2003, 2006).

In fact, if we go back roughly four centuries, the fool, a figure who typically evades rationality, inhabited an esoteric and uncanny domain of knowledge. In Shakespearean literature, for instance, it is the fool who tends to be the wisest, who holds an uncommon common sense, who sees the big picture, and who can dispense advice to those less wise characters who are infatuated by their myopic, quotidian existences (Goldsmith, 1974). Foucault also describes uncanny knowledge held by fools in his first chapter of *Madness and Civilization* (1965/1988), wherein he speaks about the ship of fools. He details how, during the Middle Ages, the insane were cast away from their homeland, exiled to anywhere else so that they weren't a drain on their respective societies. However, on a more symbolic level, they were sent on a journey—they possessed a kind of knowledge of the world, of mortality and death, that most simply weren't ready for. To say that one who is mentally different is "touched" refers to a touch of God; those who are so touched are graced with that wisdom that comes from the tree of knowledge. Similar to the Shakespearean fool, they held a kind of wisdom that seemed to come from some external plain, from an "elsewhere," and they were sent back to that elsewhere. These were indeed a "special people," different due to the uncanny knowledge that they held.

Genius and Insanity: A Thin Line

Although this esoteric knowledge is possessed by the insane, it is also this kind of knowledge that has been attributed to the public intellectual. The intellectual figure also exists on the fringes, and according to Said (1993), the "right role for today's intellectual" is that of the "outsider," a concept "best exemplified by the condition of exile" (p. 117), just as fools were exiled in the Middle Ages. Nearly a century prior, Nietzsche (1984) suggested something similar by introducing the concept of the free spirit, a Zarathustrian (Nietzsche, 2005) figure who is constantly at odds with conventional wisdom and normalcy. "Solitude encircles and engirdles" (Nietzsche, 1984, p. 9) this free spirit. This free spirit is an intellectual figure with whom Nietzsche himself identified, both apart from and a part of the public that said esoteric knowledge is delivered to. His Zarathustra figure had lived on a mountain in solitude for a decade, developing wisdom, before deciding to spread his own "truth-insanity" (2005, p. 178) to others. It should be noted that at the end of Nietzsche's life, Nietzsche crossed the line from intellectual to insane, and some of his own "crazy" ideas have been attributed to his slide into madness (Aschheim, 1993). It seems, then, that the platitude of a fine line existing between genius and insanity remains true. It seems also that intellectualism, divergent thinking, and unconventional wisdom are often married to the idea of the outsider, the exile—perhaps, even, the insane.

This begins to open a space for the neurodivergent individual to contribute intellectually. We dismiss neurodiversity because we do not recognize the kind of knowledge that it holds—but when we think about what counts as knowledge as an unstable entity, it means that anyone has the potential to be a public intellectual. We simply need to allow ourselves to view said knowledge *as* knowledge. In what follows, I attempt to answer Manning's (2016) call for attention to neurodiversity. She notes that the construction of (mental) difference often leaves such individuals impossible to "celebrate," addressing the "life of the autistic, still taught in segregated classrooms, yours, mine, the life of the schizophrenic, of the psychotic, the depressed, institutionalized and out of sight" (2016, p. 4). We fail to consider, in a generous light, those who are neurodivergent. Instead, we keep them at a distance, "out of sight."

Manning (2016) specifically mentions the autistic, and in recent conversations of intellectualism and neurodiversity, a space seems to have opened for the autistically neurodivergent. Leong (2012), for instance, criticizes the "draconian intellectualism" that understands autistic individuals as limited, and he asks that we acknowledge autistic thinking simply as unusual thinking, tending toward a creative, aesthetic cognition that can "inspire a fresh perspective for research, practice and collaboration" (p. 3). Dyck and Russell (2019) similarly seek to celebrate the autistic, suggesting that rather than identifying autism as a pathology, we allow "autistic" simply to be a kind of identity. People with autism, Dyck and Russell remind us, are still "intellectually able individuals" (2019, p. 172) who have a right to exist as autistics.

Worth noting is that Manning (2016), Leong (2012), and Dyck and Russell (2019) not only push for a tolerance for neurodivergence but also acknowledge that there is a special kind of intelligence that comes with this diversity. However, acknowledging that autistics can contribute to society via their intellectual differences focuses on one type of neurodivergence. If we are to take this neurodiversity movement seriously and if we allow for all neurodivergent individuals to contribute intellectually, then we need to focus on other kinds of neurodiversity as well. In this case, I turn to DS, a Vietnam War veteran with PTSD and early stages of dementia, as one who might be considered a public intellectual.

An Autoethnographic Disclaimer

Before I begin *describing* DS's story, I want to make clear that I do not feel I am *telling* his story. The stories that DS told me were disjointed, and it was sometimes difficult to determine how they related to one another; as such, I make no claim to his story or any ability to relay it. Ellis and Bochner (2000) suggest that this is normal for autoethnography as the researcher reflects on his or her experiences; the power of a story is not in its truth but its potential to evoke. I present here a short vignette of DS's life as I remember him presenting it to me, and I attempt to contextualize it by further describing the events that occurred between DS and his caretaker while I was meeting with him. Although another's story is present here, I feel that the important aspect is my reaction to the story; were I to call this a narrative piece, I am unable to verify it with DS given that I no longer have contact with him. Furthermore, the division between researcher and other becomes murky as we begin autoethnography—where does one's story begin when another's ends (Ellis & Bochner, 1996)? It is due to this instability in one's own narrative experience that Jackson and Mazzei (2008) suggest autoethnography break with the stable, narrative "I" in autoethnographic research. DS's story? My own? Ultimately, I characterize this as an autoethnographic piece; all information is based on my memory, even if it involves interactions with others. I further make no attempt to justify anything beyond this personal filter as authentic, accurate, or true (Jackson & Mazzei, 2008).

I feel this is a particularly appropriate approach because autoethnography is also useful for helping us to come to terms with and understand those who are different from ourselves (Ellis & Bochner, 2000), as stories and voices are shared among those that appear within autoethnographies (Ellis, 2004). These multiple filters of experience make it difficult to tell what is completely factual in my recounting. I ask that my readers suspend any disbelief regarding these accounts and entertain the potential that the stories may, in fact, be accurate—that is, forget for a moment, as I had to, that these stories originate from one who may have PTSD or dementia and instead acknowledge that these events potentially happened. I ask that readers try to find "value" in this "narrative truth based on what the story of experience does" and consider how it may be "used, understood, and responded to for and by us and others as writers, participants, audiences, and humans" (Ellis et al., 2011, p. 282).

Interacting With DS

I had joined a tutoring agency as an English/writing tutor about a year prior to my experiences with DS. This was during my time as a PhD student, and it was a way to make a little extra money as I finished my dissertation. The agency found individuals in need of tutoring and then reached out to potential tutors to make a match. The email I received from the agency said that DS was an adult learner in need of computer support, and having done similar projects before, I accepted the position. DS's caretaker contacted me a few days later. She told me that she was skeptical about hiring another tutor—the first one has crossed some boundaries that she should not have by helping him with his taxes, which was his caretaker's job. So, in addition to not whistling, I was explicitly told not to discuss finances with him. When I first met with DS, his caretaker stayed in the apartment with us to make sure that things ran smoothly. My first assignment was showing him how to make a USB-powered microscope work on his computer. The microscope itself was obsolete, and his newer laptop could not run the drivers to make the microscope work. I spent the better half of two tutoring sessions trying to figure this out, and while I was doing so, DS told me about some of his experiences in Vietnam. He told me about how he was hired as a mechanic despite no formal training or education, working on C-130s. He told me about how he was staying in the Vietnamese Embassy the night a car bomb went off outside of it. There must have been a pool or something on top of the embassy, he said, because water flooded the building. He told me about how even after the war, he went back to Vietnam to continue working as a mechanic. His caretaker would tell him to focus on what I was doing on the computer so he could learn, as though finding drivers for an outdated USB microscope fell into the realm of basic computer literacy.

She stopped attending our tutoring sessions, and I stopped worrying about helping him with "computer literacy." Instead, I suggested setting up a speech-to-text program on his computer. Our tutoring sessions became times for him to tell me about his life as they were recorded into a Word document. I began thinking of my tutoring time with him as informal interview sessions. He would talk about whatever topic he wanted to, and I would probe as he talked. He was soft-spoken, so the speech-to-text software didn't always register exactly what he was saying. He did not know that there were commands for punctuation, so after a few minutes of talking, he would have a wall of text that needed grammatical deciphering. We would stop after a few minutes and smooth out the story, correcting (or sometimes reinventing, when it was indecipherable) wording, adding punctuation, and rearranging sentences so that they seemed more narrative, less stream of consciousness.

I no longer have access to these stories, as they were saved on his computer. Over the course of a year, I have lost contact with DS. His phone number is no longer active, and he has not responded to the most recent emails that I sent him. But I will take a moment to recount one story that I found fascinating due to the impact that it potentially has for the U.S. agriculture and grocery industry, as well as the fact that it is both entirely plausible and impossible to prove or disprove:

> DS spent a great deal of time in Vietnam, even after the war. He took in much of its culture while he was there. While he was there, he began to develop an interest in agriculture and Vietnamese farming. They had a unique way of farming sprouts in Vietnam—there were heated sheds wherein the walls and ceilings were lined with sod, and they would plant vegetables along the entire area of the shed. As sprouts grew, they would harvest the sprouts from the floors, walls, and ceiling, yielding hundreds of pounds of sprouts.
>
> When he returned to the United States, he began gardening, incorporating what he had learned from Vietnam into his farming practice. A successful farmer, he started a marketing co-op and a farmers' market in a major U.S. city, growing and selling sprouts. He could grow sprouts at times of the season when others couldn't, and he always had a healthy harvest. He shared his knowledge of sprouts farming with others, and he met with local retailers to begin selling his produce. These retailers were taken with his practices and began modeling the co-op that he had developed. They also began farming sprouts, following DS's Vietnamese farming model. Years later, these retailers would incorporate as Sprouts Farmers Market, a major chain of grocery stores in the South and Southwest, which currently operates over 300 stores.

DS, then, was the brains behind a major grocery chain. Is this enough to consider him a public intellectual? His experiences abroad and general ingenuity allowed him to advance sprouts production in such a way that there now exists an entire grocery chain named after it. Perhaps it would help to think over what should or could constitute a public intellectual.

Said (1996) suggests that an intellectual must seek to move beyond ready-made answers. The intellectual must "struggle to balance the problems of one's own selfhood against the demands of publishing and speaking out in the public sphere" (Said, 1996, p. 23). DS was not concerned with publications. However, this view suggests that the only intellectuals out there are those that exist within academia, and ignores the potential "sheer ordinariness of the role of the intellectual" (Collini, 2002, p. 206).

Although his agricultural endeavors may have been "ordinary," there is still something Zarathustrian (Nietzsche, 2005) and political (Said, 1996) in his actions. DS entered a kind of exile, one in which he left his homeland behind and discovered a new piece of knowledge. Upon return, he attempted to share this knowledge with those that he had left behind. Moreover, his formation of the marketing co-op and dissemination of knowledge helped to empower a farming community and led to the foundation of a corporation that uses elements of farming cooperatives and public outreach in its business model. Recognizing this as an intellectual contribution to the public both celebrates DS as an intellectual despite neurodivergence, as called for by Manning (2016), and helps us to represent "the diverse, ordinary activities of intellectuals in the here and now" (Collini, 2002, p. 206).

It was not long into my tutoring gig with DS that I received a call from his caretaker, who told me that DS had accused her of rerouting some of his money into her own bank account without his permission. Another discursive construction: the senile, delusional old man who thinks the nurses are stealing his money. His caretaker encouraged me to cut off contact with him and stop tutoring him. The odd thing about this situation is that my tutoring had nothing to do with her or his bank account, other than the tutoring payment I received, which I eventually stopped charging anyway. Why should I stop helping him write?

Over the course of a couple months, DS would eventually have to undergo a psychological evaluation, and I began to tutor him in that capacity: helping him remember how to draw clocks and times on clocks, helping him remember basic arithmetic related to the psychological battery that he would have to pass. It took him time to figure these things out, but he could do it with a bit of prompting, and evidently, he passed the test, because I continued working with him for several months. I never heard from his caretaker again; he claims that she fled the state and had substantial gambling debts. It may be true; she was oddly concerned about me getting involved with anything remotely related to his finances. It may be false; how could he know that she was stealing his money specifically to pay off gambling debts? I do not remember her name, and it would be impossible for me to follow up on any public police reports one way or the other. Either way, DS and I stayed in contact briefly, even after I moved away from him, until his phone number no longer worked.

Considerations/Lessons Learned

It is easy to dismiss those who are neurologically different, to ignore their stories and the generativity associated with them. When one of these people makes a claim or performs a behavior that is inconvenient for us, we always have the upper hand as we occupy a space of "hegemonic power of ableism" (Lester & Nusbaum, 2018, p. 4). We may subject them to psychological testing; we may send them away because they do not meet the agreed-on criteria for what is psychologically normal, not unlike the ship of fools described by Foucault. Their stories become silent because they are no longer stories. Instead, they are ravings, bullshit, untrue. But I think of the Tim Burton movie *Big Fish* (2003), about a father/teller of tall tales and the broken relationship with his son as a result of these tall tales. As the father is dying and the son is helping him get his possessions in order, it becomes apparent that there was always a kernel of truth within those far-out stories. The line between truth and fiction falls in on itself.

In this chapter, I do not provide a strict definition of "public intellectual" because it is too slippery a term, contingent on constantly shifting ideas of what counts as intellectualism. Whatever we might agree constitutes an intellectual, however, I argue that neurodiversity is traditionally excluded from the conversation. In this case, I feel that DS offers an example of one who has contributed, in some important way, intellectually to the development of a major entity that serves public consumption. There are no records of his story or his contributions, and perhaps this story represents the dreams of a patient falling deeper into the depths of dementia. But a move toward mad studies, which seeks to promote "education, scholarship, and analysis about . . . the people who identify as: mad; psychiatric survivors; consumers; service users; mentally ill; patients, neuro-diverse; inmates; disabled" (Costa, 2014, "What Is Mad Studies?" para. 1), would tell us that we must meet DS on his own terms.

DS helps me to think about and upset notions of truth and truth telling within qualitative research. Qualitative relies so heavily on interpretation—why should I discount his interpretation of events more than another participant? I ask this not as a sympathetic plea on behalf of one who is neurodivergent, but because if he were not otherwise labeled, I would not feel the need to hold his truth to any kind of scrutiny. And ultimately, why should I?

Is there any reason to think that he has not made contributions to the agricultural industry? He had given me no reason not to trust him otherwise. My experiences with DS suggest that as a researcher, we never quite have access to a capital *T* Truth, regardless of who the participant is, and it is important to respect various manifestations of truth; doing so allows the way for intellectual contribution rather than suspicion. I believe that my experiences with DS also push the bounds of what counts as participant and scholar. In fact, I would have liked to have worked with him more closely on this chapter, including him as an author; my inability to contact him prohibits this, but there is no reason not to think of DS as a scholarly contributor to this piece, which dovetails with the larger point—neurodivergence and intellectualism are not mutually exclusive.

References

Aschheim, S. E. (1993). Max Nordau, Friedrich Nietzsche and degeneration. *Journal of Contemporary History, 28*(4), 643–657.

Banda, F., & Mawadza, A. (2014). 'Foreigners are stealing our birth right': Moral panics and the discursive construction of Zimbabwean immigrants in South African media. *Discourse and Communication, 9*(1), 47–64.

Burton, T. (Director). *Big fish* [Film]. Columbia Pictures.

Collini, S. (2002). "Every fruit-juice drinker, nudist, sandal-wearer . . ." Intellectuals as other people. In H. Small (Ed.), *The public intellectual* (pp. 203–223). Blackwell.

Costa, L. (2014). *Mad studies – What it is and why you should care.* http://madstudies2014.wordpress.com/2014/10/15/mad-studies-what-it-is-and-why-you-should-care-2/

Dreyfus, H. L., & Rabinow, P. (1983). *Michel Foucault: Beyond structuralism and hermeneutics.* University of Chicago Press.

Dyck, E., & Russell, G. (2019). Challenging psychiatric classification: Healthy autistic diversity the neurodiversity movement. In S. J. Taylor & A. Brumby (Eds.), *Healthy minds in the twentieth century: In and beyond the asylum* (pp. 167–187). Springer.

Ellis, C. (2004). *The ethnographic I: A methodological novel about teaching and doing autoethnography.* AltaMira.

Ellis, C., Adams, T. E., & Bochner, A. P. (2011). Autoethnography: An overview. *Historical Social Research, 36*(4), 273–290.

Ellis, C., & Bochner, A. P. (1996). *Composing ethnography: Alternative forms of qualitative writing.* AltaMira.

Ellis, C., & Bochner, A. P. (2000). Autoethnography, personal narrative, reflexivity. In N. K. Denzin & Y. S. Lincoln (Eds.), *Handbook of qualitative research* (2nd ed., pp. 733–768). Sage Publications.

Farrelly, M. (2015). *The discursive construction of mental health problems in Irish print news media.* (Publication no. 20763) [Doctoral dissertation, Dublin City University]. DORAS DCU Online Research Access Archive.

Foucault, M. (1988). *Madness and civilization.* Random House. (Original work published 1965)

Foucault, M. (2003). *Abnormal: Lectures at the Collège de France, 1974–75* (G. Burchell, Trans.). Verso.

Foucault, M. (2006). *Psychiatric power: Lectures at the Collège de France, 1973–74* (G. Burchell, Trans.). Palgrave Macmillan.

Glasson, B. J. (2012). The intellectual outside: Anti-intellectualism and the subject of populist discourses in Australian newspapers. *Continuum: Journal of Media and Cultural Studies, 26*(1), 101–114.

Goldsmith, R. H. (1974). *Wise fools in Shakespeare.* Liverpool University Press.

Goodson, I. (1999). The educational researcher as a public intellectual. *British Education Research Journal, 25*(3), 277–297.

Gordon, C. (1991). Governmental rationality: An introduction. In G. Burchell, C. Gordon, & P. Miller (Eds.), *The Foucault effect: Studies in governmentality* (pp. 1–52). University of Chicago Press.

Jackson, A. Y., & Mazzei, L. A. (2008). Experience and "I" in autoethnography: A deconstruction. *International Review of Qualitative Research, 1*(3), 299–318.

Leong, D. (2012). *Thinking through the body: A multimodal approach from autism* [Paper presentation]. International Conference for Research Creativity: Praxis, Baptist University of Hong Kong, Hong Kong, China.

Lester, J. N., & Nusbaum, E. A. (2018). "Reclaiming" disability in critical qualitative research: Introduction to the special issue. *Qualitative Inquiry, 24*(1), 3–7.

Manning, E. (2016). *The minor gesture.* Duke University Press.

Melzer, A. M. (2003). What is an intellectual? In A. M. Melzer, J. Weinberger, & M. R. Zinman (Eds.) *The public intellectual: Between philosophy and politics* (pp. 3–14). Rowman & Littlefield.

Nietzsche, F. (1984). *Human, all too human: A book for free spirits* (M. Faber, Trans.). University of Nebraska Press.

Nietzsche, F. (2005). *Thus spoke Zarathustra* (C. Martin, Trans). Barnes and Noble Press.

Said, E. W. (1993, Autumn). Intellectual exile: Expatriates and marginals. *Grand Street, 47*, 112–124.

Said, E. W. (1996). *Representations of the intellectual: The 1993 Reith lectures.* Vintage.

Stoegner, K., & Wodak, R. (2016). 'The man who hated Britain' – the discursive construction of 'national unity' in the *Daily Mail. Critical Discourse Studies, 13*(2), 193–209.

Wodak, R., De Cillia, R., Reisigl, M., & Leibhart, K. (2009). *The discursive construction of national identity* (2nd ed.). Edinburgh University Press.

Un/known Intellectual

Authority

Authority,
Immovable mass
Mountain range
Meticulous MENTAL
Of the multitude.
Audience,
Ultimately unstable
Cumulonimbus
Clientele
To the RATIONAL.
Popular philosophy
Prevails

Fenced

SEVEN

Intellectual Gatekeepers: Reclaiming Black Queer Youth as the Public

Boni Wozolek, Penn State University, Abington College

IN HER ESSAY "MASTER'S TOOLS," Audre Lorde (1984) argues that when Black women in general and—more specifically to Lorde's work and identity—queer Black women are called on to educate others to validate their "existence and needs, it is . . . an old primary tool of the oppressors to keep the oppressed occupied with the master's concerns" (p. 113). This point was also argued by scholars such as Anna Julia Cooper (1892), Carter G. Woodson (1933), and W. E. B. Du Bois (1903), to name a few, who wrote about the insidious nature of intellectual spaces that use the veneer of opportunity to maintain oppression. This chapter takes up the arguments similarly made by Fanon (1961), who writes that oppression is often sustained through a system of intellectual colonization, creating what he calls the "colonized intellectual." The colonized intellectual is a person who is recruited by the colonizer to learn the "essential qualities of the West . . . so that he is ready to defend the Graeco-Latin pedestal" (Fanon, 1961, p. 36), often doing so against his own people. Fanon explains that this kind of intellectualism is often a temporary consequence of colonization as the intellectual often has agency to engage with liberation through three stages explained in greater detail below.

Explicating relationships between the intra-public (Giroux, 2015; Sandlin, Schultz, and Burdick, 2010) and the colonized intellectual (Fanon, 1961), this chapter focuses on what intellectual opportunities mean for queer Black youth as they engage with/in the dominant norms and values. By intra-public, I am attending to the multiple ways that the "public" is formed through the intra-actions of its participants (Barad, 2007). As Barad (2007) argues, factors such as agency, or one's ability to act in a context, is inextricably linked to one's experiences with human and nonhuman bodies. Much like a student walking into a classroom, they[1] might have had agency prior to any intra-actions with peers, teachers, the setup of the room, or the curriculum. However, agency is formed, reformed, and often reinforced through such intra-actions. Similarly, how one conceptualizes the "public" and what makes up the "public body" is largely dependent on such intra-actions. As described in the following, the "intra" in both public and action is understood as a part of an assemblage that is often violent to and for marginalized youth in its cultural reproductions. This is important because as the data from this study argue, there are aspects of the intra-public that unintentionally seek to reproduce colonized intellectuals (Fanon, 1961) rather than encouraging identities that are in resistance or refusal (Simpson, 2014) to systemic oppression. This chapter begins with a dialogue on intellectualism as it relates to the intra-public as it intersects with colonization. It continues by presenting data from a 2-year ethnographic study with Black and Brown queer youth in an urban middle school whose schooling positioned them as colonized intellectuals within an extracurricular opportunity.

Finally, the analysis of this study discusses systems of power that raise three significant points with intra-public intellectual dialogues. First, this study asks, "If everything is always already entangled, which part of the intellectual belongs to the intra-public?" Second, this chapter argues that the onto-epistemological understandings of queer youth of color should be valued as inherently intellectual in nature. Finally, this chapter seeks to reconsider everyday oppressions that often enable all-too-familiar patterns of colonization in and across systems of schooling. If, to quote Sedgwick (1993), we are to find solutions to the indelible numbers found within queer student self-harm and suicide, this work becomes increasingly important as it seeks to center the value of Black queer youth intellectualism while attending to how gatekeepers unintentionally devalue queer youth roles within the intra-public.

The Intra-Public Colonized Intellectual

Systems of schooling in the United States have historically been, and largely continue to be, a product of colonization (Simpson, 2014; Tuck & Yang, 2012). Although often discussed as the domination of land and sociopolitical power (e.g., Said, 1979; Spivak, 1988; Young, 2001), this chapter focuses on the many ways that systems of schooling are central to the colonization process (see, e.g., residential schools and other forms of cultural and intellectual genocide that took place through public schools). Being "places designed for, populated by, and controlled by others" (Nespor, 1997, p. 91), schools are overrun by "dark suffering . . . educational systems built on the suffering of students of color" (Love, 2019, p. 29). To understand intellectual pursuits through K–12 education, then, is to understand how systems of schooling continually cause emotional, intellectual, and physical harm to marginalized students (Love, 2019; McCready, 2007; Woodson, 1933). In other words, one's ways of being and knowing through schooling are inextricably linked to becoming under systems of colonized ideologies that serve the White cis-hetero patriarchy.

To be clear, the onto-epistemological impacts of an educational system driven by hegemonic norms and values effect and affect all students. However, this chapter specifically focuses on how queer students of color are co-opted by the colonizer to maintain the status quo against their ways of being, knowing, and doing while promoting their presence in ways that maintain a false sense of opportunity for marginalized students. This focus is important for at least the following reasons: First, as scholars like Bethune (1938), Lorde (1984), and Love (2019) have noted, narratives from people of color largely make up the null curriculum (Eisner, 1985). The null curriculum is the lessons that are unintentionally not taught in schools become the notable absences of voices that do not just push queer people and communities of color to the margin but leave them out entirely. One only needs to recall how many lessons focused on women of color outside of slavery or civil rights to understand how the null curriculum functions in schools. For queer youth of color, this absence implicitly devalues their ways of being as persons of color. Furthermore, although people of color are certainly absent, queer people are even further marginalized from the school curriculum. Take, for example, James Baldwin, who is sometimes included in the curriculum, but his sexuality is rarely discussed. This exclusion of queer knowledges implicitly invalidates LGBTQ+ identities. For queer youth of color, the combination of these two absences becomes a violent echo chamber of messages that constantly and consistently tells youth that their identities have no space in schools or communities (McCready, 2007; Quinn & Meiners, 2009; Wozolek, 2018).

Queer intellectuals are still seen as problematic across spaces, but this is especially amplified as queerness intersects with K–12 schooling in the United States (Gilbert, 2014) and, by extension, conservative institutional schools of education (Gilbert, 2014; Kissen, 1996; Miller & Rodriguez, 2016; Seidman, 1994). Like many of the persons seen as problems (Du Bois, 1903) in schools, LGBTQ+ youth of color are often intellectually, emotionally, and physically tracked out (Gilbert, 2014; Love, 2019; Morris, 2016; Woodson, 1933). For youth in schools, this has been shown by the increase of LGBTQ+ youth in the school-to-prison pipeline (Morris, 2016) and the school-to-coffin pipeline (Wozolek, 2018). For professors, this is shown through the consistent elimination of spaces designed for LGBTQ+ faculty (Gilbert, 2014; Miller & Rodriguez, 2016). The intellectual absence of these voices in university spaces becomes mirrored by the absence of these youth in the school.

When LGBTQ+ youth of color are not excluded, they are consistently expected to validate their experiences, to use the masters' tools that maintain oppressive structures (Lorde, 1984). Fanon (1961) might argue that this system of oppression is a way of honing a very specific type of intellectual—the colonized intellectual. Fanon's work is particularly useful here because he not only discusses the impact of colonization on intellectual development but is also clear in his dialogue that individuals educated under such conditions have agency that can be enacted against the oppressor. Furthermore, Fanon argues that the colonized intellectual exists in three phases, rather than remaining static in her[2] colonization. Because colonialism destroys culture by teaching the colonized that they are, to quote Woodson (1933), "a curse" (p. 3), the ability to enact agency becomes all the more significant for liberation in which people reclaim their roots or, as Fanon writes, produce a new culture outside of colonized ideas and ideals that have perverted original cultural norms and values.

In the first stage, the intellectual mimics colonial ideas and ideals. Fanon (1961) uses Fodéba's (1950) poem "African Dawn" to demonstrate how those marginalized by class are often exploited physically and intellectually by colonizers. The main character in the poem, Neman, was recruited by the colonist to go to war, a decision supported by his village elders in an attempt to defend their honor to the colonists. Neman subsequently fell into colonist systems of power, only to perish at the end at the hands of the police. This, as Fanon argues, is a sacrifice that has been normalized through colonization both in Neman's need to fight for and in the colonizer's war and to defend the honor of the village—a use of the master's tools to reify oppressive structures.

In the second stage, as an act of resistance against the colonizer, his culture, and the oppressive education she received, the colonized actively resists the colonizer and the "Graeco-Latin pedestal." Fanon (1961) distinguishes this stage as an act of resistance to, rather than a refusal of, the ideas and ideals that she was taught through colonized spaces and places. In this stage, the individual might argue for the racialization of the culture. However, she finds this task difficult as her knowledge of her culture is limited and steeped in Western perspectives. She is, as Fanon (1961) writes, working from a "very narrow path where [she] is expected to demonstrate the existence of 'Negro' culture" (p. 150) rather than her own. Ultimately, she finds herself unable to find a strong foothold for resistance due to the Westernization of ideas and the "continental scope" (Fanon, 1961, p. 150) imposed by the colonist.

Finally, the colonized intellectual begins to fight for liberation through an attempt to galvanize her people. This is a refusal of colonialist cultures in an attempt to build new norms. Fanon (1961) recognizes the inherent violence in revolution, starting the book with the passage "decolonization is always a violent event" (p. 1). Returning to Fodéba's (1950) poem, violence is integral to Neman's life and to the village as they follow his experiences at war through letters Neman writes to his wife. It is crucial, Fanon argues, to have violence directed in the interests of the new nation rather than the colonizer. In this final stage, Fanon discusses the hope of developing a new culture that will inform nationhood rather than building a culture from previous racial understandings that are inherently tied to Western ideologies.

Given that K–12 schools in the United States are deeply entangled with the norms of the colonizer, all students receive an education predicated on such values. For students whose histories and resulting privilege are rooted in hegemony, this education only further reifies the power structures from which these students benefit. For marginalized students, they become the next iteration of colonized intellectuals. Similarly, Gramsci (1975) argued that because systems of power are ubiquitous, being and becoming an intellectual is often a process designed to maintain the status quo. Although both Gramsci's and Fanon's dialogues tend to miss contemporary nuance that might focus more on intersectional understandings and the potential fluidity of the class critique, both discuss the entanglements between intellectualism and power structures.

Queer youth of color experience a double(d) consciousness (Du Bois, 1903; Lather, 1991) is often formed and informed by the implicit and explicit lessons that are central to those instilled in the colonized intellectual. As previously discussed, on one hand, these norms funnel students into the school-to-prison (Christle et al., 2005; Meiners, 2016) and school-to-coffin (Wozolek et al., 2016) pipelines, both functioning as an important part of tracking students out of school. On the other hand, students' ability to move from the initial stage of colonized intellectual understandings and toward stages of liberation is often based on circumstances that impact one's ability to exercise agency—or, as I call it here, one's agentic contingencies.

The colonized intellectual is inherently connected to the "intra-public." In this case, "intra" is being defined as an assemblage (Puar, 2007; Weheliye, 2014)—or the entangled sociopolitical, historical, and cultural elements that inform spaces, places, and people across layers of scale. Although it is important to think about an assemblage's contents and what those contents produce, here I am focusing on the interrelations of the contents with the assemblage that forms the "intra" of the intra-public. This is because, as Puar (2013) argues, "specific *connections with* other concepts is precisely what gives them their meaning. Concepts do not prescribe relations, nor do they exist prior to them; rather, relations of force, connections, resonance, and patterning give rise to concepts" (p. 57). Engagement with public(s) as an assemblage therefore attends to entanglements with sociocultural and political histories as they are imbricated with contemporary contexts.

An intra-public assemblage as it is in relation to the colonized intellectual raises several important points. First, it puts into question the idea of public intellectualism. If, as Gramsci (1975) argues, all intellectualism is in some way public and that public in the United States is also knotted with colonialist histories, are intra-public intellectuals inherently tied to the colonial project? Second, are agentic contingencies surmountable for marginalized youth given the echo chamber of oppression within the intra-public?

The remainder of this chapter uses the data from a 2-year ethnographic study to think about how public education positions queer youth of color as colonized intellectuals with an arts-based project aimed at presenting students with an opportunity to express themselves and their ways of being. Engaging students in arts-based work was significant in this study because the doing of art became an emotional outlet for students, but it also created a space of possibility (Helfenbein, 2010) where students were able to find ways to express their intellectual abilities outside of traditional education.

STEAM in the City

Wozolek: Tell me a little bit about your school.

Davonte:[3] *It's a nice school. I mean, sometimes some of the things that happen here hurt, a lot. But it's a place for second chances for people like us. They do that for you. Provide second chances. And we could all use a second chance. Right? So that's a good thing.*

Eaton Middle School was located directly on the harbor. From one perspective, the school had a rather peaceful feeling, with a cafeteria looking out onto the water in a building tucked away from the main streets of a busy downtown in an urban city on the East Coast. Although this was a public school, some of the practices mirrored Montessori education, including a school garden, complete with a greenhouse and a chicken coop. Although classrooms did not boast high levels of technology, several teachers had put up posters displaying culturally diverse people that were relevant to the courses they taught. On casual observation, this small school might be perceived as engaging in practices that facilitated the emotional and intellectual growth of its majority African American and Latinx youth, many of whom lived in economically disenfranchised neighborhoods.

As I am a person who identifies as a queer woman of color, and whose scholarship focuses on equity and access for queer youth of color through qualitative research, my expertise was sought out by the school. To be clear, as a queer woman of color, I identify with some of the anxieties, emotions, and experiences of youth who are questioning. However, the social landscape has changed drastically since my middle school experiences. Additionally, although I am Brown and as a scholar engage in urban education, I was raised in a rural space and have not had a childhood experience that includes being a queer youth of color in an urban context. These differences are significant to note, as without doing so can unintentionally flatten the experiences of marginalized people. Without much discussion about the complexity of identities, the school called on me to help with what I was told was a "queer problem." This meant that some students had come out to faculty, and as a response, some teachers called and outed students to their parents/guardians. As a result, some students were kicked out of their homes while others found unexpected support with accepting parents/guardians.

After meeting with the administrator to offer antiracist, antihomophobic/transphobic training, the administration team decided that my time at the school was better served doing research with the students rather than as a resource for the faculty. The group was to serve as a "Diversity Club," rather than a "Genders and Sexualities Alliance," because there was some concern that parents would not let their middle school children participate in a group that directly discussed sexuality. Additionally, the group was to meet during the enrichment time during the school day, a time when students could participate in clubs and/or receive additional tutoring from teachers.

I arrived at the school one afternoon to learn that a teacher had worked with a faculty team to design and administer a survey to identify students who might want to join this group. This faculty team then compiled a list of students that *they* identified as queer or questioning—the "problem kids," as one teacher put it. I would later learn that some students who were included in the group did not indicate interest in participating and others who expressed interest were excluded because the teachers and administrators were worried that these students were "too much of a problem [in ways that] would embarrass the school," according to one student in the group.

The group ended up consisting of 15 students ranging from sixth to eighth graders. Despite how students identified themselves or how they were identified by adults, I decided not to ask them to share their identities unless they felt compelled to do so. Instead, per a suggestion voiced by Maria, an eighth-grade Latinx student in the group, the dialogue began with a discussion about how they understood themselves in relation to others. Along this line of inquiry, students decided that they wanted to make a podcast. During the first year, students chose podcast topics, wrote and conducted the interviews, and mixed the sound files to make two podcasts.[4] The first podcast was designed by students to help them think about school culture. Toward this end, they interviewed teachers, the school secretary, the dean of students, and the principal. The second was designed with community in mind. Students interviewed the community mentors who had been assigned to them by faculty that year.

At the end of the first year, students expressed interest in my return to the school. They asked that I help them engage in an art form that would facilitate thoughts about broader connections outside of the city context. Specifically, they requested the ability to use an art form that moved away from the portrait art they practiced in art class. Over that summer, I forged some connections with a nationally recognized art museum in the city. The mobile classroom from the art museum presented students the opportunity to participate in a project with National Geographic. This program encourages students to think about how plastics get into waterways. Students collectively agreed that this project was a good fit for their group, and with the help of the museum educator, they were excited about building sculptures that would represent their research. In a matter of weeks, students were deep into investigating plastics found in the harbor, such as straws. They wrote letters to local business owners and to the city. The letters used comparative analysis to ask businesses to switch to paper or metal straws and a second letter asked the city to invest in solar-powered trash cans. For example, the "straws group" looked at the amount of waste a restaurant would produce in one night of discarding plastics straws. They also investigated the amount an establishment would spend nightly and annually for plastic straws. They then compared the pounds of waste and the cost of plastic straws to that of paper and metal straws to include in their letters.

Toward the end of the academic year, students from Eaton Middle School engaged in a video exchange with high school youth from Madagascar who were participating in a science camp that had a similar project. The final stage was an exhibit at the museum (see Figure 7.1). Students curated the space with their sculptures, laminated letters to the restaurants and city, and short explanations of the overall process and products. The museum also offered to display the students' sound art from the previous year, and student prepared materials to accompany the podcasts that were to play on a loop near the sculptures.

The findings from this study were significant for at least the following reasons: First, students expressed that engaging in and completing the project boosted their confidence in math, science, and language arts classes. One student explained that she always felt "like the teachers were waiting for [her] to make a mistake but that this project made [her] feel like [she] could be smart." Another student remarked that he didn't know "art was connected to math and science" and that learning this made "math-relatable." Second, a few months into the first year, students began to talk about questions of sexual orientation and gender identity as they were mixing sound files. As the study progressed, such dialogue became normalized as students worked on

Figure 7.1. "Straw City"—Straws on Cardboard With Oil Paint.

their art. Findings raised questions about the spaces created during moments of artistic expression. From this, conclusions could be drawn about what that might mean for marginalized youth to have the space and place to unpack questions of their identity in the presence of, but not always in direct conversation with, an adult who shares aspects of their queer identities. Finally, and toward the focus of this chapter, findings explicated the power dynamics that became apparent when queer youth of color were given the space to express themselves.

As students began their work with podcasts in the first year, interview questions and their dialogue around the answers they received from faculty were largely in defense of the school and their education. For example, several students explained that teachers frequently implemented various types of shaming in the classroom to maintain control of the classroom and the school's principal was constantly reinforcing what he called the "number one school rule: Don't embarrass the principal." However, they also noted that the purpose of this was, as Latrell noted, to ensure "school safety because kids like [them] need to be shown how to act in order to succeed." This is not unlike Fanon's (1961) description of the colonized intellectual who defends colonized culture and, ultimately, their colonizers.

As the first year came to an end, students initially asked if they could do research into important figures who were Black/Brown and queer and paint a mural on one of the walls to reflect their research. Students noted that the stairwell (see Figure 7.2) already had inspirational murals and that they felt an image that reflected the diverse identities through historical figures would feel empowering. The administration quickly rejected this idea, citing that the wall spaces were meant for more "neutral art." When I inquired how this idea varied from the materials teachers presented in their classrooms, I was told that those images were presented within the context of the curriculum and that such art would need to be justified within those parameters and not presented as work from an outside club.

At the end of the second year, within the first hour of students exhibiting their work at the art museum, the group was told by a museum docent that they could not play the podcasts. The docent explained that although the podcasts might have been previously approved by the administration at the museum, he believed the sound of the interviews was "disruptive to the museum experience." Another docent similarly agreed and asked that the podcasts be turned off. While the docents were objecting to the sounds, the music from an acapella group spilled through the gallery from the sculpture garden. When I inquired as to why the acapella group, which happened to be an all-White group singing pop tunes, somehow produced more favorable sounds, my question was met with silence and a third request to keep our "noise down." As, in total frustration, I discussed what happened with one of the teachers, she reminded me that the project was not to "embarrass the school with those kids" by allowing their "noise" but to show what they could do through STEAM (science, technology, engineering, the arts, and mathematics).

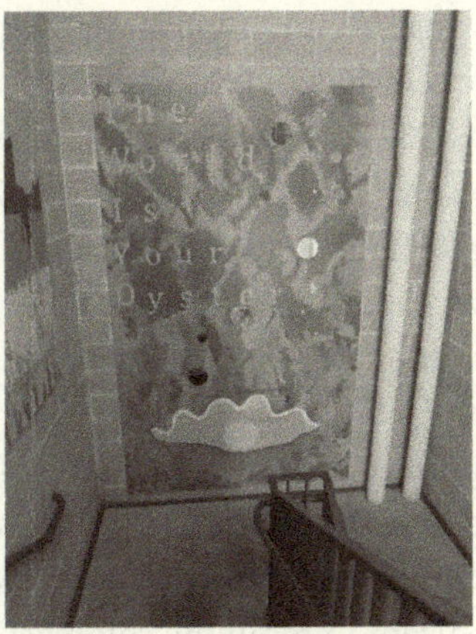

Figure 7.2. Mural in the Stairwell.

Intra-Public Colonizing/Ed Intellectuals

There are many ways to interpret the events around students' engagement in the arts. For example, there is a strong argument to be made that the consistent rejection of any art that reflected students' ways of being (e.g., the mural) and actual voices (e.g., the podcasts) can be understood as power operating to keep the status quo. Scholarly dialogues have certainly shown how these oppressive norms function over time and across layers of scale (e.g., Freire, 1970; Halberstam, 2011; Meiners, 2016).

As Fanon (1961) argues, while colonizing people and lands, the colonizer often seeks to invalidate and limit the ways of being and knowing of the colonized. As students' forms of art were limited to "appropriate forms of expression," the school and museum "distorted their aesthetics" (Fanon, 1961, p. 6). This is not unlike Du Bois's (1926) dialogue on African American forms of art being "choked away" as a form of sociocultural control. Fanon argues that this is the first stage in engendering and maintaining people as colonized intellectuals.

It can also be argued that in this study, marginalized students' work was recognized in many ways—first by being given the initial space to meet, then through an invitation to continue the group a second year, and finally through the opportunity to exhibit work at a nationally recognized gallery. Students genuinely expressed appreciation for these opportunities, especially as they had historically been identified as "problems" in the school. They explained that these spaces made them feel "like they belonged." A sense of belonging is no small thing, and this analysis is not meant to take away from that feeling.

However, each subsequent interaction with those in power made it clear that elevating the work as a STEAM project was encouraged until that project crossed into ideas that resonated with students' identities. This issue has been well documented within dialogues about power in schools. The point raised here is about how power seeks to reproduce colonized norms in a way that disproportionately impacts queer youth of color. Finally, if as argued earlier, the intra-public is a part of a larger assemblage, then even in moments when students' ideas are recognized, the intra-public is still deeply entangled with colonialist norms and values. This extends to intra-public intellectualism that is enmeshed with the colonized intellectual. If we are to redefine the role of the intellectual, it is important to recall the colonized ideals under which the status quo continues, as well as the entanglements of the intra-public within colonized norms. Otherwise, despite efforts to overcome the continued marginalization of queer youth of color through these projects, the projects themselves can, albeit unintentionally, reify colonization through those who serve as intellectual gatekeepers.

Notes

1. My use of *they* is intentional here as this chapter attends to queer theory and queer bodies. *They* is therefore used here as gender-inclusive and an attention to the gender binaries that often pervade academic writing.

2. The pronouns used in this chapter reflect a feminist refusal of traditional academic writing that is often aligned with male pronouns. Although not the intent here, it should be noted that using *she/her* can be inherently marginalizing to gender nonbinary people and groups.

3. All proper nouns are pseudonyms to protect the identities of the participants and their school.

4. To listen to the podcasts, go to http://bit.ly/BlueDragons1 or http://bit.ly/BlueDragons2.

References

Barad, K. (2007). *Meeting the universe halfway: Quantum physics and the entanglement of matter and meaning*. Duke University Press.

Bethune, M. M. (1938). Clarifying our vision with the facts. *Journal of Negro History, 7*(2), 10–15.

Christle, C. A., Jolivette, K., & Nelson, C. M. (2005). Breaking the school to prison pipeline: Identifying school risk and protective factors for youth delinquency. *Exceptionality: A Special Education Journal, 13*(2), 69–88.

Cooper, A. J. (1892). *A voice from the South, by a Black woman from the South*. http://docsouth.unc.edu/church/cooper/cooper.html

Du Bois, W. E. B. (1903). *The souls of Black folk*. McClurgand.

Du Bois, W. E. B. (1926). Criteria of Negro art. *The Crisis, 32*, 290–297.

Eisner, E. (1985). *The educational imagination: On the design and evaluation of school programs*. Macmillan.

Fanon, F. (1961). *The wretched of the earth*. Grove Press.

Fodèba, K. (1950). *Abe africaine: et autres poemes africains*. Presence Africaine.

Freire, P. (1970). *Pedagogy of the oppressed*. Continuum Books.

Gilbert, J. (2014). *Sexuality in school: The limits of education*. Duke University Press.

Giroux, H. A. (2015). Public intellectuals against the neoliberal university. In N. K. Denzin &

M. G. Giardina (Eds.), *Qualitative inquiry—past, present, and future: A critical reader* (pp. 194–221). Routledge.

Gramsci, A. (1975). *Prison notebooks, volume 2*. Columbia University Press.

Halberstam, J. (2011). *The queer art of failure*. Duke University Press.

Helfenbein, R. J. (2010). Thinking through scale: Critical geographies and curriculum spaces. In E. Malewski (Ed.), *Curriculum studies handbook: The next moment* (pp. 304–317). Routledge.

Kissen, R. M. (1996). *The last closet: The real lives of lesbian and gay teachers*. Heinemann.

Lather, P. (1991). *Getting smart: Feminist research and pedagogies with/in the postmodern*. Routledge.

Lorde, A. (1984). *Sister outsider: Essays and speeches by Audre Lorde*. Crossing Press.

Love, B. (2019). *We want to do more than survive: Abolitionist teaching and the pursuit of educational freedom*. Beacon Press.

McCready, L. (2007). Queer urban education: Curriculum and pedagogy for LGBTQI youth in the city. *Journal of Curriculum and Pedagogy, 4*(2), 71–77.

Meiners, E. R. (2016). *For the children? Protecting innocence in a carceral state*. University of Minnesota Press.

Miller, sj, & Rodriguez, N. M. (Eds.). (2016). *Educators queering academia: Critical memoirs*. Peter Lang.

Morris, M.W. (2016). *Pushout: The criminalization of Black girls in schools*. The New Press.

Nespor, J. (1997). *Tangled up in school: Politics, space, bodies and signs in the educational process*. Lawrence Erlbaum.

Puar, J. (2007). *Terrorist assemblages: Homonationalism in queer times*. Duke University Press.

Puar, J. (2013). 'I would rather be a cyborg than a goddess': Intersectionality, assemblage, and affective politics. *Meritum, revista de Direito da Universidade FUMEC, 8*(2), 51-66.

Quinn, T., & Meiners, E. R. (2009). *Flaunt it!: Queers organizing for public education and justice*. Peter Lang.

Said, E. (1979). *Orientalism*. Vintage Books.

Sandlin, J. A., Schultz, B. D., & Burdick, J. (Eds.). (2010). *Handbook of public pedagogy: Education and learning beyond schooling*. Routledge.

Sedgwick, E. K. (1993). *Tendencies*. Duke University Press.

Seidman, S. (1994). Queer-ing sociology, sociologizing queer theory: An introduction. *Sociological Theory, 12*(2), 166–177.

Simpson, A. (2014). *Mohawk interruptus: Political life across the borders of settler states*. Duke University Press.

Spivak, G. (1988). Can the subaltern speak? In C. Nelson & L. Grossberg (Eds.), *Marxism and the interpretation of culture* (pp. 271–313). University of Illinois Press.

Tuck, E., & Yang, K. W. (2012). Decolonization is not a metaphor. *Decolonization: Indigeneity, Education & Society, 1*(1), 1–40.

Weheliye, A.G. (2014). *Habeas viscus: Racializing assemblages, biopolitics, and Black feminist theories of the human*. Duke University Press.

Woodson, C. G. (1933). *The mis-education of the negro*. Tribeca Books.

Wozolek, B. (2018). In 8100 again: The sounds of students breaking. *Educational Studies, 54*(4), 367–381.

Wozolek, B., Wootton, L., & Demlow, A. (2016). The school-to-coffin pipeline: Queer youth, suicide and resilience of spirit, *Cultural Studies↔Critical Methodologies, 17*(5), 392–398.

Young, R. (2001). *Postcolonialism: A historical introduction*. Blackwell.

Enstrangled

Public

Population

Citizens of which nation?

Followers of which creed?

Society

Community

Which piper do I heed?

Does he offer immunity,

Sanctification,

Greed?

The NULL

The CURSED

Viceroy, mimic

To the queen

I need not

Your foul flavor

Yet your stripes keep me

Enstrangled

Word-ing

Does the flight signify a soaring high, becoming, lines of flight that produce generative possibilities? Or is it a fleeing away from, a flight, an escape? Do we escape into words? Do words create reality, alter reality, create alternate reality?

Words without meaning. Words cascading. Words wording…

EIGHT

The (Un)Common Intellectual: Possibilities for New Relational Bonds

David Lee Carlson, Arizona State University

What we must work on, it seems to me, is not so much to liberate our desires but to make ourselves infinitely more susceptible to pleasure.

—Foucault (1997, p. 137)

Today in the west, most of us are gonna have two or three relationships or marriages, and some of us are gonna do it with the same person. Your first marriage is over. Would you like to create a second one together?

—Perel (2018, p. 11)

Justice Anthony Kennedy opined in the *Obergefell v. Hodges* (2015) Supreme Court decision that to deny a person the choice to marry whomever he or she wishes is to deny them due process under the law and equal protection. The jurisprudence that Kennedy cites in this case relies on four fundamental aspects of a democratic society. It (jurisprudence) relies on historical and legal precedence. He contends that the ability to marry implies a certain level of autonomy that the state should not inhibit because it is one of the "most intimate decisions an individual can make" (*Obergefell*, 2015, p. 12) and can "shape one's destiny" as well as offer "freedoms such as expressions, intimacy, and spirituality" (p. 13). Second, marriage promotes a certain lifestyle based on an enduring commitment between two people. States cannot deny individuals the basic right to form intimate partnerships that seek to foster stable relationships. Third, marriage protects families and children. Finally, marriage, according to Justice Kennedy, is the "cornerstone to social order" (*Obergefell*, 2015, p. 16); without marriage, civilization and progress would cease to exist. Of course, such lofty and high-minded ideals shape the contours of marriage, but as recent statistics indicate, very few marriages live up to them. In fact, any Google search of divorce rates in the United States reveals that they remain between 40% and 50%, according to most estimates.

Clearly what makes marriage both admirable and necessary (perhaps) is the risk involved in the commitment. The risk is that they oftentimes don't work out. Marriages fail to live up to their ideal, and if as a society, as Kennedy implies in his decision, we rely on marriages to keep civilization and progress intact, then we might have to reconsider the social ties that keep it all together. In fact, many recent writers and thinkers, from philosophers to activists and psychologists, have suggested that we do. It may be time to reconsider the role that marriage plays in keeping the social fabric together.

What I would like to argue in this chapter is not so much about the choice to marry or not. I fundamentally believe that individuals should have the right to marry—but what I want to discuss is how marriage is contested on relational grounds. The ideals of marriage based on fidelity and monogamy have recently been challenged by what I would call the *common intellectual*. They are thinkers and public figures in the present moment who rely on history, philosophy, archival information, and everyday materials (journaling, letters, voice mails) to contest commonly held beliefs about the restricted and often traditional ways individuals are instructed or scripted to relate to one another. They are not scientists or professional academics but work with common people in their everyday lives, and they usually use everyday experiences of common people to problematize high-minded and idealized sentiments similar to the ones espoused by Justice Kennedy. I am particularly interested in issues related to marriage. Part of my argument is that common intellectuals lift the veil off humanist ideals that so restrict pleasures, sensualities, and erotic life. Common intellectuals act as social provocateurs to instigate a rethinking and (re)practicing of relational forms.

The purpose of this chapter is to argue that the role of the intellectual is to function as a provocateur to offer individuals choices about relationality. I rely on three contemporary writers to illustrate how the role of the intellectual is to offer people choices beyond institutional modes of relating, such as marriage, to potentially generate new ways of relating to others. I wonder sometimes if institutions dictate the parameters for our erotic and sensual lives. In this instance, then, marriage, or traditional monogamous marriage, offers a certain buffet of erotic experiences with one person. For the couples therapist Esther Perel (2018), marriage is an institution that has too many demands placed on it. Monogamy remains the key feature of a marriage, and thus, cheating and affairs will remain part of its fold. She relies on sessions with hundreds of couples to contend that infidelity does not have to be the end of marriage but the start of a new one with new possibilities for both partners. According to advice columnist and sexologist Dan Savage, these rather prescribed and prearranged sensual and sexual offerings produce too much stress and strain on a relationship, and finally, for the late French intellectual Michel Foucault (1997), institutions such as marriage should be abandoned altogether. In his mind, there is no need for such institutions anymore. Marriage as an economic and highly gendered institution historically marginalized other erotic experiences and pleasures. The gay rights movement in the 1970s and 1980s ushered in the new possibilities for revitalizing those once lost or discarded erotic experiences. Why would anyone want to return to marriage when new relational potentials remained on the ongoing, ever-experimental horizon? Thus, these three common intellectuals offer us a series of invitations to question our own ways and modalities of relating, as well as provide opportunities for new social orders that are more specific to place rather than governable in their generalities. These thinkers, I would argue, represent the intellectual because they provide people with alternative ways of relating—to generate new potentialities of pleasure and potentially a new social order.

Esther Perel: Marriage-in-the-Making

If marriage holds society together, as Kennedy opined in the Supreme Court decision (*Obergefell v. Hodges*, 2015), then perhaps he should read Esther Perel's books and watch her TED Talks. The institution of marriage makes a promise, she asserts, to its participants that it is just unable to keep. According to the couples therapist Esther Perel, marriage comes with a whole litany of expectations. She explains that in the contemporary moment, most people have a romantic ideal, one person to fulfill all of our endless list of needs along with a sense of being the "one" unique perfect fit for the other person. Each partner gets to demand that the other one fulfill their every need (intellectual, emotional, erotic etc.; Perel, 2018). Such demands create a relationship fraught with fragility. It's like putting too many groceries in one bag; it becomes too easy for the bag to break. Paradoxically, what distinguishes marriages from other types of relationships, such as friendships, for example, is the level of intimacy one gives a partner. Marriages are intimate relationships and tend to involve sharing many aspects of oneself with another person. Central to this intimacy is trust and commitment. Marriages are contractual, intimate relationships based on trust and commitment. The fragility of marriages necessitates trust between partners and the need for mutual commitment. If marriages hold civilization together, through mutual bonds, then it (civilization) is tethered together by tenuous sinews. As she states, cheating and affairs are here to stay. They are not going away. As long as marriages are based on monogamy, cheating will remain a possibility. And the fact that cheating remains the central fold for marriage isn't the interesting part of her research. We don't need a couple's therapist who has listened to hundreds of couples confess their marital problems to tell us that cheating is endemic. The contribution her research makes on our understanding of marriage are the reasons why people cheat—even individuals in satisfying marriages and, more important, what couples do after the cheating is revealed.

Perel's (2018) research, based on countless hours with hundreds of couples, shows the married partners cheat for a variety of personal, marital, and existential reasons. Sociologically, she asserts that the current moment suffers from luxuries and comforts of living in a highly advanced and technological Western society. Paradoxically, advanced societies offer their citizens the ability to pursue happiness at every turn. Many of us live in a world where we believe that our own happiness is a right, exemplified in the phrase that she so commonly hears: "I deserve to be happy." Simultaneously, we understand at a fundamental level that we need to be with others and, in this case, oftentimes in marriage. The marital bond offers so much potential in terms of solving key human concerns, such as security, closeness, intimacy, financial quality-of-life issues, and many others. However, the sense of entitlement to happiness can cause one partner to stray. When things go awry or when certain needs get neglected or when problems arise, one's right to happiness can trump one's commitment to the other person (Perel, 2018). One's need for happiness can blind one to the benefits of marriage. In fact, Perel argues that staying in a relationship is the new shame. Choosing to remain committed to a marriage when it's difficult or going through a rough patch is the new shame. One's individual happiness is more important in many instances than staying in an unhappy marriage. Such a paradox puts pressure on the marital bond (and the other partner) to always keep each other happy, which is quite impossible. Certainly, people in unhappy marriages cheat on their partners.

They often calculate that being single would be in the imaginary more fulfilling than remaining with their partner. And it should be noted that we're not talking about abusive relationships here. Partners, for whatever reason, begin to feel unfulfilled and unhappy in a marriage tend to find other avenues to find that fulfillment and happiness, and oftentimes, it includes having an affair. But what about partners in happy and fulfilling marriages? Why do they cheat? How do couples generally recover from infidelity? The results of her research might surprise the reader.

Perel's (2018) research indicates that partners in happy marriages, even those who have been inclined to be in monogamous relationships their whole lives, tend to cheat for existential reasons including as a way to try to cheat death. Having an affair or cheating on one's partner offers the person a sexual intensity that gives them autonomy and a sense of freedom they haven't experienced in a long time. Perel's research also indicates that people who cheat locate a part of themselves they felt had been lost for many years. Having an intense sexual encounter permits them to get in touch with that lost self. Most people who cheat report "feeling alive" again, and according to Perel, they don't regret having the experience but regret the pain it caused their partner. For some, too, cheating is a chance to try to beat back death. After being monogamous for many years, her clients reported raising questions such as "Is this all there is?" "Will I ever feel that way again (like when we first fell in love)?" and "Am I going to go on like this for another 25 years?" An affair or an episodic cheat gets rid of the deadness, the commonality, the boredom in a marriage, and brings the person back to life again. Cheating and having an affair, Perel asserts, are less about sex and more about desire—and about being desirable, again. The stability and certainty of marriage, again based on trust and commitment, can turn on itself and can produce the opposite of what it was intended for.

So what happens to couples after the affair or cheating escapade is over? How do they recover? Perel's (2018) research indicates that some couples don't recover. In this instance, the marriage was already fractured to begin with, or the act of betrayal caused such a gulf between the partners that they just couldn't trust each other again. Yet, in other cases, the act of betrayal can reinvigorate couples into new relational possibilities. Most often, the betrayed partner reveals that they, too, were unsatisfied in the relationship or were so involved in the relationship that they lost a sense of their own identity.

The betrayal offers the betrayed partner an opportunity to reclaim a sense of identity and gives them an opportunity to redefine the relationship on terms that are more suited for their happiness. Additionally, the fear of loss generates a new kind of passion for their partner. Partners can rekindle what brought them together in the first place and rebuild their relationship again. Perel states that when she meets with a couple for the first time, she informs them that most couples in the West are going to have two to three significant relationships in their lifetime. Sometimes, it is with the same person, and sometimes, it is not. For the second one to work, the cheater needs to become the protector of the relationship by rebuilding trust again and allow the betrayed partner to build some self-worth again and gain some independence from the relationship. Couples can rebuild from betrayal, but it takes work and a conscious effort.

What makes Perel a common intellectual is her use of everyday people in their daily lives as material to contest commonly held beliefs about the marriage institution. Her research shows that monogamy may not be the best contractual agreement for every couple and that cheating and affairs seem to be part of the necessary fold of monogamy. Cheating and affairs show us that marriage can be fragile when too many expectations, often chimerical or ideal ones, are placed on it. The affordances of modern life, including but not limited to technology, can be both advantageous and disadvantageous to marriage as a relational modality. The advantages are that they offer individuals more choices in partners and more opportunities to find a partner who fits. The disadvantage is that they offer the ideal desire or right to always being happy. This means that people can keep shopping without settling on one or always searching for a better one. Happiness, the real fragile and evanescent sentiment, can fracture social bonds. What Perel's (2018) research reveals is that marriage needs to be given the flexibility to be modified between couples. Couples can no longer keep making demands of marriage that it is unwilling and unable to keep.

While Perel tries to find ways to keep a marriage together, sexologist and advice columnist Dan Savage (2006) argues that marriage doesn't have to be based on monogamy but can be based on mutually agreed-on terms. Building on its contractual roots, Savage (2006) argues that two people can predetermine and change the terms of their agreement, including but not limited to being or not being monogamous.

Savage Love: Dan Savage and the (IL)Logics of Monogamy

Ostensibly, it may seem that Dan Savage endorses chaotic, even anarchic social order. If we apply Justice Kennedy's standards that marriage functions as an institution that provides the glue that keeps civilization and progress needled together, then Savage's views on marriage and particularly monogamy may make the Supreme Court justice wince and groan. Savage (2006) does argue that monogamy is an outdated necessity of marriage. Rather than being the focus or the center of the marital bond, monogamy can be one of many negotiated components of a commitment. In fact, such negotiation can occur throughout a relationship. Monogamy, Savage states, only became the center of marriage about 100 years ago. In fact, men and women married for economic and gendered reasons, not for love and/or passion. In fact, men often had whores, concubines, and side pieces to channel their need for love and passion (Savage, 2006).

Monogamy entered the stage when women left the home and began to assume their own economic needs and reproductive health in the discovery of contraception (Savage, 2006). Marriage didn't need to be part of the equation. Instead of granting women the freedoms once given to men, men gave up their concubines and began to marry for love and passion with the explicit rule to maintain monogamy. Infidelity, once seen as necessary for men to remain in a relationship, now is seen as the ultimate betrayal (Savage, 2006). Marriage then became the enclosed unit guarding against the temptations of the rake and mistress. This focus on monogamy places too much stress on the relationship, and the emotional toll it takes often forces couples to break up. The idea, Savage proclaims, that once you marry, one no longer will be attracted to or want to be sexual or erotic with another is excessive and chimerical. One's ability to remain monogamous in a marriage equates to the amount of love one has for his or her partner. Savage asserts that to be monogamous is not only not normal but also not healthy (Savage, 2006). Instead, what needs to occur in marriages, and relationships in general, is communication about one's erotic life. One's partner, Savage asserts, does not own the other's erotic life—the individual does.

Moreover, a partner cannot and probably will not be everything for the other. As he states frequently in his writings, "There is no 'the one.' . . . You'll meet a .64 or two if you are lucky . . . and it's your job to round that motherfucker up to one" (see Savage, 2015, para. 1). Rounding up is the risk, the excitement, and the gift couples give to each other in a relationship. Marriage does not have to be a situation in which both people try to fit themselves into a corset but one that involves continual negotiations about one's and each other's erotic life and pleasures. Thus, instead of equating monogamy with virginity, perhaps we need to think of it as akin to sobriety. If one falls off the wagon, they just get right back on it. In these ways, then, Savage proclaims to be a conservative. He's trying very diligently to maintain marriages and honor committed relationships, but they can't be based on humanist idealisms of "the one" and monogamy.

What happens to marriage and relationships generally speaking if we think of pleasures and erotic life as playful, experimental, and creative rather than domination, control, and enclosure? How might erotic and sexual lives offer other ways of relating and communicating with others? How might negotiating one's sexual desires with one's partner expand your understanding of yourself or of pleasures themselves? How might we consider building a different social order not based on an outdated modality that fissures many marriages and relationships? How might we think about marriage if we didn't let an infidelity break it up but as an opportunity to reevaluate, and recommit, and reimagine our erotic lives? How might our relationships look different if we remained committed to our partner and not so much to the ideals of monogamy? These provocative questions Savage encourages us to consider, and as a common intellectual, he forces us to reimagine our relational bonds and new possibilities for coupling.

One person who did consider them is the late French intellectual Michel Foucault. He argues that getting rid of marriage as an institution offers potentially new modalities for erotic and sensual life (Foucault, 1997).

Polyhedronic Relationalities: Michel Foucault as Intellectual

The choice to include late French intellectual Michel Foucault in a discussion about the common intellectual may seem odd. His philosophical works seem to be anything but common. But his personal biography and political activism speak to his interests in ground-up mobilization against various forces of power/knowledge, particularly against sovereign power. Forces of power/knowledge operate in strategic networks that operate through the body of both individuals and groups. As such, it is not uncommon to locate instances of heightened political activism in Foucault's biography. For example, events of May 1968 prompted Foucault (1977/1980) to assert that the intellectual does not know more than local people. In this instance, he was referencing the general intellectualism of Sartre and Zola. Instead, Foucault endorsed a more local, specific intellectual, or what I'm calling a common intellectual. Here, the intellectual makes specific interventions in local settings based on specialized knowledge and provided alternative ways of potential relating to others. In this vein, then, Foucault's genealogical studies were not simply fancy historical footwork designed to offer new perspectives but were strategic indictments on various forms of power/knowledge that also provided readers with different modalities of relating to power, to see the machinations of knowledge in relation to power, and opportunities to reconsider self-creation as a work of art. His political activism throughout his life, from the riots at Vincennes to the composition of the *Le Groupe d'information sur les prisons* (The Prisons Information Group, or GIP) and his journalistic endeavors in what was thought to be the people's revolution in Iran, Foucault's scholarly work and his biography reveal a rather profound connection between his scholarly works to his guerrilla warfare on the streets.

In relation to sexuality and relationships, Foucault made significant contributions to our understanding. In his works on the *History of Sexuality*, Foucault (1976/1990) revealed the relationships between sexual acts/practices and truth were knitted together by false assumptions, faulty science, and a violent moralism that privileged normalization over human experimentation and creation. Moreover, he argued that sex could be utilized and problematized to produce an *ascesis*, or working on the self, to produce a life as a work of art. Rather than renouncing the self or hedonistically giving into the pleasures of the body or relying on Reichian psychology to explain neurosis and psychological disequilibrium, Foucault contends that sexual practices can be used to continually build a life as a work of art as part of a variety of techniques of the self. And although he remained continually fascinated with the post-Stonewall era of gay liberation and the openness of gay culture in the United States that took place in the 1970s and 1980s, he never thought that gayness, or homosexuality, was necessarily about liberating one's sexual desires in order to build or construct a stable identity but was rather a potential to practice self-creation and self-experimentation as a continual in-the-making. Sex and sexual practices were not an endpoint but were a collection of possible techniques of the self that provided the potential to build new relationships and alliances that could shift power/knowledge into more expansive and inclusive ways to see how sexual practices could be used to build one's life as a work of art. The role that sex could play in the construction of one's life as a work of art was explained in an interview he gave to the newly formed gay magazine *Le Gai Pied* and later titled "Friendship as a Way of Life" (1997).

In this interview, he wonders more about why a group of people so demonized by the institution of marriage would ever want to be a part of it (Foucault, 1997). Foucault argues that rather than opening up marriages and fostering a new way of being in the world while maintaining old institutions the gay rights movement and the subsequent coming out of gays and lesbians offered people the opportunity to build different types of relationships. Rather than men interacting with other men based primarily on institutional ways, such as military, sports, and bromances, Foucault (1997) argued that social intimacies could be based on friendships. Friendships could serve as the basis for new relationalities that fostered a desire in uneasiness and could therefore be an ascesis. In his mind, friendships could be opportunities to test oneself based on pleasures of the body that would aid someone to build a life as a work of art. Thus, pleasure in friendships could serve as tools to help a person fashion oneself as a work of art. As he states in the interview,

> Homosexuality is a historic occasion to reopen affective and relational virtualities, not so much through the intrinsic qualities of the homosexual but because the "slantwise" position of the latter, as it were, the diagonal lines he can lay out in the social fabric allow these virtualities to come to light. (Foucault, 1997, p. 138)

Homosexuality is not necessarily an identity with specific intrinsic qualities but is a social position. Homosexuality is an invitation to reconsider the traditional lines endemic in the "social fabric" through "slantwise" relationalities. Bodies and pleasure become useful in terms of reimagining, even inventing, relationalities in the social fabric. Instead of maintaining institutional ways of relating, Foucault argues that homosexuality could invite individuals to reimagine their relationships. Such invention and reimagining would make homosexuality "not a form of desire but something desireable" (1997, p. 136).

Thus, instead of channeling bodies and pleasures toward marriage anchored by monogamy, Foucault makes a convincing argument to employ bodies and pleasure to reconsider relationships and to build a life as a work of art.

Conclusion

The common intellectual utilizes on-the-ground experiences, observations, conversations, diaries, and other common sorts of data to subvert institutional ways of relating. Additionally, they use these data to contest idealized purpose, and reasons for relating in institutionalized ways offer people new possibilities. In this instance, marriage and coupling seem to be an important aspect of social life, but they do not need to be the main threads that tie social cohesion together. It can be one among many, and as Savage (2006) reminds us, it can look different from traditional marriage based on monogamy. Partners can determine the contours of their marriage based on their ongoing and changing needs and desires. If marriage is to remain a vital component of social life, it must be flexible to change. Marriage must adapt to social life. Although all three of these common intellectuals challenge the purpose and effects of marriage in social and relational life, they all agree that other ways of bonding must be permitted in social life. Sensual and erotic lives may need variety and sometimes that is with one person for life, sometimes it involves multiple partners for life, and sometimes it is a combination. Although each of these common intellectuals contests traditional marital bonds, in their efforts to propagate multiplicities, they must make room for traditional marriage based on monogamy. Monogamy must be a serving on the proverbial buffet of possible sensual and erotic possibilities. Marriage based on monogamy offers certain affordances purposefully suited for some. But they do provoke us into reconsidering the reasons and purposes for getting into certain bonds and not others. They also provide options for many to become more open and susceptible to spontaneous moments of ecstatic pleasure that can potentially redefine who we think we are and redesign social lines based on social and personal affinities.

A final word about expertise and specifically as it relates to academia. Common intellectuals tend to not be detached from the social world or try to remain objective and unbiased. They are quite the opposite. They practice a type of scholarship that may defy traditional or positivistic notions of validity and reliability. Common intellectuals seek answers to complex social problems from common people in their everyday experiences and lives. They are attuned to social changes and try to offer suggestions about ways to expand erotic and pleasure experiences based on new relational bonds. Their expertise comes from their willingness to challenge themselves (and others) to be different relationally in the world. Social order can't be based on one modality of relating, and institutional forms of coupling such as marriage, but on freedom.

References

Foucault, M. (1980). Truth and power (A. Fontana & P. Pasquino, Trans.). In C. Gordon (Ed.), *Power/knowledge: Selected interviews and other writings 1972-1977* (pp. 109–133). Pantheon Books. (Original work published 1977)

Foucault, M. (1990). *The history of sexuality: An introduction* (R. Hurley, Trans.). Vintage. (Originally published 1976)

Foucault, M. (1997). Friendship as a way of life. In P. Rabinow (Ed.), *Michel Foucault: Ethics, subjectivity and truth* (pp. 135–140). The New Press.

Obergefell v. Hodges. 576 U.S. 644 (2015).

Perel, E. (2018). *The state of affairs: Rethinking infidelity*. HarperCollins.

Savage, D. (2006). *The commitment: Love, sex, marriage, and my family*. Penguin Books.

Savage, D. (2015, August 18). Savage love letter of the day: The boyfriend is out-should I get out. *The Stranger*. https://www.thestranger.com/blogs/slog/2015/08/18/22720327/savage-love-letter-of-the-day-the-boyfriend-is-outshould-i-get-out

Ideas take flight

Multi-voicing

Book authors: In our chapter we encourage readers to re-story their own research practices through the nonlinear and enmeshed collective action of soil.

Reader 1: I am not sure I follow you. What do the earth and soil-matter have to do with public intellectualism? How might human-centered narration enable more intense interactions with soil and matter? What can be accomplished via narration and storytelling in the more-than-human world? What might collective soil action intellectuals do?

Reader 2: Very enjoyable chapter! Too often intellectuals forget the role of public, avoid, and maybe dismiss public spaces (of transformation). I think that public science is the most relevant science when it comes to the transformation potential and intellectual work that can make a difference in sustainable ways. Why would one engage in science without practical and communal implications? Furthermore, this chapter prompts questions about why and how scholars and intellectuals are engaging in their mundane activities to enhance their scholarly and intellectual processes. It also troubles the division between thought and action, and it calls for intellectual actions that care and function in culturally responsible ways.

Book authors: Mundane activities matter in ecological and cosmic ways. The water set in the desert; the building of peace doves; the countless phone calls, errands, and chairs set up and taken down. Activities resonate with other activities, lives intersect, and actions transpire other actions. During these interactional and relational activities, organizational idea-practices move, pattern, and ongoingly become.

Reader 3: Patterns often develop unintentionally through assemblages. Intellectuals might watch temporal rhythms of idea-practices and draw from different scales of lifeways. Multiplicity of mattering and living matter. Tsing (2015) proposed that it is time to focus on nonscalable life objects for description and unthinkable provocations of theory. Today could also be the time of multiple temporalities and revitalizing imagination. The arts of noticing the ignored and nonfitting can make a difference and stimulate different (communal) practices.

Book authors: Rhizomatic connections of intellectuals and matter might function similar to fungi growth; speedy uncontrollable relational force into multiple directions. Natural processes could parallel more the ways public intellectuals and intellectualism work as well. In our chapter we state that "fungi can often grow in what is considered barren soil, soil that is not much more than very fine rock. In doing so, fungi create conditions for other organisms to grow. For example, soil bacteria find it difficult to survive the arid conditions of rocky soil, but fungi can provide moisture in the form of a mucosal layer around its networked body." Where might fungal intellectualism go and what might it reach?

Reader 1: As soon as we think we know the direction of growth, intellectual movement, and fungi, another turn happens and another pattern and collective intellectual formation emerge.

Tsing, A. (2015). *The mushroom at the end of the world.* Princeton University Press.

Entangled

Angled
Tangled
Lines
Interrupted
Erupted
By air
Flower
Leaves
Shade
Light
Entangled
Crisscrossed
Lines
Leading out
Leading in
Angled
Animate
Inanimate
Tangled
Entangled
Lines
Pulsating
With energy
Leaves
Throbbing
With atoms
Lines
Vibrating
With electrons
Leaves
Dancing
With the lines
Leaves
Lines
Tangled
Entangled
Animate
Inanimate
Tangled
Entangled.

NINE

Soil Storying of Public Intellectualism: Ideas Mattering Through Care and Collectivity

Nicole Bowers, Arizona State University
Adam T. Clark, Arizona State University

Figure 9.1. Mural at the International Day of Peace Sponsored by the International Sonoran Desert Alliance. September, 21, 2019.

In this chapter, we seek to expand the notion of the public intellectual and go beyond public intellectualism as communicating knowledge produced toward the mattering of ideas. When asked to consider the notion of the public intellectual, it seems most natural to start with the question, "What is a public intellectual?" We contend that this question limits our ability to rethink public intellectualism as it predefines a category that has been traditionally occupied by academics who engage a nonacademic public through speaking and writing. It only permits exploration and representation of what others traditionally considered public intellectualism. Instead, we start with two related questions: "What do public intellectuals do?" and "What can public intellectuals do?"

Some public intellectuals produce knowledge through academic research and communicate that knowledge to audiences that do not do academic research. The intellectual here is a professional knower, one who engages the public. Other public intellectuals may challenge the status quo through speaking truth to power or activating new ways of thinking in society. The latter seems much less transactional than the action of the public knower, and this action captured our imaginations, spurring us to our work.

By tracing the actions of challenging the status quo, we are no longer limited to the work of academia. We assume that to challenge the status quo, alternative ideas must be put into play so that the movement of new thoughts and ideas becomes bound up in this challenging. We further contend that the point of challenging the status quo is to change it, to create new ways of moving through the world, and to do that ideas must *matter*; ideas must cling to hands and run into eyes, becoming part of the visceral experience. We see local activists, community organizers, and their organizations as participants in challenging the status quo with the mattering of ideas.

Our proposition is simple. Academics are not the only parties involved in resisting the status quo. We invite the reader to consider community organizations and their complex work of caring embedded in their actions of resistance. The following work raises issues around the asymmetry of power in research–community partnerships and suggests an alternative story line to understanding work in community organizations. To go beyond the highly valued production of knowledge and communication toward social change, we believe caring and collectivity also need to be valued and experienced, and we present this case here.

In the sections that follow, we outline the extant literature around traditional research community partnerships. We then discuss community partners as public intellectuals in the traditional sense. Then we transition into our own experiences engaging with community organizations and alternative imaginings of public intellectualism through soil storying.

Traditional Community–Research Partnerships

It may help to first look at the way academic fields and communities traditionally interact. Serving community partners has become quite common in academia. On the surface, this trend seems to be caught up with putting ideas in play, mattering, but it remains quite linear with notions of putting research into practice—a unidirectional flow that holds the researcher to be the professional knower. Conceptualizing this relationship unidirectionally establishes an asymmetry power dynamic. Over the past 20 years, community–research partnerships have surfaced as a way for researchers to make an impact with their research in various fields, from Indigenous studies (Castleden et al., 2008) and health research (Spoth & Redmond, 2002) to more generalist accounts of research institutions' roles in partnerships (Curwood et al., 2011). However, these impacts seem to imply a collision of the researcher's knowledge with the public, causing changes in public practice, a kind of ballistics report of ideas. In fact, our own institution has developed several partnerships based on embeddedness in the community. For example, a local affordable housing high-rise for seniors partnered with our institution to expand existing services that involve health screenings (blood pressure checks, disease prevention programs, etc.) to include counseling, community assistance, and educational and cultural opportunities. The linearity of this relationship is pedagogical—in that this partnership also has institutional benefits: it helps to train future nurses and health care providers.

In practice, the history of these partnerships has been laden with inequity. Traditional researcher–practitioner partnerships often privilege the intellectual savvy of the researcher over their nonacademic partners (Fuller & Kitchin, 2004; Somekh & Zeichner, 2009). More recently, as we see in some of the preceding examples, this has morphed into researchers addressing community needs in a discourse framed by researchers and community organizers/organizations fixing community problems (Ferman & Hill, 2004). This discourse encourages researchers to codesign studies with their community partners to involve partners in data collection and analysis, but even within this approach, many community partners continue to feel the lesser. For example, in a rare look at the community-side perspective of research–community partnerships, Ferman and Hill (2004) asked various leaders from 14 organizations about their experiences with academic research partnerships and found that although they cited benefits such as access to resources and networks, they often reported feeling "devalued, ignored, or otherwise disrespected" (p. 248). We contend that what is being "devalued, ignored or otherwise disrespected" in these partnerships is not only the intellectual knowledge production of these community organizations but also the important care-oriented, mundane work that allows ideas to take shape and affect the world (to matter).

Community Partners as Public Intellectuals in the Traditional Sense

Although, traditionally, community organizations are not thought of as intellectual, we find that they do engage in processes typically reserved for public intellectuals. We agree with Melzer (2004) that public intellectuals who help to transform society exhibit the three qualities in Table 9.1.

Table 9.1. Aspects of Transformative Public Intellectuals. (Melzer, 2004)

1. Reciprocally engaging with the public
2. Passionate devotion to a nonfinite idea
3. Engagement in practices for social transformation

In this chapter, we rely on our experience with and knowledge of local community organizations where we have volunteered. As such, we have seen the processes in Table 9.1 in action within these organizations. With regard to reciprocally engaging the public, these organizations often do so at their inception by responding to issues they see in their communities. For example, Kimber Lanning, the founder of Local First Arizona (LFA), began her organization because many of the young artists who frequented her record store moved out of state due to the lack of opportunities for a career in the arts in Phoenix, Arizona (PBS, 2017). The founders of the International Sonoran Desert Alliance (ISDA) formed as a tricultural environmental conservation organization in an effort to support environmental action in the Sonoran Desert (Arizona Public Media, 2017). Both organizations eventually evolved, reciprocally engaging with the public (Melzer, 2004). LFA's dedication to changing policy that favors big business and in support of small business arose from the additional needs that Lanning and her group experienced within the community as they continued to grow their organization (PBS, 2017). The ISDA extended its mission to include supporting sustainable entrepreneurship, community education programs, and food networks in response to the voices in their community (Arizona Public Media, 2017). Both began with passionate devotion to a nonfinite idea (Melzer, 2004), another criterion for public intellectualism. Both organizations continually engage in practices for social transformation (Melzer, 2004), rounding out our conceptualization of the practice of public intellectualism. Additionally, many social movement researchers have shown that community organizers and their organizations are important knowledge producers, a function typically considered a monopoly among academics (Choudry & Kapoor, 2010). Important for critical inquiry, Novelli (2010) argues that social movements, activists, and community organizers can engage with counterhegemonic knowledge production that creates and maintains narratives that are important for socially just action to be imagined and accomplished.

Although part of our argument contends that many community organizations can certainly be considered public knowledge producers, intellectuals in their own right, we argue that they have strengths that surpass those of traditional public intellectuals, but those strengths remain difficult to identify through research that remains predefined and prioritizes the production of knowledge in specific ways. Through our volunteer engagement with community organizations, we came to experience community organizations as spaces of caring, collectivity, and idea mattering. We share the following vignettes to provide a glimpse of the processes and experience with community organizations that go beyond knowledge production.

Vignette: Dove Children (First Author)

It was cool for September, only 96 °F, as I stood out on the street corner waiting. Beside me, in two cardboard boxes, sat four cases of bottled water that I retrieved from the local bank standing behind me offering no shade to my sun-drenched position. To my right, lining the street, community members sat in a variety of portable chairs they carted with them, and like me, they waited. By the time spectators lined the street, I had been standing in the desert sun for about 45 minutes. Occasionally, people would come by, with longing looks at the boxes of water, and I would hand them a few bottles. Finally, the parade came around the corner, and all the anticipation released into applause and hoots of enjoyment. People supporting poles attached to the head, wings, and tail of doves of peace made from sheets and papier-mâché ambled past. Marching bands played, dance troupes danced, and elementary school children festooned with paper plates transformed into dove masks walked by; one dove child marched by clutching a papier-mâché heart emblazoned with the word *peace*. I ran water bottles out to dove children, fire truck drivers, and the law enforcement officers stopping traffic on the only road that runs through town. After only 20 minutes, the parade's caboose moved past my position, signaling the end of my water vigilance, so I handed out as many water bottles as spectators would carry, then hefted the remains into the bank and went to join the festivities.

Every year since 2008, the ISDA hosts a festival in Ajo, Arizona, for the International Day of Peace. This festival celebrates "the idea of community as Ajo chooses to bring its three cultures—Hispanic, Tohono O'odham and Anglo—together in a fun, celebratory way that highlights respect for its diversity" (ISDA, 2020b, para. 2). The ISDA (2020a) supports many projects and events, and they are "committed to fostering communication, understanding and cooperation among the diverse cultures residing in the area" (para. 1). Anyone is welcome to volunteer; I simply went to their office, and they assigned me to a water post. Since then, I have worked on other projects with this group that involved carrying equipment, researching in the local newspaper's archives, and creating graphics for flyers.

Vignette: Coworking Space (Second Author)

In my volunteer efforts, I saw the administrative side of local activism. I should also preface this by saying that I found my volunteer experiences in less directly helpful ways than that of my coauthor. Most of my experiences stemmed from a coworking space in Phoenix that I joined to get some writing done outside of the "coffee shop–home–school distraction zone." In my initial search for a removed, focused place to work, I toured a lot of spaces that seemed to be an afterthought. One was attached to a real estate brokerage and seemed to just be an overage of square footage labeled a "coworking space"; another was attached to a coffee shop and was part of a large national chain geared toward corporate nomads. The place I finally settled on was one that had started in Phoenix and had moved several times around the valley.

The most recent move was to a building that the coworking space owned, financed by donors and founding partners who intended to use the space as an office. The space is a Matryoshka doll of activism. In the outer layer, the coworking organization itself is devoted to helping small and local businesses thrive by providing space and a sense of supportive community. It does this by supplying all the normal office services, utilities, and space while also providing business seminars, networking events, and community events. Inner layers are the various businesses and nonprofits that exist in the space. They vary wildly from youth voter registration and criminal justice reform to local produce/food-scarcity work and social activism or political lobbying. Mixed into the nonprofits are tech start-ups, freelance web designers, real estate assessors, and other small business owners.

Not much of the work of each was done in the actual workspace. If I wanted to venture out with each organization, I could register college students to vote, visit a prison, distribute food, and canvass for 2020 electoral ballot initiatives, among many other opportunities. The work that I actually did seems paltry in comparison.

I'm a member of this coworking space; I pay a monthly fee for access to a desk, the internet, and coffee so I can write, which is arguably what I do for a living. However, after several months of doing this, I was slowly integrated into the work of the space. Sometimes, when the community manager needed to leave for something, I would cover the front desk and field any questions from members and people off the street ("How do I . . . ?" "Where is . . . ?" etc.). This included giving tours of the coworking space and enrolling others in the vision of the space as it related to developing entrepreneurs and activists. It was easy because at this point, I believed in their mission.

Collectively Caring: Ideas Come to Matter

Although a simple explanation of our arguments may convince our readers to position community organizations as forces of public intellectualism, we add these vignettes to evoke for our readers what occurred simultaneously, enmeshed, and entangled in our inquiry experience. We invite our readers to carry these vignettes through the remaining parts of the chapter.

Through the preceding sections, we have often referred to community organizers, activists, and their organizations. This is rather a bulky way to refer to the who/what we might think of performing as a public intellectual. It is tempting to think of the founder or most active organizer as the intellectual and all the other members of the organization or movement as the public. Perhaps in the strictest sense, the founder, the visionary who begins the movement, deserves the moniker intellectual, but it does not actually *matter* as this moniker does not carry the force of ideas that affect the world. We agree with Haraway (2016) in "that bounded individualism in its many flavors . . . has finally become unavailable to think with" (p. 5).

This is the fourth aspect that we propose to add to Table 9.1, the collective flourishing of an idea (Nagel, 1972) bound no longer to individual actions and achievement.

Community organizers and activists already understand and embody Haraway's (2016) sentiment. They already understand that their ideas cannot affect the world without others and without mundane, material workings. We (the authors) came to understand this through our own embodied experiences within these organizations as illustrated by our vignettes. In the following section, we wish to re-story, with the help of soil, what could easily be a narrative of exceptional individual leadership. We take examples from LFA and the ISDA, two organizations familiar to the first author through volunteering, to set the stage for an alternative narrative that honors care and collectivity.

Kimber Lanning, of LFA, looks to be a perfect candidate for community organizer as public intellectual. She is a rousing speaker, practiced at conveying her ideas to the public, and spends much of her time, now, doing just that; we could have easily written extensively about her intellectual prowess and engagement with the public at that level. But to focus on the rather charismatic aspects of Lanning as most valuable would minimize important work that nurtures and sustains ideas, giving them a body in the world.

Before Lanning founded LFA, she owned and ran a local record store. Here, she became concerned with the exodus of local artists; to fill a community need, she turned her record store walls into an art gallery and hosted local musicians five nights a week. Her walls and small stage were booked sometimes more than a year in advance. This activity spurred her to buy a small building on Roosevelt Street in a dilapidated part of Phoenix with the idea of creating a venue for local artists to showcase their work—a springboard for early- and mid-career artists to develop their practice (Sum and Substance, 2016).

In one speaking engagement, she relays the story of creating this venue. She bought the building that no one really wanted and gathered a coalition of 50 local artists, asking them to help her renovate it. When renovations began, only six showed up. Lanning's advice to burgeoning community organizers and activists is "to find that thing where you are one of the six" (Sum and Substance, 2016, 13:25). Her vision of creating a refuge for developing artists would have remained only an idea if not for others.

Today, the office of LFA is a hive of activity with volunteers stuffing envelopes and answering phones. Volunteers at LFA events direct traffic, help people compost leftovers and recycle, and set up and tear down the many events hosted by LFA. The vast majority of actors in community organizations like LFA spend their time in these mundane and laborious activities, and without these activities, the ideas that the community organizations are seeded with do not *matter*.

Maria Puig de la Bellacasa (2017) would characterize these activities as caring. She writes that

> to care contains a notion of *doing* . . . this is because understanding caring as something we do materializes it as an ethically and politically charged practice . . . in this vision, to care joins together an affective state, a material vital doing, and an ethico-political obligation. (p. 42)

Community organizations perform and practice through everyday mundane labors: the water set in the desert; the building of peace doves; the countless phone calls, errands, and chairs set up and taken down. These activities are the stuff of the organization's movement, these practices of care, small and undervalued in academia, become the ground for ideas' becomings.

Sustainability remains an important aspect of care. Puig de la Bellacasa (2017) begins her book *Matters of Care* by citing Tronto's generic notion that care is "everything that we do to maintain, continue, and repair 'our world' so that we can live in it as well as possible" (p. 3). She goes on to elaborate that "in the world as we

Activist Ecologies

A farmer
Cultivating,
Maintaining
A pretense
Of domination.
Harnessing
Dirt

Soil
Entangling
Fertile
Collective
The always-already-present
More-than-one
In process.

Fungus,
Resilient
Network-body.
Generative,
Reproductive
Bacterial highway.

Humus,
Unexpected,
Unpredictable,
Incorporate my DNA.
Entangle me
In your activist ecology.

know it, this involves tasks that make living better in interdependence but are often considered petty and unimportant, unproductive, however vital they are for livable relations" (Puig de la Bellacasa, 2017, p. 55). In the week leading up to the ISDA Internal Peace Festival described earlier, local artists came together to maintain the peace murals that are posted around the town's central plaza during the festival (Figure 9.1). In 2013, local artists designed the murals and community members, young and old, painted them. Over time, they became sun-faded and well worn; this year in a caring act of sustainability, artists repainted the placards, not creating them, not changing them, but maintaining and repairing them (ISDA, 2020b).

It is this type of work that is undervalued and unmentioned in discussions about public intellectualism. Caring is vital to collective flourishing, "we all need this work, but we predominantly continue to value more the capacity to be self-sufficient, autonomous, and independent from others" (Puig de la Bellacasa, 2017, p. 55). Now we are back to Haraway's (2016) argument that "we require each other in unexpected collaborations and combinations, in hot compost piles. We become-with each other or not at all" (p. 4). In the following section, we employ soil as a narrative guide for the actions of public organizations related to public intellectualism.

Soil: The Collective Body of Care

We move in this section to the use of soil as a narrative partner. Soil/earth/ground has been described elsewhere as

> the collection of natural bodies on the earth's surface, in places modified or even made by man of earthly materials, containing living matter and supporting or capable of supporting plants out-of-doors. Its upper limit is air or shallow water. At its margins it grades to deep water or to barren areas of rock or ice. Its lower limit to the not-soil beneath is perhaps the most difficult to define. Soil includes the horizons near the surface that differ from the underlying rock material as a result of interactions, through time, of climate, living organisms, parent materials, and relief. In the few places where it contains thin cemented horizons that are impermeable to roots, soil is as deep as the deepest horizon. More commonly soil grades at its lower margin to hard rock or to earthy materials virtually devoid of roots, animals, or marks of other biologic activity. The lower

> limit of soil, therefore, is normally the lower limit of biologic activity, which generally coincides with the common rooting depth of native perennial plants. (United States Soil Conservation Service, 1975, p. 1)

Both Haraway (2016) and Puig de la Bellacasa (2017) develop the idea of soil in their writings about collectively creating new futures and embodying natureculture. Soil provides an apt narration partner to understand the nonlinear, entangled process of aiding new life to flourish or, in our case, new ideas to become bodied and affective. The mysteries of soil rest not only in organisms and interactions that the human eye cannot detect unaided but also in the lack of individual action and linear causation; in other words, soil is always more-than-one and more process than static body. What's more, there are varieties of soil that enhance the growth of life in different ways. The shape, color, moisture level, density—all indicate qualities of the soil in terms of fertility and production (Witty & Arnold, 1987). The soil of the community organizations that we have engaged with is entangled in "soils" highly contingent on a number of local factors around them.

If we look at Lanning's story as an example, it is tempting to say that she created the idea of an arts venue in Phoenix, she enlisted others to help her, and she (and her followers) fought to keep the arts district from becoming corporate buildings, allowing other people access to the district for more galleries, local restaurants, and businesses. In the course of this, she created another idea around the need to protect local business interests in the face of unfair subsidies granted by the city and state to large national and multinational corporations (PBS, 2017).

Our Western minds seem soothed and attracted to this domino-like action of causation that prizes the individual, Kimber Lanning, as progenitor and activist. A soil story of LFA takes more patience and recognizes the lack of central characters and simultaneity of action. In this story, Phoenix, with all its buildings, regulations, people, and organizations, seethes and writhes with unseen processes. Without the artists who sought a venue, without the building in the arts district that Lanning and her six renovated, without other local businesses—without any of these, Lanning's ideas may never have formed at all. We cite her as an example because she was working with the bodies already entangled, and her organization has grown and thrived across Arizona (PBS, 2017).

If we consider Lanning to be extraordinary in any way, it might be that she seems more fungal than bacterial or insectoid in her interactions within the soil story. Soil fungus acts as a mysterious and resilient organism whose body creates a network that is part of the soil and runs through the soil as a collective network body, creating interactions that change the soil's composition and allow other, less resilient organisms to thrive—who, in turn, change the soil and so on. The presence of soil fungus acts as both an organism and a vast structure of nonhierarchical connections within the soil (Macfarlane, 2019).

Fungi can often grow in what is considered barren soil, soil that is not much more than very fine rock. In doing so, fungi create conditions for other organisms to grow. For example, soil bacteria find it difficult to survive the arid conditions of rocky soil, but fungi can provide moisture in the form of a mucosal layer around its networked body as it secretes enzymes and acids that dissolve rocky particles into a gooey substance in which these smaller bacteria can thrive (Frey-Klett et al., 2011). Furthermore, because fungi act as a vast highway, bacteria can travel, meet other bacteria, exchange DNA, and create new processes and bodies (Berthold et al., 2016).

We do not mean to simply say that Lanning is analogous to soil fungus and her volunteers are analogous to bacteria. Oh no, fungus is far more complex than that. It is almost impossible to tell where one fungal organism begins and another ends. Fungus has no real gender or singular body; it is a conglomeration of DNA transfer and resilient structure. We suggest that Lanning became part of that always-already present conglomeration of soil carrying a tiny bit of novel DNA, her intellectual idea and passionate devotion, that itself evolved in the soil of Phoenix that preexisted her body/process and transformed that soil.

So, in the first part of her imagined linear story, she created an idea of an art venue in Phoenix; in a soil story, Lanning's entanglement with art, Phoenix, and other people created the art venue (idea and physical body). It was realizing the idea that mattered, not the origin, and that was made possible by a universe of bodies that included Lanning. This mattering is not a series of steps but a churning of interacting bodies. The second part of the linear narrative, that she enlisted others, may be better understood as a transfer of DNA containing her ideas to others' bodies much like the lateral transfer from one fungal hypha (the long, branching filaments of the fungal body) to another. This transfer does not mean that the other bodies become clones but that the other bodies uniquely incorporate that DNA into their own. The development of the arts district, which Lanning herself refuses credit for, may be better understood as the growth of an arts district in now-fecund soil that found its way into being from the processes described earlier (Sum and Substance, 2016).

In the linear story of Lanning, we might imagine her as a gardener or farmer, planting and tending seeds and coaxing them into distinct bodies with the help of others. This seems like a story of care, but in our twisting, entangled version of care, the soil (in all its heterogeneous, processual glory) cares. The real work of flourishing happens when something barren transforms into something life-giving through a myriad of interacting bodies. Lanning did not plant an idea and tend it; she, as part of a vast soil-like under-ecosystem, became part of the changing conditions that allowed something new to live and thrive.

Understanding the laborious action, the slow growth/change enacted by soil bodies that are barely distinguishable as individuals, allows us to think through caring differently. Caring as soil is slow, it collectively works with conditions/bodies/processes at hand, it remains practically invisible, and its results are often unexpected and unpredictable. Soil, once seemingly barren, can spring to life, its processes of generation hidden from view. Once the soil becomes fertile, even more diverse bodies can flourish and, in return, change the soil again.

Our own process of engagement and research is also a soil story. Within the soil of communities and their organizations, our own research morphed and became. These organizations drew us in as we participated fully as members, and our "research" emerged through a lack of predefined notions and the everyday practices of the community organization. We found that taking ideas mattering as the point of public intellectualism illuminated that it's not helpful to focus on individual actions or series of steps or the production of knowledge, traditionally viewed as research. Rather, we identify with the unpredictable becoming of soil fertility and the actions that surround it as a process for mattering ideas. Many community organizations have this as a strength, quite clearly, in the development of their collective caring. This ethos is something that can and should guide the public intellectualism of others.

We encourage the readers of this chapter to reflect on and narrate their own research practices with soil storying. How might we transform barren rock into life-giving soil? Are we fungal enough in our approach, or are we superfluous or, worse, parasitic? We believe that these types of reflections accompanied by soil storying's generative capacity may help to guide our ethico-political decision making as we strive to matter ideas.

References

Arizona Public Media. (2017, October 16). *The Curley School in Ajo, Arizona* [Video]. YouTube. https://www.youtube.com/watch?v=PhwYedi9KFo

Berthold, T., Centler, F., Hubschmann, T., Remer, R., Thullner, M., Harms, H., & Wick, L. Y. (2016). Mycelia as a focal point for horizontal gene transfer among soil bacteria. *Scientific Reports, 6*, 1–8.

Castleden, H., Garvin, T., & Huu-ay-aht First Nation. (2008). Modifying Photovoice for community-based participatory Indigenous research. *Social Science & Medicine, 66*(6), 1393–1405.

Choudry, A., & Kapoor, D. (2010). Learning from the ground up: Global perspectives on social movements and knowledge production. In A. Choudry & D. Kapoor (Eds.), *Learning from the ground up: Global perspectives on social movements and knowledge production* (pp. 1–16). Palgrave.

Curwood, S. E., Munger, F., Mitchell, T., Mackeigan, M., & Farrar, A. (2011). Building effective community–university partnerships: Are universities truly ready? *Michigan Journal of Community Service Learning, 17*(2), 15–26.

Ferman, B., & Hill, T. L. (2004). The challenges of agenda conflict in higher-education-community research partnerships: Views from the community side. *Journal of Urban Affairs, 26*(2), 241–257.

Frey-Klett, P., Burlinson, P., Deveau, A., Barret, M., Tarkka, M., & Sarniguet, A. (2011). Bacterial-fungal interactions: Hyphens between agricultural, clinical, environmental, and tood microbiologists. *Microbiology and Molecular Biology Reviews, 75*(4), 583–609.

Fuller, D., & Kitchin, R. (2004). Radical theory/critical praxis: Academic geography beyond the academy? In D. Fuller & R. Kitchin (Eds.), *Radical theory/critical praxis: Making a difference beyond the academy?* (pp. 1–20). Praxis (e)Press.

Haraway, D. (2016). *Staying with the trouble: Making kin in the Chthulucene.* Duke University Press.

International Sonoran Desert Alliance. (2020a). *Home.* https://isdanet.org/

International Sonoran Desert Alliance. (2020b). *Signature events: International Day of Peace.* https://www.isdanet.org/signature-events

Macfarlane, R. (2019). *Underland: A deep time journey.* W. W. Norton & Company.

Melzer, A. M. (2004). What is an intellectual? In A. M. Melzer, J. Weinberger, & M. R. Zinman (Eds.), *The public intellectual: Between philosophy and politics* (pp. 3). Rowman & Littlefield.

Nagel, T. (1972). Aristotle on Eudaimonia. *Phronesis, 17*(3), 252–259.

Novelli, M. (2010). Learning to win: Exploring knowledge and strategy development in anti-privatization struggles in Columbia. In A. Choudry & D. Kapoor (Eds.), *Learning from the ground up: Global perspectives on social movements* (pp. 121–138). Palgrave.

PBS (Producer). (2017, December 4). *In focus: Kimber Lanning, founder of organization* [Video]. In *Arizona Horizon*. https://www.pbs.org/video/12042017-in-focus-kimber-lanning-founder-of-organization-5zzqhd/

Puig de la Bellacasa, M. (2017). *Matters of care: Speculative ethics in more than human worlds.* University of Minnesota Press.

Somekh, B., & Zeichner, K. (2009). Action research for educational reform: Remodeling action research theories and practices in local contexts. *Educational Action Research, 17*(1), 5–21.

Spoth, R. L., & Redmond, C. (2002). Project family prevention trials based in community–university partnerships: Toward scaled-up preventive interventions. *Prevention Science: The Official Journal of the Society for Prevention Research, 3*(3), 203–221.

Sum and Substance. (2016, May 4). *Kimber Lanning* [Video]. YouTube. https://www.youtube.com/watch?v=WOgzRjTi-us

United States Soil Conservation Service. (1975). *Soil taxonomy: A basic system of soil classification for making and interpreting soil surveys.* Soil Conservation Service, U.S. Department of Agriculture.

Witty, J. E., & Arnold, R. W. (1987). Soil taxonomy: An overview. *Outlook on Agriculture, 16*(1), 8–13.

Connected

Mind------------Body------------Soil

Scattered

Shadows
Disintegrate
Pulling apart
Blowing apart
In the wind
Or the
Explosion
Violent
Violating

Coyolxāuhqui
Taking apart
The human
Integral
Whole
Which was never
There
Hole
Hollow

Hallowed
Haunted
Shadows
Split up
Scatter
Blowing
In the wind
Like so many
Dry leaves

TEN

Enacting Anzaldúan Spiritual Activism: Intersecting Personal and Collective Shadows in Public Intellectualism

Kakali Bhattacharya, University of Florida
Mildred Boveda, Arizona State University

THIS CHAPTER IS FRAMED BY an Anzaldúan conceptualization of the seven stages of conocimiento,[1] in which one deals with the shadow monster. Conocimiento means knowledge and wisdom. The seven stages of conocimiento offer a pathway for attaining wisdom by embracing one's shadows and understanding the relationship between personal and public shadows. Engaging with these stages brings forth notions of transnationality, standpoint feminism, and decoloniality.

We begin with a brief introduction to the seven stages of conocimiento and then offer personal narratives and theorization about each author's journey, informed by these stages. These discussions explore how we engage with the shadow in both personal and public intellectual spaces. We conclude by identifying key ideas from these narratives and reflecting on the implications of engaging with a collective shadow within a space of public intellectualism.

The discourse on decoloniality is too vast to describe fully in this chapter. However, any understanding of colonialism must integrate not just invasion of lands or settling in lands that are not one's own but also the consequences of such settling and the ruins left behind, even after colonizers leave or are ousted. We cannot think of colonialism as land issues only but must also understand how other power structures contribute to environmental injustice, wars that displace people and lead to human trafficking, and the proliferation of corporations, patriarchy, neoliberal education systems, epistemic hegemony, and other infrastructures that sustain colonial forces and give rise to fascist governments worldwide (McClaren, 2017).

We lean on Bhattacharya's (2009, 2013, 2015) conceptualization of de/coloniality with a slash to capture the inevitability of being in relation to colonial forces while engaging in the decolonizing imagination of freedom. The slash represents hybridity, shuttling, a movement between resistance to and complicity with colonizing and other interlocked oppressed spaces and the imagination of utopian futurism absent all colonial relations and forces. These arguments of de/coloniality represent the pervasiveness of colonial and other interlocked structures of oppression that become the terrain upon which public intellectualism is located. Moreover, Anzaldúa (2015a) teaches us that colonialism (in addition to other structures of oppression) cultivates spirit-draining experiences that we must understand in order to engage in spirit-nurturing activism.

We learned from bell hooks (1994) that the personal is always political, and Gloria Anzaldúa (2015d) taught us that at the intersection of the personal, political, and public exists the individual and collective parts of ourselves that we have disowned, repressed, or found too hard to face, damaging our spirits. A de/colonial framing of personal and collective shadow requires understanding the colonial forces at work with other oppressive structures to cultivate shame, guilt, and repression. We disown parts of ourselves and subsequently project them to the world when they become too much to contain within. To navigate interlocked oppressive structures, women of color and other multiply-multiply minoritized people consistently enact the various forms of border crossings, shifting identities, and hybridism that Anzaldúa (1987/1999, 2015c) marks as strategies for decolonization.

For Anzaldúa (2015b), decolonizing our lived realities consists of an understanding that "reality is a composition" (p. 43) and "unlearning consensual 'reality'" (p. 43) is seeing through reality's roles and descriptions by what Don Juan calls "acts of not-doing" (p. 44). She recommends various decolonial strategies of imagination to disrupt the sociocultural understanding of identity as they are grounded in our programmed understanding of reality, culture, self, and Other. Imagination, for Anzaldúa, is a necessary catalytic agent of transformation within the entangled personal, political, communal, and sociocultural terrain. To activate imagination is to activate creativity, think beyond restrictive boundaries, and courageously manifest dreams, intuitions, and memories of a freedom-laced futurism.

However, Anzaldúa cautions that unlearning is difficult work, as we contend with what we have repressed within ourselves and projected onto the collective as our personal and public shadows, respectively. Borrowing from Jung's

(2014) notion of the shadow archetype, Anzaldúa conceptualizes a shadow beast. This beast arises from what we do not want to know about ourselves, from desconocimientos, the "ignorance we cultivate to keep ourselves from knowledge so that we can remain unaccountable" (Anzaldúa, 2015f, p. 2).

Engaging the shadow beast entails illuminating the parts of ourselves we have disowned or fragmented due to pain and trauma and calling them back, despite the shadow beast's tenacious effort to keep us in ignorance. Anzaldúa (2015f) names this process

> the "Coyolxauhqui imperative": a struggle to reconstruct oneself and heal the sustos resulting from woundings, traumas, racism, and other acts of violation que hechan pedazos nuestras almas, split us, scatter our energies, and haunt us. The Coyolxauhqui imperative is the act of calling back those pieces of the self/soul that have been dispersed or lost, the act of mourning the losses that haunt us. (p. 1)

While recalling our disowned, repressed, fragmented parts, we understand our own shadow and its relationship to the collective consciousness and its shadows. We begin relying on our inner knowledges; connecting with imagination to other knowledges, ideas, and insights beyond the material realm; and understanding the interconnectivity among the living and nonliving. Our personal shadow work can also reveal the illusory nature of identity based on the associated sociocultural programming. If reality is constructed, so is identity, and therefore in calling back parts of ourselves, we would discover the instability of certain identity labels. Such insight building reconfigures our previous understanding, as Anzaldúa (2015a) explains:

> In an instant of insight/conocimiento, your life and its dismembered parts get reconstituted. You enact a healing. The myth of our lives struggles to be heard. Each of us has a story within us; we can speak it through the various disguises and voices of our different personas. (p. 189)

The Coyolaxauqui process, in conjunction with de/colonial strategies, reveals the shadow beast's individual and collective hold. Our collective shadows are structures of desconocimiento (and oppression) that lead to racism, ableism, patriarchy, transphobia, homophobia, xenophobia, violence, consumerism, and irresponsibility toward one another, the environment, and all living beings. Repressing shadows for prolonged periods harms our bodies, relationships, culture, and environment. Creativity, channeled through imaginative journeys that lead to storytelling, offers a modality of healing that we enact in this chapter.

Anzaldúa (2015e) recommends doing shadow work by navigating the seven stages of conocimiento. The first stage, *el arrebato*, jerks us[2] out of our previously held worldviews, creating a sense of betrayal and breach of trust. It invites us to relinquish previously held assumptions and reconfigure our understandings of the world.

Responding to this invitation, we land in the second stage, the liminal space of *nepantla*, in which one negotiates competing truths regarding worldviews and identities—those that have been broken and those that call for new knowledge and wisdom. Here one learns the fluidity of reality, truth, identities, worldviews, and meaning-making at the personal and collective levels; in this challenging space, one confronts contradictions, chaos, and instability. This can lead to Stage 3, *the Coatlicue state*, in which we fall back into familiar patterns of existing, retreat to our previous skin, and sink into depression, self-loathing, addiction, and more.

In the fourth stage, *the call, el compromiso*, we move beyond depression to discover spaces and paths of insight. Relinquishing established coping strategies, we shift our consciousness by opening ourselves to larger realities of the universe informed by our own wisdom traditions. The fifth stage, *putting Coyolxauhqui back together*, highlights our need to make meaning as we sort through previously lived stories; scan our interiority; and engage with books, media, and wisdom-knowers.

The sixth stage encompasses a *clash of realities*, as a newly reconfigured worldview confronts the material world's resistance, and we test the veracity of our new insight(s). This stage may create another round of crisis, of navigating through the stages of conocimiento, of confronting one's own shadow beast at war with the collective shadow. Moving through this stage with utter honesty and raw vulnerability illuminates the path to the last stage, *shifting realities, acting out the vision or spiritual activism*, in which we enact a vision that connects the mind, body, spirit, and individual and collective shadow or shadows (Anzaldúa, 2015e, pp. 122–123).

Addressing the (personal and public) shadow beast requires recognizing the isolation and separation created by dominant ontology and its practices. This necessitates an expansive understanding of philosophy that integrates various cultural and wisdom traditions embracing spirit, alchemy, mythic figures, ancestral guides, and more. Anzaldúa uses "shamanism, curanderismo, alchemy, and the indigenous philosophies they reflect to substantiate and illustrate her transformational ontology and aesthetics, including her insistence on language's material(izing) properties" (Keating, 2015, p. xxxii).

Moving outside Enlightenment-based and/or Eurocentric ways of thinking to access cultural treasures allows Anzaldúa to mark a path for *ontological decolonizing* (Keating, 2015, p. xxxii). These journeys teach us that we can fall apart and reconfigure ourselves, if we truly contend with our individual and collective shadows. Through such shadow work, moreover, we illuminate freedom-inspiring possibilities, understand our resistances, and create resonances.

We posit that excavation work requires deep contemplation to juxtapose personal and public shadows historically, racially, nationally, internationally, and across other social categories to understand the intergenerational genealogies of these shadows (racism, patriarchy, xenophobia, homophobia, transphobia, ableism, and more), akin to performing a kind of historiography. Mapping intergenerational knowledge transmission illuminates how personal and public shadows function, especially in academic spaces, allowing us to dismantle binaries and think in terms of limits, possibilities, incongruencies, resonances, imagination, freedom, and healing. In the next section, we share narratives of our navigation and how it is informed by Anzaldúa's framing.

Mildred—"Who's Afraid of the Dark?" Brokenhearted Returns To Informal, Non-Westernized Sources of Credibility

Both as a child in the United States and on visits to the Dominican Republic, I was amazed by how easily my mother moved through the dark. When I called for her at night or while we waited for family members to light candles when the frequent apagones shut down electrical grids throughout Santo Domingo, I witnessed how swiftly Mami got around without tripping or bumping into furniture. While I was paralyzed by the dark, Mami appeared activated by it.

I aspired to someday be as agile and unbothered by darkness as Mami seemed to be.

Mami showed me what can be accomplished in spite of the dark—and by intentionally remaining within shadowy spaces. People like Mami learned early in life to move without being seen or heard. These navigational skills were transmitted to the next generation by elders who recognized a demonstrable truth: When the imperialist white supremacist capitalist patriarchal gaze focuses on our swarthy bodies (and the language, thoughts, and spirits they contain), it demands even more than it has already extracted. To be productive and secure, we learned, sometimes we must lay low.

Given my transnational experiences, "shadow work" for me evokes women, children, and men from around the world, especially those from the Global South who are dark-skinned, impoverished, and multiply marginalized. *Billions* have been relegated to living and working within colonialist- and imperialist-induced shadows. Take, for example, the countries the U.S. president referred to as "shitholes." Many public intellectuals were outraged at the anti-Blackness and deficit imagery pronounced by this world leader. Ugandan American poet Mildred Barya (2018) reacted differently. She understood the amazing functionality of the unglorified, concealed locations of our bodies and the material world. She wrote:

> Consider the shithole:
>
> It does not envy the hand for being the hand, it does not envy the feet for their gift of movement, it does not strike against other body parts, but in humility and pride carries on its duty without complaint, aiding bodily functions, enabling the health of the body as a whole. You can know the health of the people by the way their shitholes function.
>
> Consider the shithole literally. What we may call a toilet. A latrine. A dump pit . . . Who can live a day without a visit to the shithole? An absolute necessary place that contains our waste, what we no longer need, what our bodies cannot keep inside for our own wellbeing. We may as well confer upon the shithole the title, "the greatest containment." (Barya, 2018, para. 1–3)

Without romanticizing marginalized and obscured positionalities, I acknowledge that it is precisely within shadowy spaces—the shitholes the most powerful deem least worthy—where many perfect the skill of traversing darkness to create space for themselves and others. Yet were it not for my U.S. birthplace, training in prestigious universities, and ability to speak and write in English, my scholarship highlighting the importance of ways of being and knowing developed by Mami and others like her might never have achieved its current audience or reach.

As a devoted student of Mami, I have grown to embrace dark and shadowy places. Avoiding the white gaze triggered by the (lime)light, however, may seem impossible for scholars of color in the Global North who are now, more than ever before, incentivized to demonstrate their scholarly impact. The reward systems of the westernized academy emphasize citation counts, public and media engagements, prestigious awards, and other metrics that highlight and center scholars. My shadow work thus involves a constant de/colonial reminder. Although westernized and monstrous notions of meritocracy announce, "*You deserve* to speak and be heard!" a de/colonial light reminds me, "*You're privileged* and thus have the *responsibility to tell* those stories forged in the shadows."

As a doctoral student, I was disillusioned by witnessing senior scholars of color using their platform to make authoritative public statements about trending topics on social media or in public discourse without any evident expertise (Boveda & Bhattacharya, 2019). For example, an academic with limited knowledge about the Dominican Republic felt compelled to write a blog about the country's racialized identities. She went so far as to compare the country to Rachel Dolezal, a white woman who falsely presented herself as Black.

This was done in the name of . . . decolonizing education? Public intellectualism? But who invited her to write about the Dominican Republic? She was not the only scholar of color to move as if she had the "academic freedom" to speak on all narratives of marginalized people. When I witnessed junior colleagues of color navigating against whiteness while embodying internalized dominant narratives about what a doctorate bestows on its recipients, predictably, they were targeted by Fox News and fascist watchdogs. When they complained about being surveilled, I was confused. Their outrage following their prolonged academic engagement with white supremacy left me wondering, "What did you expect? This is precisely how white supremacy works when 'we' fall within its purview."

And yet, despite the endarkened moves I learned from Mami—and my purposeful (self-congratulatory) evasion of the limelight—the effects of the white and academic gaze have caught up with and devastated me. In 2016, struck by racial battle fatigue enacted within my institution, I was admitted to the hospital with broken heart syndrome (Boveda, 2019). Mami gave me many usable tools, but without access to formal education, she could not prepare me for the disrespect I encounter regularly as a Black Latina academic working in the master's house (Lorde, 1983). Thus, when a "mentor" suggested that my best chance at obtaining an academic position was a diversity hire, I landed in an emergency room two days later with a palpable response to her statement.

As I retreated and stayed home to mend my broken heart and spirit, I articulated for the first time an awareness I had long avoided. I had allowed myself to psychically and professionally bond with people with whom I would have never connected outside the academy. Meeting the demands of the westernized university had left me isolated and fragmented to the point that I allowed the absurd words of multiply-privileged women to affect my body and spirit. Questions about my credibility and worthiness had taken their toll. Yet I could not afford to isolate myself further, nor did I want to deny myself access to the abundant resources hoarded within hostile spaces.

The scholars whose public engagement brought me spiritual fatigue seemed to perform for people of color yet ultimately used the master's tools (Lorde, 1983) to highlight their expertise and edify the master's dominance. The gatekeepers who managed to gain my trust would eventually question my credibility, reminding me of the pervasiveness of the collective shadow's distorting function. We must maintain awareness that the casted shadow that produces marginality does not go away once we achieve terminal degrees . . . or tenure . . . or whatever marker of merit we are incentivized to pursue.

Our system demands transparency, public announcement of scholarly achievements, and posting of syllabi and vitae for surveillance and disciplinary purposes. How can I creatively manipulate the dark and shadows to my advantage, as Mami showed me, while I am subject to the evaluations of those who know nothing of the marginality that birthed my way of being? How can marginalized people know that moves are happening on their behalf unless those actions are communicated publicly, despite the threat of surveillance?

Chela Sandoval (1991) offered a way for women like me, multiply marginalized yet in the midst of the epistemic, imperial power of the westernized university, to do our work without feeling constrained by the power structures surrounding us. In describing U.S. third-world feminism,[3] Sandoval suggests that multiply-marginalized people have differential consciousness that "operates like the clutch of an automobile: the mechanism that permits the driver to select, engage and disengage gears in a system for the transmission of power" (p. 14). Sometimes, we must publicly speak truth to power, and sometimes, it is wisest to slow down and strategize in the shadows. When we reach the Anzaldúan stage of compromiso, it is precisely this negotiation of our multiple consciousness that propels us to move despite once feeling stuck.

In other words, the "oppressed" have found ways not only to be productive in the shadows but also to navigate hypervisibility. As a focus of both the public and academic gaze, faculty of color are subject to the constant scrutiny of the collective shadow. As such, Sandoval's (1991) insights on the tactical subjectivity that differential consciousness affords can be used, in conjunction with Anzaldúa's (2015e) stages of conocimiento, to de/center aspects of ourselves that make us more/less vulnerable to attacks. Recognizing our personal shadows provides the means to build coalitions with marginalized colleagues who have different vulnerabilities.

Kakali—From Cellular to Collective Pain: Enacting the Coyolxauhqui Imperative

I distinctly remember falling apart when the press released the trial verdict of George Zimmerman, a neighborhood watch coordinator who shot and killed Trayvon Martin, an unarmed Black teenager, for looking suspicious in his predominantly white gated neighborhood. I was instantly transported to the emotional state of this young man who went out for iced tea and Skittles, only to be attacked for breathing the same air as Zimmerman. What must he have thought and felt in his last moments? How scared must he have been to die on the sidewalk, alone, as retribution for walking back to his father's home wearing a hoodie?

For years prior to that, I understood racism, experienced it in many shades, even conducted doctoral research investigating how Indian graduate students negotiated their first year of graduate school at a predominantly white institution. Racism and its entanglement with other interconnected structures of oppression were not new to me. But this—this was what Anzaldúa (2015e) identified as the first stage of conocimiento, *el arrebato*, in which one's established worldview is destroyed. Trust in oneself, other people, and the universe are compromised, and one is irrevocably changed. With this verdict, racism was no longer something I intellectualized or crafted critical arguments about. It was as if I understood at a cellular level that suffering and struggles for liberation worldwide are inescapably intertwined.

After the verdict, I had to acknowledge that each time I articulated personal or collective racial acts through nuanced, measured intellectual perspectives, I dismissed the cold, hard fact that there are people who would readily kill others, including me, simply for breathing the same air. The recognition that humanity can harbor so much hate broke me, bringing me to this stage of conocimiento. The shadow I had repressed, our personal and collective capacity to hate, loomed large before me. Seeing white colleagues and friends justifying Zimmerman's actions on social media illuminated the entanglement of the private and collective shadow. I felt devastated, broken, deep in sorrow and pain. I wrote multiple incomplete poems about Trayvon to deal with the shards of my fragmentation.

Out of Breath
Fiery bullet of fear
Blazing from one
Heart to another
Going straight through
Faded pages of history
Forty-four days till arrest
Forty-four years
After MLK's death
Yin wrestling yang
Wrapped around
Bashing, smashing
Punching, kicking
Mounting, surrendering
Bleeding on a puddle
of melted rainbow sweetness.

Trayvon
There's a hole in your heart,
Fear fired,
Where love ran out,
And the rainbow candy
In your hands, dye
Washed in winter rain,
Mixed colors and blood
Brown together in cold
Gravel of Floridian suburb.
The streetlamps grieve and bow,
And cast their orange light
Into the misplaced Black
Skin of your hoodied head.
For fear, we will call this
An expected loss.

To look at certain people, individually or collectively, with the suspicion that they will do harm ran counter to my being. Yet I could not ignore the enormous hate Zimmerman must have possessed to resort to murder. And Trayvon's murder is not an isolated incident: The pattern of white supremacy, colonialism, and racism permeates multiple historical periods and spaces (Call-Cummings & Martinez, 2017; Moraga & Anzaldúa, 2002; Turner et al., 2008).

Oppression is inherently a spirit-breaking force, and I had to release previous perspectives that thwarted an embodied, cellular-level understanding of suffering. I felt exposed, disoriented, and vulnerable, unable to navigate a world so hostile to me. I entered what Anzaldúa (2015e) calls the *nepantla*, the in-between, liminal space. I had to negotiate understanding the broken parts of myself, either by reassembling them or opening myself to an alchemic shift.

Anzaldúa's (2015e) depictions of the stages of conocimiento might be expressed in a linear format in published spaces, but she does not proclaim the experience of these stages as linear. I moved in and out of multiple stages, alternately feeling lost and found, stable and disoriented, confident and confused. Anzaldúa (2015e) states that being in the *nepantla*, especially in contradictions that cause us pain, puts us in *the Coatlicue state*, in which we shut down, retreat from the world, and engage in addictive behavior—all indicators of remaining in desconocimiento (ignorance), refusing the cost of knowing and remaining in darkness.

For weeks, I could do nothing but cry and sleep. I did not want to be in a world that felt so exceptionally cruel to so many. If I talked to my partner, then it was mostly in the form of screams and long monologues, after which I would walk away and hide under the covers. I feared that once I allowed my consciousness to grasp the extent of cruelty at a cellular level, everything I held dear would fully break apart. What would I hold on to then? Afraid of existing in and navigating the ruins, I stayed in the dark.

Anzaldúa (2015e) would say that behind my self-imposed isolation lay the opposite—"a smoldering desire for love and connection" (p. 130). Not wanting to live with suspicion toward certain groups, as I would not want others to live suspicious of me, I opened up to the fluid nature of my being. I did not want to exist in desconocimiento, refusing to connect with the personal and public shadow of suffering from various forms of oppression.

Through existing in paradox one might hear the call of the next stage, *el compromiso . . . the crossing and conversion*. Existence in chaos permanently is unsustainable; we have a need to make meaning. Thus, Anzaldúa (2015e) suggests cultivating new insights, understandings, and narratives, writing a new script for ourselves and the world, fully aware that this too can fall apart. I recognized that I must engage with my personal shadow before I could understand the nature of the public shadow in various spaces of public intellectualism and existence.

Over the years, I have engaged in public intellectualism through streamed public talks, webinars, and social media. My efforts have received both cheers and jeers. I have looked toward my wisdom tradition in undergoing this journey, scrutinizing over my wounds, mapping a new form of existence, and understanding some aspect of my life's purpose in this time, at this moment.

I am under no illusion that the fear and hate Trayvon experienced is gone or that a new narrative script can make that more palatable. It remains painful, and as I write this, my eyes well with tears. But understanding my own shadows means recognizing that we exist with these shadows, and only by illuminating them can we discover what lies within/behind them.

Those who accept the invitation will undergo their own process of falling apart and coming back together. For me, this journey illuminated how sociocultural discourses limited my identity. I am more than the categories with which I am labeled or label myself. I am light and dark, connected to every living and nonliving being. My existence obligates me to care for people, animals, or nature, and spiritual activism provides my path to healing.

In the fifth stage of conocimiento, *putting Coyolxauhqui together . . . new personal and collective "stories"* (Anzaldúa, 2015e, p. 138), I began to distinguish which stories no longer served a purpose for me and which stories I wanted to write into the present to create a different future. I explored these fragmented narratives through a mixed-medium art project, excavating and finally releasing the stories by painting over them after making peace with the past (Bhattacharya & Payne, 2016). At this turning point, Anzaldúa (2015e) says, we can intersect the personal with the collective and theorize through critical, de/colonial, hybridized, creative means.

I embrace the knowledge that multiple cycles of falling apart and putting myself back together have cultivated the conditions for a "keener mind, stronger spirit, and a wiser soul" (Anzaldúa, 2015e, p. 138). At this stage, I began to ask how I could make my work matter, what I could illuminate for myself that could be extended to public intellectualism. I engaged in various social media spaces with other scholars, students, and those who left academia, as they individually and collectively dealt with their shadows and pain.

Anzaldúa's (2015e) sixth stage encompasses *the blow-up . . . a clash of realities*. In this newly constructed space, I was subjected to the erasure whiteness, colonialism, and other interconnected structures of oppression cause in academia's intellectual spaces. In dissertation meetings, my students of color were attacked for being "too angry," while I was labeled intimidating, intense, and aggressive. When I won a mid-career scholar of color award, a white colleague commented, "I wish there was an award for white males."

I was told to "stay in my own lane" repeatedly when I advocated for students and faculty from underrepresented communities or disrupted incestuous hiring practices. Liberal white, postmodern, and poststructural feminists promoted radical interconnectivity while connecting only with scholars who looked like them, broadcasting Black criminality in social media spaces, and remaining silent about the brutality against Black and Brown and colonized people. When I raised the issue publicly, they gaslighted me and said my scholarship was shit by inserting a poop emoji in publicly viewable spaces.

A white colleague who invited me to submit an article for her edited special issue asked that I discuss how I navigated my career as a qualitative methodologist. Upon receiving my manuscript detailing my experiences of academic bullying causing me to relocate to another institution to obtain tenure, she commented, "What's the big deal about tenure? We all have tenure." This colleague now promotes herself as a critical scholar.

Yet I did not want to be the wounded woman, using victimhood and oppression as my currency. Wounds bond me to the oppressor. The oppressor has little to no incentive to really engage in perspective taking and make the necessary move for *my* healing or the healing of the collective. Nevertheless, I admit that such daily oppressive acts trigger my shadow beast, and I fear another cycle of falling apart and coming together, especially when I desperately want to preserve the calm, balanced, wiser version of me, despite the unsettling caused by experiencing and bearing witness to multiple forms of conflict, oppression, trauma, and rage.

As someone who moves in and out of various worlds, crosses thresholds, and builds bridges, my work lies in positioning myself "exposed and raw—in the crack between these worlds, and in revealing current categories as unworkable" (Anzaldúa, 2015e, p. 148). I can reject the oppressor/oppressed binary and reconfigure my identity narrative through other relationalities, such as being descended from wisdom-makers and wisdom-seekers. I can connect to other realms of consciousness through deep meditation to mitigate my isolation in the material world. My connection to the rise and fall of waves, the flight of birds, and the undulating moves of snakes reveals other ways of relating to existence. The work ahead of us is to nurture spirits in personal and public intellectual spaces, choose reciprocity over transactionalism, and create alliances among individuals and groups invested in transforming communities.

Anzaldúa's (2015e) final stage of conocimiento, *shifting realities . . . acting out the vision or spiritual activism*, reminds us that we gain insight into interconnectivity by journeying through the stages of conocimiento. Yet this does not suggest that as a public intellectual, I must place myself at the receiving end of toxicity, violence, or oppression. Burnout and fatigue are real, material consequences of doing this work. Thus, the call is for clarity while engaging in shadow work, understanding my spiritual stance, and manifesting it in personal and public spaces of intellectualism. Either shadow work opens one to multiple possibilities or the fear of such work erects a barrier, perpetuating ignorance.

Shadow work excavates wounds by leaning into one's pain, creating a conduit of light, insight, and compassion for oneself and others. Anzaldúa (2015e) recommends rituals and spiritual practices of conocimiento, noting that

> praying, breathing deeply, meditating, writing—dropping down into yourself, through the skin and muscles and tendons, down deep into the bones' marrow where your soul is ballast—enabled you to defuse the negative energy of putdowns, complaints, excessive talk, and verbal attacks, as well as other killers of the spirit. Spirituality became a port you moor to in all storms. (p. 154)

This practice offers self-compassion that can extend to others within interpersonal relationships, and to a larger collective within the public intellectual spaces in which I exist, in congruence with my spiritual stance. I invite those who bear witness to my stance to engage with their own shadow beasts and spiritual stances.

Personal and Collective Shadows in Public Intellectualism

We have situated our negotiations of personal and collective shadows within western academic spaces using Anzaldúa's (2015e) seven stages of conocimiento. Mildred disrupted negative understandings of the shadow, highlighting its value in offering freedom from surveillance and disciplinary apparatuses. When the center does not know what the margin is doing, it cannot discipline the margin.

Acknowledging the value of endarkened spaces disrupts the light/dark binary, as we move between both to create strategic possibilities as women of color, from colonized backgrounds, in hostile academic spaces. Mildred speaks of falling apart in multiple ways, leading to her hospitalization, when she had to contend with the illusion of previously held perspectives about some academic actors. Falling apart and reconfiguring oneself while negotiating personal and collective shadows can illuminate possibilities for healing, for sacred conversations and relationships, and for a spiritual calling that exceeds the boundaries placed on our bodies.

Kakali discussed how the seven stages of conocimiento illuminated suffering as an interconnected phenomenon, shifting her intellectual awareness to a cellular level of experience following the verdict in Trayvon Martin's death. Her description of negotiating personal and collective shadows highlighted the illusions that hold us together, resistance to being vulnerable, raw, and honest with oneself and of the possibilities we create by attending to repressed parts of our consciousness. Such journeying, juxtaposed against the collective, illuminates the entanglement of the personal and collective shadow where discourses of bigotry, prejudice, and oppression are privileged, maintained, and proliferated.

Doing shadow work or working within endarkened spaces requires reconfiguring our relationship with reality, connecting to our wisdom traditions for spirit nurturing and strengthening, and inviting our imaginative selves to exceed the boundaries placed on us. Only through such border crossings can we envision and manifest a freedom-inducing future. Such work requires understanding the function of shadows from multiple cultural perspectives and making friends with the shadow so our energies are not depleted. In doing so, we accept all parts of ourselves, allowing us to recall the fragmented and dispersed parts. Even with our bodies in multiply-hostile spaces, we can then reconstruct ourselves in ways that build capacity to engage our spirits in doing the activist work in material form in personal and public intellectual spaces.

Notes

1. Following Anzaldúa, to disrupt anglocentric ways of reading we do not italicize Spanish words. Additionally, where possible we capitalize Black and Brown but not white or whiteness. This de/colonial and critical stance critiques the pervasiveness of whiteness and centering of colonial sensibilities in academic practices, including language use.

2. *Us* encompasses those who accept the invitation to engage with shadow monsters and remain open to the possible paths illuminated through shadow work.

3. We do not promote the worlding of people, and *third world* is not our preferred term. However, at the moment in which Sandoval wrote (1991), this was a commonly used and sometimes disrupted term. We use this term to represent Sandoval's use and its associated arguments.

References

Anzaldúa, G. E. (1999). *Borderlands la frontera: The new mestiza* (2nd ed.). Aunt Lute Books. (Original work published 1987)

Anzaldúa, G. E. (2015a). Appendix 4: Alternative opening: Chapter 4. In A. Keating (Ed.), *Light in the dark/Luz en lo oscuro: Rewriting identity, spirituality, reality* (pp. 180–189). Duke University Press.

Anzaldúa, G. E. (2015b). Flights of the imagination: Rereading/rewriting realities. In A. Keating (Ed.), *Light in the dark/Luz en lo oscuro: Rewriting identity, spirituality, reality* (pp. 23–46). Durham, NC: Duke University Press.

Anzaldúa, G. E. (2015c). Geographies of selves—reimagining identity: Nos/otras (Us/other), las nepantleras, and the new tribalism. In A. Keating (Ed.), *Light in the dark:/Luz en lo oscuro: Rewriting identity, spirituality, reality* (pp. 65–94). Duke University Press.

Anzaldúa, G. E. (2015d). Let us be the healing of the wound: The Coyolxauhqui imperative—La sombra y el sueño. In A. Keating (Ed.), *Light in the dark:/Luz en lo oscuro: Rewriting identity, spirituality, reality* (pp. 9–23). Duke University Press.

Anzaldúa, G. E. (2015e). now let us shift . . . conocimiento . . . inner work, public acts. In A. Keating (Ed.), *Light in the dark/Luz en lo oscuro: Rewriting identity, spirituality, reality* (pp. 117–160). Duke University Press.

Anzaldúa, G. E. (2015f). Preface: Gestures of the body—Escribiendo para idear. In A. Keating (Ed.), *Light in the dark/Luz en lo oscuro: Rewriting identity, spirituality, reality* (pp. 1–8). Duke University Press.

Barya, M. (2018, January 15). *In praise of shitholes*. http://mildredbarya.com/in-praise-of-shitholes

Bhattacharya, K. (2009). Othering research, researching the Other: De/colonizing approaches to qualitative inquiry. In J. Smart (Ed.), *Higher education: Handbook of theory and research* (Vol. 24, pp. 105–150). Springer.

Bhattacharya, K. (2013). Performing gender as "Third-World-Other" in higher education: De/colonizing transnational feminist possibilities. *Creative Approaches to Research, 6*(3), 30–47.

Bhattacharya, K. (2015). The vulnerable academic: Personal narratives and strategic de/colonizing of academic structures. *Qualitative Inquiry, 22*(5), 309–321. doi:10.1177/1077800415615619

Bhattacharya, K., & Payne, R. (2016). Mixing mediums, mixing selves: Arts-based contemplative approaches to border crossings. *International Journal of Qualitative Studies in Education, 29*(2), 1100–1117. doi:10.1080/09518398.2016.1201163

Boveda, M. (2019). Intersectional competence within diverse Latinx communities: Conceptualizing differences at a Hispanic serving institution. In N. D. Hartlep & D. Ball (Eds.), *Racial battle fatigue in faculty: Perspectives and lessons from higher education* (pp. 101–114). Routledge.

Boveda, M., & Bhattacharya, K. (2019). Love as de/colonial onto-epistemology: A post-oppositional approach to contextualized research ethics. *The Urban Review, 5*(1), 5–25.

Call-Cummings, M., & Martinez, S. (2017). "It wasn't racism; it was more misunderstanding": White teachers, Latino/a students, and racial battle fatigue. *Race, Ethnicity, & Education, 20*(4), 561–574.

hooks, b. (1994). Theory as liberatory practice. In W. Kolmar & F. Bartkowski (Eds.), *Feminist theory: A reader* (pp. 28–33). Mayfield Publishing.

Jung, C. G. (2014). *Collected works of C. G. Jung, Volume 9, Part 1: Archetypes and the collective unconscious* (2nd ed., G. Adler & R. F. C. Hull, Trans.). Princeton University Press.

Keating, A. (Ed.). (2015). *Light in the dark/Luz en lo oscuro: Rewriting identity, spirituality, reality*. Duke University Press.

Lorde, A. (1983). The master's tools will never dismantle the master's house. In C. Moraga & G. E. Anzaldúa (Eds.), *This bridge called my back: Writings by radical women of color* (2nd ed., pp. 98–101). Kitchen Table Women of Colour Press.

McClaren, M. A. (Ed.). (2017). *Decolonizing feminism: Transnational feminism and globalization*. Rowman & Littlefield International.

Moraga, C. L., & Anzaldúa, G. E. (2002). *This bridge called my back: Writings by radical women of color* (3rd ed.). Third Woman Press.

Sandoval, C. (1991, Spring). U.S. third world feminism: The theory and method of oppositional consciousness in the postmodern world. *Genders, 10*, 1–24.

Turner, C. S. V., González, J. C., & Wood, J. L. (2008). Faculty of color in academe: What 20 years of literature tells us. *Journal of Diversity in Higher Education, 1*(3), 139–168. doi:http://dx.doi.org/10.1037/a0012837

Suffering, Burning

A chorus of sirens
The public ablaze
We search for water
To dampen the flames

As ash rises high
A shrouded sun
We strike the cracked ground
To let the buried trauma run

The suffering is immense
And we fall apart
As the fire burns
It chars the edges of our hearts

But it's this endarkened space
A place for love to paint
That forms monsoons of transformation
The smell of summer rain

Shadow Work

Shadow Work

Rear shadow beast
Arise from ignorant depths
Tear your talons
Into flesh
Drop me out of
Desconocimiento
Leave me
Dismembered
Daughter of the priestess
Painted, with bells
Painted with blood
Seeping from shadow
wounds
Spirit-draining
Draining
I blink

As a furious gust
Jerks me
To a border crossing
Repressing racism
Intellectualizing hate
Until Trayvon's
Face on screens
Iterates
I ring-a-round the rosie,
We all fall apart.
El compromiso
Transformation
Productive in shadows
Navigating
Hypervisibility.
Imagination

Re-creating
My story
Our story
Manifesting
Spiritual.
Shadow monster
Break
Bones
Breathe
Fire
Illuminating
My darkness
Through
Your shadow work
I/We
emerge

Contributors

Marina Basu is a doctoral student in the Learning, Literacies, and Technologies program at Arizona State University. With a background in teaching and teacher education in nontraditional settings, including a Krishnamurti Foundation India school, Marina has rich experiences in creative and integrated curriculum and pedagogy. Her research interests span elementary education, feminist philosophy, biopolitics, and critical qualitative inquiry, including art-based approaches.

Kakali Bhattacharya, PhD, is a multiple-award-winning professor at the University of Florida. Housed in the Research, Evaluation, and Measurement program, she serves as a qualitative methodologist for the College of Education. For the last 15 years, Dr. Bhattacharya has explored qualitative research through critical, de/colonial, creative, transnational, and contemplative perspectives. She is the 2018 winner of the American Educational Research Association's (AERA's) Mid-Career Scholar of Color Award and the 2018 winner of AERA's Mentoring Award from Division G: Social Context of Education. Her coauthored text with Kent Gillen, *Power, Race, and Higher Education: A Cross-Cultural Parallel Narrative*, won a 2017 Outstanding Publication Award from the AERA (SIG 168) and a 2018 Outstanding Book Award from International Congress of Qualitative Research. She was recognized as one of the top 25 women in higher education by *Diverse* magazine for her significant contribution to social justice work and efforts to de/colonize qualitative research.

Mildred Boveda is an assistant professor of Special Education and Cultural and Linguistic Diversity at Arizona State University. In her scholarship, she uses the terms *intersectional consciousness* and *intersectional competence* to describe teachers' preparedness to address intersecting equity concerns. Drawing from Black feminist theory and collaborative teacher education research, she interrogates how differences are framed across education communities to influence education policy and practice. Dr. Boveda earned an EdD in Exceptional Student Education at Florida International University and an EdM in Education Policy and Management from Harvard Graduate School of Education.

Nicole Bowers is a doctoral candidate at Arizona State University, Mary Lou Fulton Teachers College. Her research interests include qualitative methodologies, sustainability education, and collective social action.

David Lee Carlson is an associate professor at Mary Lou Fulton Teachers College at Arizona State University. He writes in the areas of qualitative inquiry, queer theory, and curriculum studies. His most recent articles appear in the *Journal of Curriculum and Pedagogy*, the *International Journal of Research in Qualitative Inquiry*, and *Qualitative Inquiry*.

Adam T. Clark (PhD, Arizona State University) is a researcher at Mary Lou Fulton Teachers College (MLFTC) at Arizona State University. His research focuses on the internationalization of higher education, international student success, language program evaluation, and qualitative research methodologies. His most recent study explored the internationalization networks of university English-language programs and the unique and highly localized connections they develop between departmental and community actors. Before joining MLFTC, Adam was an English instructor and program administrator in various university language programming environments, working on program accreditation and helping learners with their language goals using technology.

Jonathan W. Crocker is a PhD student in Curriculum Studies at Texas Christian University. He works at the intersection of education, politics, and rhetoric and explores the possibilities of antiauthoritarian pedagogy and curriculum within neoliberal society and public culture. His work also appears in the *International Journal of Žižek Studies* and *The Encyclopedia of Educational Innovation*.

Joshua Cruz is an assistant professor in the College of Education at Texas Tech University, teaching qualitative methods and theory courses to doctoral students. His academic interests include critical and poststructural theory, college readiness, writing, and a myriad of other projects. He also instructs the student-led capoeira club at Texas Tech. His personal interests include martial and circus arts and cooking.

Mathew D. Evans graduated from Mary Lou Fulton Teachers College at Arizona State University. He focuses on the intersections of adult learning, design, and public engagement with science. He can often be found at the nearest board-game café trading sheep for ore.

Brian Grant is a dad, lover, and artist exploring sustainability education through posthumanism, creativity, and somatic practices. Currently, he is a PhD student in the School of Sustainability at Arizona State University.

M. Francyne Huckaby is an associate dean of the School of Interdisciplinary Studies and a professor of Curriculum Studies at Texas Christian University (TCU). She's a former director of TCU's Center for Public Education and current president of the Society of Professors of Education. She works (as pedagogue, curricularist, and scholar) to create openings and spaces for anti-oppressive discourses and practices. She is most interested in spaces where divergent worldviews coexist. These, she argues, are sites of power relations that are educational and political. Her scholarship on community organizing and resistance to neoliberal education reform puts filmmaking to work as a form of inquiry and making public—publicaré—research and sites of resistance and struggle. Her books include *Researching Resistance: Public Education after Neoliberalism* (2019), with its companion website scalar.usc.edu/works/publiceducation, and *Making Research Public in Troubled Times: Pedagogy, Activism, and Critical Obligations* (2018). She is the author of numerous peer-reviewed journal articles and book chapters. Her honors include the Claudia V. Camp Faculty Research and Creative Activity Award, the TCU Deans' Teaching Award, TCU Mortar Board Preferred Professor, Straight for Equality from Fort Worth's PFLAG chapter, and the American Educational Research Association's Outstanding Dissertation (Qualitative Research). In 2017, her work was the feature article for *Fort Worth Weekly*, https://www.fwweekly.com/2017/03/29/documenting-school-rights/.

Taylor M. Kessner is a PhD candidate in the Learning, Literacies, and Technologies program at Mary Lou Fulton Teachers College in Tempe,

Arizona. His research focuses primarily on the intersection of the learning sciences, history and social studies education, and games scholarship. Taylor taught history and social studies to middle and high schoolers for 4 years. He resides in Arizona with his wife and daughter.

Mirka Koro (PhD, University of Helsinki) is a professor of qualitative research at Arizona State University. Her scholarship operates in the intersection of methodology, philosophy, and sociocultural critique, and through her work, she aims to contribute to methodological knowledge, experimentation, and theoretical development across various traditions associated with qualitative research. She has published in various qualitative and educational journals, and she is the author of *Reconceptualizing Qualitative Research: Methodologies Without Methodology* (2016), published by SAGE, and coeditor of *Disrupting Data in Qualitative Inquiry: Entanglements With the Post-Critical and Post-Anthropocentric* (2017), published by Peter Lang.

Lauren Mark is a critical intercultural researcher and performer situated in the field of human communication. Her work looks at issues that explore embodied negotiations of race, power dynamics, and surveillance in relation to political ideologies and interpersonal relationships. She works to accomplish these goals through critical, postcolonial, and performative epistemological and methodological approaches. One of her approaches to this work explores the effects of microaggressions when traveling across surveilled borders and within power dynamics. Another approach expands and complexifies lesser represented forms of diaspora through a variety of approaches that have included rhythm analysis, affect, arts-based methods, and autoethnography. All her research questions are rooted in lived and witnessed experiences of fellow immigrants and global nomads navigating new environments, cultures, and power structures.

Jorge Sandoval is a doctoral student in the Learning, Literacies, and Technologies PhD program at Mary Lou Fulton Teachers College, Arizona State University.

Joseph D. Sweet (PhD, Arizona State University) is an assistant professor of English education at the University of North Carolina at Pembroke whose research interests include pedagogies of gender equity in secondary English-language arts, qualitative inquiry, arts curriculum, and masculinities. Joe served as a secondary English and theater teacher for 9 years.

Marek Tesar is an associate professor and associate dean international at the University of Auckland, New Zealand. His research is focused on philosophical methods, childhood studies, and early childhood education, with expertise in the philosophy of education and childhood. His latest research is concerned with the construction of childhoods, notions of place/space, and methodological and philosophical thinking around ontologies and the ethics of researching these notions, in China, Indonesia, New Zealand, and Australia.

Anani M. Vasquez is a graduate student in Mary Lou Fulton Teachers College's Learning, Literacies, and Technologies PhD program. She comes to the program as a veteran elementary school teacher with certifications in elementary and special education and endorsements in bilingual and gifted education. Anani has dedicated her career to better understanding the needs of underserved populations, promoting differentiated instruction in the regular classroom, and implementing problem-based instruction. Anani's goal is to develop and promote effective teaching practices for neurodiverse classrooms, including practices that develop students' individual strengths, passions, self-awareness, and self-direction. In alignment with this goal, she defines her areas of specialization as neurodiversity and creativity in education and research methods.

Timothy C. Wells (PhD, Arizona State University) is a faculty associate in the Mary Lou Fulton Teachers College at Arizona State University. His work resides in the fields of educational foundations and qualitative inquiry, bringing a critical interdisciplinary framework to the study of social and affective experience in schooling. Currently, his research considers the historical production of the acting out student and the social and political functions of qualitative inquiry. He has published in *Teachers College Press*, *Qualitative Inquiry*, and *Discourse: A Journal of Culture and Education.*

Boni Wozolek is currently an assistant professor at Penn State University, Abington College. Her work considers questions of equity and access at the intersections of race, genders (with their multiple expressions and identities), sexual orientations, and qualitative research. Dr. Wozolek is the recipient of several awards, including the James T. Sears Award, the Outstanding Dissertation Recognition Award for American Educational Research Association's Division B, and an induction into the Kent State University Hall of Fame for alumni. Future publications include a book with Routledge that focuses on how violence can be understood through an assemblage and an edited book with SUNY Press on Black Lives Matter and education.

Permissions

Word Fall - 2019
Kate Fitzpatrick
Cut paper and thread on a black backdrop
12 feet (height) 4 feet (width)

About the piece: "Word Fall" is the manifestation of how language is made up of symbols. Meaning is malleable through our own understanding of the world. Sign systems play a crucial part in the social construction of our reality and we often cannot separate these sign systems from our own experiences. Reproduced with permission from Kate Fitzpatrick, Word Fall, Alexandria, Virginia, 2019.

Jigsaw - 2020
Purvai Aranya
Lasercut of digital artwork
12 inches by 10 inches

About the piece: "Jigsaw" is a digital artwork made into a physical object using a laser cutter, exploring the interconnectedness of human bodies in private and public spheres. Reproduced with permission.

Dis-integrating

i
in
intellect
effectual
ineffectual
intellectual
i
disintegrating
integrating
publics
numerous
i
eyes
multitude
spilling out
infinite
finite
in effect
tell
elect
ritual
in
i

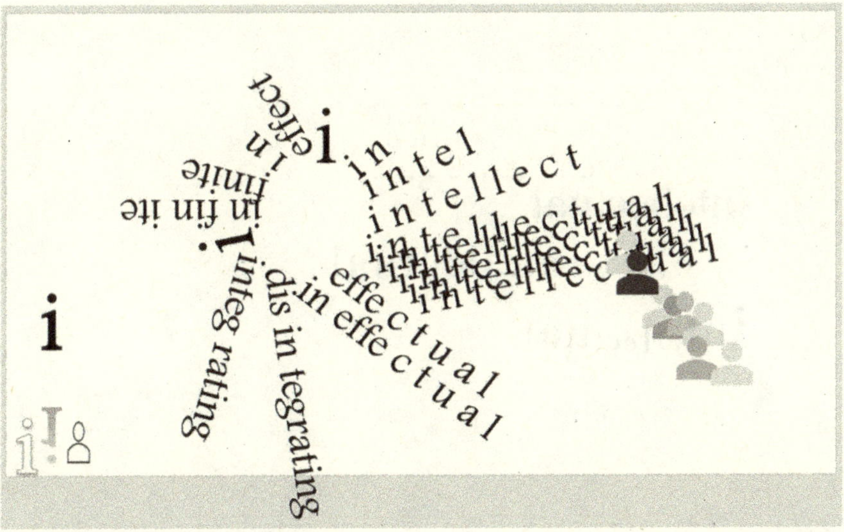

Interludes

			J				
			O				
	M	I	R	K	A		
	A		G		N		
	R		E		A		
	I				N		
	N		B	R	I	A	N
	A						

						B		
				J	O	R	G	E
		M				A		
		A	N	A	N	I		
		R				N		
	M	I	R	K	A			
		N						
		A						

					J			A
					O			N
			M	A	R	I	N	A
			I		G			N
			R		E			I
			K					
B	R	I	A	N				

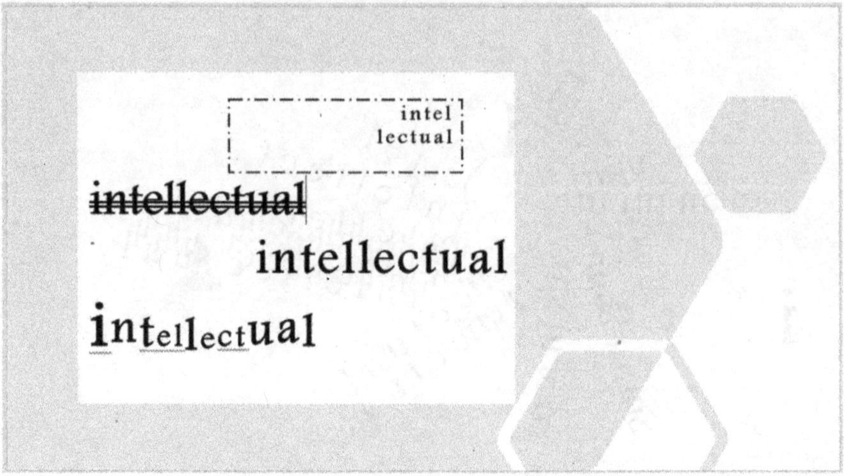

Send your feedback to
mitslew@gmail.com

Index